Beyond Calypso

Beyond Calypso

Re-reading

SAMUEL SELVON

Edited by Malachi McIntosh

IAN RANDLE PUBLISHERS
Kingston • Miami

First published in Jamaica, 2016 by
Ian Randle Publishers
16 Herb McKenley Drive
Box 686
Kingston 6
www.ianrandlepublishers.com

© Malachi McIntosh
ISBN: 978-976-637-861-5

National Library of Jamaica Cataloguing-In-Publication Data

Beyond calypso : re-reading Samuel Selvon / edited by Malachi McIntosh

    pages; cm
    Bibliography : p.
    ISBN 978-976-637-861-5 (pbk)

1. Selvon, Samuel – Criticism and interpretation
2. Trinidad and Tobago – In literature
3. West Indies – In literature
I. McIntosh, Malachi

813.54   dc 23

Cover Design Notsirk
Photo © Alma Jordan Library University of the West Indies
Book Design by Ian Randle Publishers
Printed and Bound in the United States of America

For Stephanie Decouvelaere

CONTENTS

ACKNOWLEDGEMENTS

This book is a product of the conference *Beyond Calypso: New Perspectives on Samuel Selvon*, held at The University of Warwick on 2 July 2011. Three of its chapters, "The Other Selvons", "The Island and the World: Kinship, Friendship and Living Together in Selected Writings of Sam Selvon" and "*A Brighter Sun*: 'I Still Want to See How the Story Unfolds'", are edited versions of articles which appeared in the *Journal of West Indian Literature* special issue *Re-Reading Selvon* (20.2), a collection of some of the *Beyond Calypso* conference papers. A fourth chapter, "'A Man Who Knows His Capabilities and His Limitations is Benign to Papa Bois': On Omniscience, Autonomy and Paternal Authority in *Turn Again Tiger* and *Those Who Eat the Cascadura*" also featured in the issue but in a significantly shorter form. Chapter six, "Symptoms of Malaise: Diagnosing Post-War Caribbean Identity" is an expansion of the argument presented in "Beyond the Colonized and the Colonizer: Caribbean Writing as Postcolonial 'Health'" in *Postcolonial Literatures and Deleuze*. I am thankful to Victor Chang for facilitating the reappearance of the *Journal of West Indian Literature* articles in this collection and am thankful, too, to the Institut d'Etudes Transtextuelles et Transculturelles at Jean Moulin Université Lyon 3 and the Humanities Research Centre, the Research Student Skills Programme, and the Centre for Caribbean Studies at the University of Warwick for their initiation of the process that resulted in this volume through their joint funding of the *Beyond Calypso* event.

Several people have been wonderfully helpful at all stages of the completion of this project. Christine Randle believed instantly that Selvon deserved another collection bearing his name; Alison Donnell and Kenneth Ramchand provided insightful keynotes at the *Beyond Calypso* conference that inspired or helped to develop much of the thinking featured here. Kriston Chen, after much hand-wringing and fretting on my part, designed a fantastic cover with only my ham-fisted guidance. I am very thankful to all three and this book is better for their help. Thanks must also be offered to the *Geographical Magazine* for permission to reprint the images featured in chapter four, and to the staff of the Harry Ransom Center at the University of Texas, Austin, and the Alma Jordan Library at the University of the West Indies, St Augustine, for their aid in finding and reproducing a variety of archived material. Of the latter I am particularly indebted to Maud-Marie Sisnette for her assistance with images and visits. Research for my contributions to this volume was funded by King's College, Cambridge and by a Smuts Memorial Project Grant and I am grateful both to the Smuts committee and to the college for their support. I am also thankful to Arathi Papineni for all of her help with most things, not least the odd bit of funding.

I first encountered Samuel Selvon's work as a postgraduate student through his first novel, *A Brighter Sun*. Like many of his readers, I was struck by the warmth of Selvon's representations and the concision of his writing style, and intrigued by interviews where he conveyed a sense that writing was a part of a process of working out his own position in the world. After moving from Selvon's words to the words of his scholarly readers, I felt increasingly that the Selvon I read about in critical studies did not quite match the Selvon that I read. I was very lucky to meet another PhD student, Stephanie Decouvelaere, who felt much the same way. Within the space of a conversation over cold sandwiches and warm juice at the 2010 Society for Caribbean Studies conference, Stephanie and I decided to develop our shared recognition into a call for papers for the *Beyond Calypso* event. In the years that followed, working alongside Stephanie led to several chances to deepen my knowledge of Selvon, Trinidad and Tobago and the Caribbean as a whole. Although she has since left academia, she remains the inspiration for, impetus behind and shadow presence within this collection. Co-organizer and co-conspirator, I am indebted to her for all of her help developing what has become *Beyond Calypso: Re-Reading Samuel Selvon* and hope this book finds her well in the publishing world.

INTRODUCTION

On Re-reading Sam Selvon and "Beyond"

Malachi McIntosh

Despite Samuel Selvon's status as one of the most important writers in the field of Caribbean literature, his works, when considered as a body, are relatively unknown. Author of novels, screenplays, poems, radio plays and a range of non-fiction texts, Selvon's reputation and readings rest, as Kenneth Ramchand argues in detail in the following chapter, on the fact that he was the author of two seminal texts, *The Lonely Londoners* and *A Brighter Sun*. This volume aims to redress this. It unites scholars from Canada, Britain, and Trinidad and Tobago, the three sites where Selvon spent his writing life, to assess the author's often neglected texts in order to showcase the insights they provide into Selvon's influences, interests and aesthetic.

The Need for Re-reading

To call Samuel Selvon "one of the most important" writers from the Caribbean is to register a newly attained but firmly held status in English-language literature. Where Bruce MacDonald was able to argue in 1988 that the author was largely overlooked, presented in critical studies "merely [as] a reference point in the debate over the use of English in the West Indies" (173), over a quarter of a century later that is clearly no longer the case. From the year of MacDonald's assertion onward, the sustained efforts of a small collection of critics rescued Selvon's work from the neglect it suffered toward the end of his writing life.[1] Susheila Nasta's 1988 publication, *Critical Perspectives on Samuel Selvon*, in which MacDonald's article appears, paved the way for single-authored studies by Clement Wyke in 1991 (*Sam Selvon's Dialectal Style and Fictional Strategy*), Mark Looker in 1996 (*Atlantic Passages: History, Community and Language in the Fiction of Sam Selvon*), Roydon Salick in 2001 (*The Novels of Samuel Selvon: A Critical Study*), Maria Grazia Sindoni in 2006 (*Creolizing Culture: A Study on Sam Selvon's Work*), and Roydon Salick once more in 2013 (*Samuel Selvon*). The release of *Critical Perspectives* also opened the avenue for two subsequent essay collections on Selvon's work compiled by Susheila Nasta and Anna Rutherford in 1995 (*Tiger's Triumph*) and by Martin Zehnder in 2003 (*Something Rich and Strange: Selected Essays on Samuel Selvon*). Alongside these books have come chapters in edited volumes, journal articles, and the re-issue of several of Selvon's texts, including the rebirth of *The Lonely Londoners* and *Moses Ascending* as Penguin Modern Classics. All of this activity has lifted Selvon to the status of a central figure writing in Britain in the 1950s, '60s and '70s; it has seen him hailed as the "father of Black Literature" in the country (qtd. in Nasta "Setting up Home" 82), praised for heralding "new multiracial London" in work that "describe[d it] into existence" (Dyer 129), and ushered into consideration within curricula at a range of stages of education in the US, Canada, the Caribbean and the UK.

Despite the heights reached in his recent re-ascension, Selvon is most often read as less than all he produced, his works consulted in pursuit of a handful of themes in the two major works referenced above. The vast majority of his Anglo-American critics seem concerned only with the creation of "one of the key literary texts in the representation of the Windrush generation of immigrants from the Caribbean" (Bentley 41), *The Lonely Londoners*; his Caribbean critics and the minority in the Anglo-American orbit supplement this interest with considerations of *A Brighter Sun*. Not only has this led to the neglect of a great deal of Selvon's writing, it has also caused, due to the investment of several minds over several decades in the techniques of just two texts, an unusual tendency to trace and re-trace the same themes, in similar terms, in numerous critical works.

Nowhere is this clearer than in the abiding scholarly fixation on the author's debts to calypso. A calypso heuristic dominates engagements with *The Lonely Londoners*, in particular, and has bled into assessments of Selvon's whole oeuvre. "Calypso" is everywhere, from Ashley Dawson's assessment of the "calypso aesthetic [that] saturates" *Londoners*, which he argues is "most evident in the novel's apparently loose-knit string of humorous anecdotes depicting the lives of flamboyant characters" (33); to Nick Bentley's assertion that the representation of women in the same text "corresponds to the appropriation of the calypso form, which traditionally produces negative images of women" (43); to Simon Gikandi's flagging of a "calypso idiom" in Selvon's writing (116); to Michel Fabre's assertion that "the calypso style" unites Selvon's England and Trinidad-set fictions ("Moses" 389); to Maria Grazia Sindoni's claim that the "image of the Calypsonian" is a repeating trope across all of Selvon's works (72); to much else besides.

Calypso-inspired analyses have, of course, provided some insights into Selvon's use of language and the episodic structure of his novels, as well as helped to sketch the larger artistic context in which he began his career; nonetheless, not only do studies focusing on similarities between Selvon's writings and calypso music almost necessarily feature repetitions of ideas already framed, they also, more worryingly, recall the practice of the author's first and largely condescending Anglo-American critics.[2] These first readers used "calypso" as something of an analytic shortcut, one taken as much to praise innovation as to invoke a staunch Caribbean Difference.

Early readers cheered, for example, Selvon's "primitive calypso tempo" (Benson), his "easy calypso rhythm" (Edmondson "Easy Calypso" 12), and, in concert with this, his "vivid, racy language", language presumed in one description to be shared amongst all of "the coloured, colourful Londoners who came from Jamaica and Trinidad and Barbados" ("The Secret London"). While later readings detach from these clearly stereotypical depictions, they nonetheless reflect the impulse of the early assessments to compress fragmentary, often multi-referential texts into a fairly restrictive container. Moreover, and in like manner to Selvon's first reviewers, they threaten to make uniform both Selvon's diverse works and an equally eclectic stock of calypso music whilst also implying that a Trinidad-specific lens is best suited for the study of a writer who spent almost his entire adult life abroad.[3]

Perhaps even more threatening to our understanding of Selvon's work, though, has been the relative silence about the author's mid-career novels, *I Hear Thunder* and *Turn Again Tiger*; his later novels, *The Housing Lark*, *The Plains of Caroni*, and *Moses Migrating*; and his radio plays and poems.[4] This logic of this practice is a tacit sentiment that these works have very little to offer to us, another belief that echoes the explicit ideas of Selvon's earliest readers. These individuals, on both sides of the Atlantic, took the author's later works as clear failures worthy of little word, as pale reflections of what preceded them.[5] In this tradition, Mervyn Morris wrote in 1967 that:

> [i]n some [Caribbean] writers, what began as an honest examination of roots becomes more and more an exploitation of the exotic. The classic and saddest instance of this is in the work of Samuel Selvon: in standard English he declines from the sensitive *A Brighter Sun* to the meretricious *I Hear Thunder*; in dialect from the wry humour of the short stories in *Ways of Sunlight*, and the gentle puzzlement and fun of *The Lonely Londoners*, to the cheap triviality of *The Housing Lark*. ("Some West Indian Problems" 128)

A similar dismissal can be found in Eric Roach's reflection, after admitting that "[e]veryone fell in love" with Selvon's first novel, *A Brighter Sun*, that

> [t]he critic may [now] say Sam writes badly [...] [h]e may say Sam is some sort of political or racial idiot [...] [a]fter 20 years of hard labour in the wilderness outside [of the Caribbean], Sam must certainly be growing old and weary. His writing has not fetched very much. He has not the stature of the elder Naipaul. He is of little significance to the world outside (6).

The concept of decline which both Morris and Roach present, coupled with their questioning of the relevance of Selvon's later writing, reveals its legacy through the scant attention paid to the mid-to-late Selvon – the writer's final few novels, in particular, rarely granted attention, most often only touched en passant as evidence of his "disenchantment" (Sandhu 148).

More than a Calypsonian

This lack of interest in the mid- and late-career works, coupled with few readings of Selvon's creations in genres beyond the novel, has pre-emptively frustrated our understanding of the author. Within Selvon's wider biography – beyond the moment of initial migrant departure/arrival – and in his full bibliography – which includes works, like his radio plays and non-fiction, which are rarely touched – are several thus-far understudied "other Selvons", as Ramchand calls them in chapter one, with pictures very different from the standard image of the comedic calypsonian. These "other Selvons" complicate the common image of the man and his work and are present everywhere in the texts that are in danger of becoming a Selvonian apocrypha.

As soon as we wander past Selvon's first and third novels, we cannot avoid encountering "others" everywhere: in his wider work, the "calypso" novelist takes his famously light, comedic tone and either drops it altogether or complicates it; his "stereotypical" female figures vanish; the author famed for his lack of anger and political quietude takes on a fierce and direct tone, most overtly in the opening pages of *The Plains of Caroni*, but also at points in *Those Who Eat the Cascadura* (see chapter eight), *The Housing Lark* (chapters four and nine) and *Moses Migrating* (chapter ten); the episodic, ballad narratives we know best are supplemented with longer arcs, Freytag structures, and play with other forms including romance, farce and magical realism. While Selvon's works are markedly recursive – in their redeployment of characters' names, restaging of certain scenes, replay of phrases, and their grounding, almost always, in the environs of London and Port of Spain – the mid-career, later works, short stories, poems and scripts break apart and recombine what precedes them in order to present a range of other ways of seeing. A recognition of the presence and value of the "other" in these pieces – channelled into a desire to see the presence of that "other" elsewhere – facilitates our ability to see something new in the familiar; to note, for instance, in the *Londoners* Selvon a fixation on the British state's decay (chapter nine), to see in the *Brighter Sun* Selvon an interest in the resistance of Indian-Trinidadians to his celebrated ideas of creolization (chapter five); to recognize in all of Selvon a philosophy of living in and with difference (chapter four) and, through all of this, to question if Selvon's oft-granted spokesman status as voice of "folk" concerns was ever a good fit (chapter two).[6]

Going Beyond

The eleven essays that follow turn to the neglected and the under-read to facilitate a deeper understanding of Selvon's body of writing. Most were drafted in response to direct requests to new and established critics to return to and reassess Selvon's texts, a handful finding their first expression in papers presented at the conference, *Beyond Calypso: New Perspectives on Samuel Selvon* held at the University of Warwick on 2 July 2011.[7] Regardless of their inspiration, all of the chapters share the sense that there are several significant impasses in analyses of the author beyond which we must progress. It is important to note that not a single critic included here evidences a strong desire to abandon "calypso" altogether as a useful heuristic tool – in fact both Alison Donnell and J. Vijay Maharaj draw directly upon it in their contributions. Nonetheless, and collectively, the chapters all assert that studying Selvon requires more than many "calypso" readings have offered us so far: both more specific, detailed analyses of the concrete features of Selvon's aesthetics and also wider frameworks to situate his writing in relationship to his peers, his readers, philosophy, literary theory and a range of historical events.

In pursuit of the "other", these essays invert common critical practice and make only passing reference to Selvon's most often studied novel, *The Lonely Londoners*, from which our familiar image of the author is most regularly drawn. Nonetheless, and almost irresistibly, several of the chapters touch upon themes that have been explored in *Londoners'* readings but which Selvon's critics, so far, have not studied as assiduously in relation to his other works. These include his representation of Caribbean and English women (chapters two, three, four, seven and eight), his linked fixation on modes of masculinity (chapters three and seven), his use of humour (chapters one, four and ten), and his various attempts to portray creolization and mixed communities (chapters two, four and five). Other essays consider themes wholly absent from Selvon's most famous text, such as his diagnosis and disparagement of post-Federation Trinidad (chapter six), his consideration of the state management of Caribbean citizens in 1970s and '80s Britain (chapter nine) and his efforts to represent mutually-fulfilling love relationships and Hindu faith (chapters two and eight).

While there are clear fixations in Selvon's writing that appear and re-appear in the chapters of this collection, this book does not present or even attempt to offer a comprehensive new view of a single "other" Selvon and his literary work: instead, its essays act as a series of pathways into new perspectives on the author's writing and life. Insofar as we understand the fields of literature and criticism as "space[s] of possibles", of potentially realizable aesthetic choices and critical responses to those choices, then this collection points towards more interpretative "possibles", through its "others", recognizing with Pierre Bourdieu that potentials irrupt in a field in response to new discoveries, new information, and new targets of attention (261). It is no coincidence that several chapters here draw heavily upon archived, never-published and long out-of-print works by the author currently held at the Alma Jordan Library at the University of the West Indies (St Augustine), the Harry Ransom Center at the University of Texas (Austin), and elsewhere. To find "others" it is necessary to go beyond the sources that critics have consulted and re-consulted so far to discover evidence that we have either had limited opportunities to date to consider or which alterations in the field have encouraged us to forget.

Re-thinking the Caribbean Field

Samuel Selvon was a seemingly restless writer. When taken as a whole, his works reveal all the conflicts in positioning self and subject matter that a career in search of certainty and form, rather than fixed within a clear sense of either, seems to have demanded. Many of Selvon's texts fail to "fit with any of the grand narratives governing contemporary criticism" (MacLeod 177), but all of them reflect Selvon's own social location and respond to a changing globe.

This book itself emerges at a time of change. Several readers concerned with the ways that critics, texts and markets have concretized a Caribbean field have recently re-shaped our understanding of Selvon's era and are currently building upon and complicating the writing of the scholars of previous decades. These new readers have returned to the *Windrush* generation to ask questions thus far unaddressed, querying representations of resistance, authenticity, gender, sexuality and nationhood, working together to force more "possibles" into Caribbean studies. This book aims to make a contribution, however small, to these efforts by inspiring engagements of all kinds with the arguments its chapters present. In response to recent changes, and in anticipation of a future of many more, it offers a single, simple overarching argument: Selvon's texts – all of them – demand our attention and demand too to be read and re-read.

NOTES

1. See Harney, *Nationalism and Identity* (95), and Clarke, *A Passage Back Home* (140), for further details.
2. I am thankful to J. Vijay Maharaj for highlighting this connection to me as a product of her archival work.
3. In contrast to this practice, Peter Kalliney makes clear in his reading of *The Lonely Londoners* that we are as or more justified in applying the term "modernist" to Selvon's episodic, demotic works as we are applying "calypsonian", or in fact any other appellation linked to "folk" form ("Metropolitan Modernism" 96).
4. In the case of the poetry, critical neglect is understandable, as Selvon's verse has only recently seen light in a single collection, *The Poems of Sam Selvon*, edited by Roydon Salick (2012).
5. See Walcott, "The Action is Panicky"; Quigly, "New Novels"; Naipaul, "Caribbean Voices" and "Turn again Tiger"; and Redding, "Sex in Trinidad".
6. Both Selvon's "other" works and Selvon himself call into question the idea of the author as folk spokesman. The *Samuel Selvon Collection* at the Alma Jordan Library contains several interesting unpublished autobiographical pieces in which Selvon

differentiates himself from both the Caribbean migrants in Britain and the workers in Trinidad and Tobago for whom he was and commonly is understood to be a straightforward representative. Where, for instance, Eric Roach says that Selvon "and the base are one" (6), Selvon himself writes "'to tell you another truth, I have to confess that after a time I became a bit fed-up of being taken for the mouthpiece of the coloured community. It wasn't that I didn't feel concerned, but the circumstances of my own personal life were far removed from that of the hustling immigrant in a factory. All well and good for me as a writer to sit back and voice my opinion: but how honest could it be, unless I made a point of being in touch from time to time with the coloured man who conducted the bus, or swept the streets, or worked overtime in the factories to make ends meet?" ("Autobiographical Essay 3" 7). Elsewhere, in contrast to the life of the average Caribbean labourer, he describes an upbringing that featured house servants and the fact that "the lower class had to approach [the family home] with some caution, and be prepared to go away unreceived if my mother was busy inside" ("Autobiographical Essay 5" 1–2).

7. See Acknowledgements for details.

CHAPTER ONE

The Other Selvons

Kenneth Ramchand

This chapter is an edited version of the keynote address delivered at the conference Beyond Calypso: New Perspectives on Sam Selvon *held at Warwick University on 2 July 2011.*

I begin my exploration of the theme "the other Selvons" by outlining what is generally agreed about Samuel Selvon's work. This will allow me to notice some of the overlooked Selvons who reside in and invisibly shape the familiar one. It will also allow us to see if criticism and commentary have been thorough enough even on the agreed fronts and will be the ground from which I argue for a side of Selvon radically different from the Selvon we accept and know.

Samuel Selvon began as a philosophical writer, a poet of love and a searcher with a religious yearning for meaning, value and transcendence. His religiosity made him respond to entities both as they impinged upon his senses and as forms of the Absolute. The familiar Selvon, the Selvon that critics and ordinary readers recognize, emerged from two of his first four books, namely the first, *A Brighter Sun* (1952) and the third, *The Lonely Londoners* (1956). His second work, *An Island Is a World* (1955), is largely unread, and his fourth, *Turn Again Tiger* (1958), is taken as read; simply imagined to be a continuation of *A Brighter Sun* with no new strands of its own. Between 1963 when he published *I Hear Thunder* and 1983 when *Moses Migrating* arrived, Selvon wrote seven extended fictions. In 1989, most of his early prose writings were reprinted in *Foreday Morning: Selected Prose 1946–1986*. In 1993, *An Island Is a World* was re-issued. But apart from Roydon Salick's re-classification of the fictions in *The Novels of Samuel Selvon*, there has not been any attempt to adjust the view of the writings or the writer that derived from the first and third works.

The credits justly associated with these two books are:

i. *The installation of a peasant hero*

In what can be read as a political statement about colonialism's limiting view of subject persons and as a response the kind of heroes that West Indian school-children were exposed to until well into the 1960s, Selvon's *A Brighter Sun* made an ordinary person, and a West Indian one, a convincing main character in a novel written to be read by West Indians. Celebrating one of the remarkable achievements of some of the West Indian writers of the 1950s, and with Selvon very much in mind, Lamming declared in *The Pleasures of Exile*:

> Unlike the previous governments and departments of educators, unlike the business man [sic] importing commodities, the West Indian novelist did not look out across the sea to another source. He looked in and down at what had traditionally been ignored. For the first time, the West Indian peasant became other than a cheap source of labour. He became, through the novelist's eye, a living existence, living in silence and joy and fear, involved in riot and carnival. It is the West Indian novel that has restored the West Indian peasant to his true and original status of personality. (38–39)

At this early stage in his career and life, Selvon's belief in the possibility of the wholeness of the person informs the kind of characterization that is effected in *A Brighter Sun* and in *The Lonely Londoners*. For many readers, Tiger is solid and knowable and real, and can be imagined living on outside the confines of the book, like V.S. Naipaul's Biswas or Earl Lovelace's Aldrick.[1]

ii. *An unforgettable rendering of the West Indian immigrant experience in London*

In *The Lonely Londoners* and in a number of short stories of the 1950s and 1960s, Selvon wrote poignantly and in a comic vein of the problems and possibilities, the hopes and disappointments, the excitement and the disenchantment of the first generation of immigrants, often dubbed "the *Windrush* generation", to the United Kingdom. The majority of the characters in *The Lonely Londoners* are vivid and memorable for certain defining traits, but they are not presented in depth of Moses, the main character. Moses in *The Lonely Londoners* is as memorable and emblematic as Tiger and he recognizes the fragmenting of the person in the impersonality of the metropolis, while sustaining a nostalgia for wholeness. This book establishes him as Selvon's second emblematic and solid character.

iii. *A major linguistic achievement*

The third achievement for which Selvon is celebrated drew raving attention to itself in *The Lonely Londoners* where he used the Trinidad language as the language of all the characters, including Jamaicans, Barbadians and other islanders. He also used it as the language of the narrating voice, using that voice to gather in with compassion and find pattern in the lives of the scattered immigrants. Selvon's chosen language animated and made vivid the encounters, episodes and ballads through which the figures in that book are presented. This achievement continues to be described with reference to terms like "nation language", "modified dialect", "the demotic", all of which point to Selvon's participation in the unfinished nationalist project of claiming the identity and the languages colonized peoples were taught to despise. But we have to go further even if we seem to digress.

Selvon's linguistic achievement, which announces itself in *The Lonely Londoners,* starts before his third novel and continues beyond it. It contains two main processes that may be described as follows:

(a) The meeting of orality and writing: A way of putting into words that allows us to analyse the work of many other writers from the region, and to appreciate not only what Selvon effects in *The Lonely Londoners* but also his calculated use and misuse of different kinds of orality and different kinds of writings to enhance the meaning in what Maureen Warner-Lewis brilliantly describes as the "linguistic extravaganza" of *Moses Ascending.*

(b) The intuitive use and acceptance of the Trinidadian "tone of voice": "Tone of voice" is more extensive and subtle than "accent" and more available to be picked up by a native reader than by a non-native as a mark of cultural and linguistic identity. The significance of "tone of voice" to social groupings is made easy to understand in the fifth chapter of David Crystal's *The English Tone of Voice.* Even without Crystal's explanations, it is clear that some elements of tone (pitch, quality, strength, modulation, intervals) have distinctive national or cultural shading which invisibly make subtle semantic distinctions and add functional meaning for native speakers.

From the beginning of his career, Selvon had an ear for the Trinidadian tone of voice. The following passage from *A Brighter Sun*, decidedly not a "dialect" passage, illustrates this. It looks like Standard English in places and towards the end the spelling recognizes a speaker of dialect but the Trinidadian tone of voice gears smoothly from one to the other and back. In this section of the novel, Americans are building a road in wartime Trinidad to link their Port-of-Spain base to Wallerfield:

> A tractor leveled down the beds on which he had planted lettuce at one time; he saw earth where melongene and tomatoes grew change shape, scooped up into the air and flung to one side. And he thought how after one time, is another. In one week the landscape was showing the colour of the naked brown earth and the deep impressions of the tractors. Landmarks familiar to him—a coconut tree near the edge of the swamp, a ricefield—were buried under the powerful machinery as they advanced.
>
> "You mean" Tiger asked a fellow worker, "that that bulldozer could root anything from out of the ground?"

"Well, no. I uses to work down in de base, and it have some root dat so deep in de ground dat we had was to blow dem up wid dynamite. Dat was big time work, boy. [...] Dem scraggy tree, looking desperate, is nutting for de bulldozer to lick down." (146)

In *A Brighter Sun* the establishment of the Trinidadian tone of voice is facilitated by the narrating voice's sympathetic involvement with the characters, something reflected in the fluid way in which it moves in and out of consciousness and modulates between comment, analysis and accommodating reportage.

Selvon's modified dialect might not have worked as a language if he hadn't had such control of the Trinidadian tone of voice.

iv. *Humour*

Words like "funny", "hilarious", "comic" "farcical", "riotous" "ribald" all point to humour, the fourth characteristic for which Selvon's writing is universally praised. Humour is a Selvonian strength but criticism has been very slack in its thinking about it.

In the first place, as Victor Ramraj indicates in his Selvon entry for the *Dictionary of Literary Biography (Canadian Literary Humorists)*, it is in the four London novels and the short stories set in London beginning with *The Lonely Londoners* that humour impresses itself as a defining attribute of Selvon's writing. In these works the association between humour and dialect/modified dialect is the norm. We can add that it is here too that the sense of the writer as a genial and happy-go-lucky person fixes itself.

Ramraj reminds complacent readers that "Selvon's reputation as a humorist rests on these [London] works" ("Samuel Selvon" 230) and not on *A Brighter Sun*, *An Island Is a World*, *Turn Again Tiger*, *I Hear Thunder*, *The Plains of Caroni*, and *Those Who Eat the Cascadura* which are all set in Trinidad. The last three of the Trinidad novels, he notes

touch on aspects of race, class, education, and materialism that threaten Selvon's romantic vision of a harmonious Caribbean world. His tone is still genial and tolerant, but in *The Plains of Caroni* it has an uncharacteristically satiric bite when he describes the exploitation of sugar workers. There is not much authorial humour in these three novels; even less is displayed by the protagonists. (232)

In his analysis of humour in the London books, Ramraj makes a distinction between the different kinds and uses of humour, a distinction not made by many commentators. At the risk of simplifying, I summarize Ramraj thus: *The Housing Lark* is Selvon's most hilarious work but it is farce without moral judgment; the largely verbal humour in *Moses Ascending* serves the cause of comedy, treating with a conflicted or confused Moses's ambivalent feelings about Britain and the English language and culture; and in *Moses Migrating* the humour shifts from comedy with a social purpose to farce, slapstick and ribaldry played mainly for laughs.

We don't have to agree completely with the details. What is quite fertile is that Ramraj traces a progression in the use of humour from *The Housing Lark* to *Moses Migrating*. This has significance for how we interpret each book. As I have suggested in my "Comedy as Evasion", the reduction in the scope of comedy in *Moses Ascending* and its descent into farce and ribaldry in *Moses Migrating* have implications for the standard description of the author as happy-go-lucky raconteur and for how the writing responds to the changing world.

In addition to providing relief from stressful experiences, and offering amusement, delight and entertainment, humour when worked into the shape of comedy has great social and human value. A benchmark moment in Selvon's writing is the closing movement of *The Lonely Londoners* where the author deliberately directs Moses to make an observation about the presence of the serious or tragic, the underside of comedy that gives poignancy and purpose to the comic and the humorous:

> Under the kiff-kiff laughter, behind the ballad and the episode, the what-happening, the summer-is-hearts, he could see a great aimlessness, a great restless, swaying movement that leaving you standing in the same spot. (141)

Critical Issues

However we construct or elaborate them, the four features identified above are the undeniable bases of Selvon commentary and criticism, and rightly so. They have led, however, to certain imbalances in our appreciation of the oeuvre and in our "reading" of the author and his books. Here is a bare count of the imbalances:

i.   A repetitiveness in the criticism which fine-tunes and extends but also, unfortunately, prejudices discussion towards the four topics mentioned above.

ii. More attention to the novels, and little attempt to relate them to the short stories, the poems, the radio plays and the early non-fiction and semi-fictional writings, such as those collected in *Foreday Morning*.

iii. A cringing refusal to consider the impact of Selvon's practice on the form (structure and texture) of the novel. This practice includes the use of orality and oral narrating strategies and narrative stances, the episodic quality, the use of digressions, and the crossing of conventional boundaries between prose and verse and between the short story and the novel. The early West Indian novelists who began as poets and short story writers have stretched and complicated the form of the conventional novel and Selvon stands strong with Wilson Harris among the innovators.

iv. Emphasis on the "folk" and "proletarian" elements and the exclusion of writings based in the middle class to which Selvon belonged. In addition to *An Island Is a World* the middle class works include *I Hear Thunder*, *The Plains of Caroni* and the short story "Rhapsody in Red", all of which widen our appreciation of Selvon's use of the Trinidadian language, his satire on the dead end and mimic aspirations of the middle class, and his concern about the fate of the artistic and/or thinking person in Trinidad and Tobago society.

v. Insufficient recognition of the fact that in addition to his portrayal of the black experience of West Indians in London, Selvon constructs from "Cane is Bitter" (1950) and *A Brighter Sun* (1952), *Turn Again Tiger* (1959) to *I Hear Thunder* (1963) and *The Plains of Caroni* (1970) through to *Those Who Eat the Cascadura* (1972) a socio-economic and cultural history of sugar and the descendants of Indians in an evolving Trinidad and Tobago.

vi. Neglect of the seminal, second "philosophical" novel *An Island Is a World* which points to themes that will emerge and to the darkening mood of the later writings.

vii. Delay in relating developments in Selvon's later practice to the thinking and feeling and the anxieties of the poems most of which were written by 1950 and the early prose pieces collected in *Foreday Morning*.

The Other, Early Selvons

I want to look now at the poems and the early prose pieces and to highlight some of the "other Selvons" to be found in them. In the early prose pieces, Selvon is the poet of nature and the human heart, and a cultural nationalist urging his countrymen to see action, adventure and drama in their own lives and in the lives around them; he advises them to turn for romance not to the Hollywood heroine but to the far more entrancing "lass around the corner"; and for stunning images from nature they should "go to St Ann's, and stroll along the road where tall bamboos criss-cross the sky in moving lines of green" (*Foreday Morning* 28). These pieces show the novelist-to-come immersing himself in place and investing in the persons there as subjects worthy of respectful representation.

Among the short stories now found in *Foreday Morning*, "What's the Use" chafes at the fear that prohibits a pair of lovers from voicing their love and at the inability of language to siphon out into the open the strong feelings they have for each other. In "Passing Cloud", Dan returns from his four years of law studies abroad to find that Elsie is now married. She agrees to meet him and he reproaches her for not waiting for him and for throwing away the happiness together that they had talked about. The final conversation before Elsie walks out of his life touches on questions that haunted the early Selvon:

> She cried, "Hush, Dan, don't say such things to me."
>
> I looked down in the bubbling stream, and suddenly my heart went limp. I felt ashamed. I thought, a lawyer…
>
> "Do you remember we used to wonder about happiness, what life was all about? We never found out." Elsie was saying slowly. "Time makes a great difference. I began to think differently when you went away […]."
>
> "Are you happy?" I asked.
>
> She looked at me with depth. She shrugged. "What is happiness?" (*Foreday Morning* 103)

As we shall see, such questions are the staple of his poems.

Above all, in these early writings, Selvon is the natural philosopher thinking his way into an understanding of love, life, time, death, and friendship.[2] Though the past vanishes as the ink dries on a piece of paper, the mind must continue to go over the jumbles of yesterdays, todays, and tomorrows. Caught up in life and time, man must cultivate the ironic and compassionate stance of a god gazing down on the vagaries of the human heart. The grave-digger in the grim "In the Cemetery" hears the cry of anguish every day and marks how the forlorn girl bringing flowers to the grave comes no more and leaves the beloved dead to weeds and grasses. In "As Time Goes By", a man who has not found the fulfilment he sought in America where "the snow lost its freshness and skyscrapers became a common sight" (*Foreday Morning* 24), returns after three years to find that he has travelled in a circle, that homecoming has quickly lost its lustre, and it is as if he had never made the journey.

Although written as separate items at different times, the poems published between 1945 and 1950 have affinities with Derek Walcott's "Epitaph for the Young" (1949) in which the precocious teenager is found grappling with the meaning of life, the intensity of his emotions, and the discouragements of life in a philistine colonial society. In 1950 Selvon read together on the BBC Caribbean Voices programme a poem in three parts entitled "Triad", and a fourth item which had been published in 1948 under the title "Sun". The BBC script gives the title "Discovering Tropic" to the whole offering and the four pieces are published under this title in John Figueroa's collection *Caribbean Voices*. It is not clear whether the titling was the work of the BBC editor or of Selvon himself and the poems are presented separately in Roydon Salick's recent *The Poems of*

Sam Selvon. While Selvon did not number "Sun" as (iv) to follow the (i), (ii), and (iii) of "Triad", he did read them in that sequence and this invites us to think of the four works as linked, forming a kind of Odyssey in which the almost militant poet traces the lineaments of his much put-down country and challenges his countrymen to break away from the image of the tourist island and the status of being culturally inferior. Under "Caribbean compulsion" the exuberant poet sings of cedar trees "Skeletoned against the sky with seeds" ("Discovering" 162) and inherits incredible powers:

> Sometimes I straighten rainbows
> Pitch like sea-water skyward
> In the path of a Westerly wind;
> Climb stalks of rain when clouds weep
> And discover their origin. (163)

But the negative forces are strong and he finds himself in reality "Circling the Colonial prison-yard / Wherein we squeeze, jostle for position" (163) in never-ending slavery. This is the limiting frame within which the poems strive in spite of prohibition "To heighten consciousness, philosophise, / Devise morals, solve mysteries" (162).

In "Fear", the poet confesses that he is "deeply afraid of life" and that he has found "uncertainty / Creeping, / Lurking just a little way off". He is afraid that "Faith might be insufficient" and he finds all his support systems falling apart:

> I build little vague gods:
> Those vague gods in the deep
> Of night
> Or of the shallow day.
> But they all come tumbling
> Down. (*The Poems* 7)

In "Consolation", he tries to come to terms with a condition in which all he can do is react to things, suspecting that the reflex is only that, just a reflex. He wonders whether life itself might be just a reaction

> This split-second existence
> In the eternity of Time
> Might be the first reaction,
> And when we die, will come
> Wiser realms, soberer thoughts—
> The truth of life. (*The Poems* 11)

Despairing of this world and plagued by his "lucubrations" he longs in "Wings of Thought" for transcendence, for the "intensest zero" of soul touching world, "Unbarricaded by thought". He yearns for a quiet victory without the trumpet's blare:

To be naked,
And look at the sun's nakedness;
To walk freely in freedom;
To be mud in mud
Raw and thoughtless as a sod.
Yet, not straw in wind
But the existence of a straw in wind. (*The Poems* 12)

But he is too much of the world to privilege soul over body, the abstract sphere over the features of his island. Tropic remains to be discovered. He can exult in the landscape and the pattern of death and renewal in nature. He can satirize the living death of the exploiters who serve "Lucky Lucre", show up the pretensions of "Modern Art" (*The Poems* 24, 22). And he can set up against the rising doom and, in spite of the torture of lost dreams and lost love, fashion a stabilizing relationship with Droupadi, whom he married in 1947:

Droupadi,
It will always be you,
My ship has anchored
At your port for keeps,
And a home, a bed for two;
Blazing-flowered garden
Are links in my anchor chain. (*The Poems* 17)

The imagery in this positive poem betrays the need for stability and respite from a tormented existence and shows the poet willing himself into a human answer to the relentless spinning of the indifferent world. The third stanza ominously infiltrates the possibility of his resolve being swept aside:

Droupadi,
If anything should happen –
And life is happening
Know it is so I think of it.
Not the greatest love story
But humble life with you
Humble love. (*The Poems* 17)

I want to end this excursion into the Selvon of the early short pieces by looking briefly at a poem and two short stories. The poem is called "At Tacarigua" and it was published in 1947. It is in part a poem about the difficulty of expressing thoughts and feelings in words, but it closes with a concern about the relationship between the artist and his wife or love. The poet is "Whelmed by the inability / To express" (*The Poems* 18), but he has noticed that wind, water and trees speak secretly and find ways of expressing "wordless thoughts". The poet ends with an ominous prayer for his love to "understand" and to be able to "share the impression / I am unable to express."

The issue is more explicit in the 1947 short story "Echo in the Hills" in which a widow keeps a promise to deliver to a young man on his twenty-first birthday a letter written for him by his artist father shortly before his death 14 years ago. He acknowledges in the letter that Nancy had little regard for the arts and took no comfort out of being muse or object of worship. He accepts that it was so and there was nothing to be done about it:

> *Maybe my mistake was in thinking of her as a source of inspiration and so I never gave her the things she wanted from life. It is too late now for me to go her ways or she mine. I have much work to do....To me she was the wind, and the sun. I never realized that glorifying her was not giving her happiness.* (*Foreday Morning* 64–65, original emphasis)

The theme recurs sensationally in another of Selvon's middle-class stories reprinted in *Foreday Morning*, "Rhapsody in Red" where a musician is shattered when the hostility of his wife reveals itself as jealousy of the artist's possession by his art. As late as 1957, in the haunting "My Girl and the City", Selvon was still grappling with futility, with the uncertainties of self-expression, still in pursuit of the reluctant muse:

> So now I weave, I say there was an old man on whose face wrinkles rivered, whose hands were shapeful with arthritis but when he spoke, oddly enough, his voice was young and gay.

> But there was no old man, there was nothing, and there is never ever anything.

> My girl, she is beautiful to look at. I have seen her in sunlight and in moonlight, and her face carves an exquisite shape in darkness. (*Ways of Sunlight* 176)

The Novels' Other Selvon

After the early period of writing in the shorter forms, Selvon published three novels that differ from one another in social setting, use of language, subject matter and in the person of the main character. On the surface he is entering another phase. The first novel, *A Brighter Sun,* has for its central character a person we can identify as of Indian origin who moves from the countryside associated with cane to a fruit and vegetable farming community not far from Port of Spain. The second novel, *An Island Is a World,* has at the centre a person we eventually think of as of Indian origin, a character with no fixed place who wanders in the North and in the South and who spends three years in England vainly looking for a life. The third work, *The Lonely Londoners,* has at the centre a character of African origin and the bulk of the characters are people of African descent. They have come to London from the islands of their birth and colonial upbringing and had it not been for their irrepressible capacity for life their journey to expectation would have been voyages in the unrelieved dark.

These novels have more in common than the above descriptions might suggest, and one of the things that binds them is that they continue to elaborate, through the form of the novel, the preoccupations of the writings from the period before 1950. They are also alike in that the social world in which their characters are located is clearly defined even when, as in *An Island Is a World,* their boundaries are elastic. Above all they are alike in the similarity of their heroes, and in the kind of characterization Selvon is still able to practice in these novels.

The preoccupations of the early period appear most directly in the broad canvas of Selvon's longest book, *An Island Is a World.* In a personal communication of 1994, Selvon refers to this book as "my most ambitious novel in scope and theme, which does not mean to say the object was accomplished. It falls short, but of all the books I've ever written it is the only one in which I set out consciously to express or try out some of my beliefs". It is Selvon's most directly philosophical novel.

All the early reviewers recognized that the central character Foster was a troubled man. A reviewer in *The Spectator,* rushing to closure, referred to him as "a vaguely disturbed, spoilt, talented young man at odds with life till he finds the right girl" (Quigly 109). In *Bim* he was picked out as a man who is "at once fascinated and frightened by the depths and uncertainties of life" (Holder 202) and in a BBC *Caribbean Voices* broadcast, V.S. Naipaul fastened on Foster as "a symptom of the intellectual malaise that is eating away at Trinidad and the rest of the West Indies" ("Caribbean Voices" 110). Foster's mind is confused and his will paralyzed by his sensitivity to all the activity going on inside of himself, outside of himself, in his society and in the spinning world beyond. The benevolent figure Father Hope recognizes that Foster is pursuing truth and wants "a faith, a hope, a destination that will make your life worthwhile" (*An Island* 218). This seems to me to be the mission of the heroes in Selvon's first four books.

I have written elsewhere that on the surface, the middle-class Foster is different from Tiger, the Indian peasant hero of *A Brighter Sun,* and from Moses, the Afro-Trinidadian centre of consciousness in *The Lonely Londoners.* I want to indicate again, however, that:

> each of them has a capacity for wonder, a longing for clarity, and a penchant for asking awkward and literal questions. Each of them takes on the burden of consciousness and attempts to think originally (however homespun the terms) about what it is to be a person in the world, what it is people live for, and what principle, creed or belief should give direction to a life. (Ramchand "Introduction" vi)

Foster is the most relentless seeker of both an absolute creed and a lasting consolation, but the main characters in Selvon's first three books, and in the fourth *Turn Again Tiger,* may be summed up as characters looking for something to believe in and to belong to. Foster self-pityingly confesses to this on seeing bands of former indentured Indians taking up their option of repatriation. He upbraids Andrews for being critical of the Indians' wish to return to India; to Foster these returning Indians had something to return to, they had a country. Unfortunately, although he too is of Indian origin, he cannot feel the way they do; they have a home and they are going back to it but, "[h]e had nothing. He had been brought up as a Trinidadian—a member of a cosmopolitan community who recognized no creed or race, a creature born of all the peoples in the world, in a small island that no one knew anything about" (211).

It is a striking characteristic of Selvon's first four books that the author's own feelings can be detected in his main characters. They believe in life's possibilities, so does he. They believe that they have a *self* that is the basis of their continuity and development and so does he. They are aware of fragmentation but they are determined to find wholeness. They feel restlessness and agitation but never give up on the quest for harmony. The author shares in his characters' belief in the possibility of belief.

But for Selvon, by the 1960s, things had undeniably fallen apart. In *The Mimic Men*, V.S. Naipaul allows the central figure Ralph Singh to describe his reduction in London, "this feeling of being adrift, a cell of perception, little more" (26); "the panic of ceasing to feel myself as a whole person", the disfiguring effect of the great city where "[t]hose of us who came to it lost some of our solidity; we were trapped into fixed flat postures" (27). Later on, Ralph Singh is made to connect these phenomena to the end of "the [short-lived] empires of our time" and to declare his wish as an author "to give expression to the restlessness, the deep disorder, which the great explorations, the overthrow in three continents of established social organizations, the unnatural bringing together of peoples" had brought about; and Singh, without quite realizing it, falls in with other refugees from other upheavals sheltering in London (32).

Although Selvon's *Londoners* balances the pleasures of exile with the harshness of immigrant life it is clear as the book progresses that Selvon's fiction of 1956 is already registering the great disorder and the reductions explicitly named in *The Mimic Men* ten years later. In the famous "The old Moses, standing on the banks of the Thames" passage at the end of the book, Moses sees "a great aimlessness, a great restless, swaying movement that leaving you standing in the same spot", he imagines "black faces bobbing up and down in the millions of white, strained faces", and he penetrates to the nameless, "a kind of misery and pathos and a frightening – what?" (142).

I put this extremely and bluntly because discussion is necessary. It seems to me that after 1956 the Selvon preoccupations of the early writings were returning and with a vengeance. Belief was receding. A cynicism was taking hold. The disorder and the diminution of the person that lurk in *The Lonely Londoners* enter the writing in *Moses Ascending* and *Moses Migrating*; in these two books, Selvon has lost faith in the existence of people like Tiger, Foster and the first Moses who are believers in the existence of a self and in the fulfilment of life's possibilities. When Selvon returned to the Moses figure after nearly twenty years, the use of pastiche and parody, the farce, the burlesque, the bawdiness and the slapstick, the extravagant linguistic concoctions all speak of a writer and a man increasingly aware of the breakdown of order, purpose and value. Selvon's art of characterization in these two books changes drastically. Nobody can know the character and the character doesn't know himself. Selvon is writing less about the person than about a challenging situation in which language itself has broken down and the notion of the old stable ego of the personality has receded. The Moses figure is a device for expressing dislocation, fragmentation and disorder. To understand the other Selvon of these later works, and the depth of achievement in the first four books, we have to go far back to the passionate believer of the very early works.

NOTES

1. This fact is borne out by Vahni Capildeo's discussion of reader response in the following chapter.
2. For examples of this, see "As Time Goes By", "He Is Going to Die", and "The Life of a Day" in *Foreday Morning*.

CHAPTER TWO

A Brighter Sun:
"I Still Want to See How the Story Unfolds"
– Conversations with a Novel

Vahni Capildeo

S amuel Selvon's achievement deserves celebration. A creator promoting his country, he loosens form, distilling language. Austin Clarke, hearing Selvon's broadcasts, gave thanks: "all this was to make us feel 'we was people, too'" (Clarke et al. 16). This piece presents a stylization of the reactions of non-academic women readers familiar with *A Brighter Sun*'s environment to the book itself.[1] Their perspectives register the ever-recalibrated balance of a work during the process of reading and re-reading.

I.

Roydon Salick, in the introduction to his study of Selvon's novels, soon mentions occasional "anomalies" in Selvon's work; notably in *A Brighter Sun,* the young hero Tiger's wedding, apparently Hindu, is fêted with cattle slaughter and a meat feast: impossible in a context of ritual vegetarianism. Salick, recalling Selvon's later admission that he preferred not to describe what he did not know, asserts that "Selvon's fiction is such that the inaccuracies and anomalies do not destroy or taint our aesthetic pleasure, although they may raise niggling issues of authenticity, especially for cultural purists" (*The Novels* 4). There are, however, aesthetic grounds for objecting to these "anomalies". Such slips encourage readers who know the novel's world to stop enjoying and start fact-checking, refocusing on intentionality and the author/narrator. In such instances, the novelistic creation re-presents itself as documentary and its point of failure in factual accuracy is where knowledgeable readers lose access to the fiction's pleasures. Such a group of readers as a target audience could not have existed at the time of publication (1952): literacy in English was low among the community the novel reflects. However, inheritor-readers – Tiger's descendants – become co-writers, searching memory, composing unrecorded parallels. Reader and book split into an "us" and an "it", the artefact before the reader's eyes thus displaces itself. There is a sense that, whatever this novel achieves, the novel remains unwritten that would represent the quotidian life and hopes of a tranche of the islands: the diverse Indian communities, which were creolizing in their own fashion, though not necessarily by focusing on urbanization or the erasure of Hinduism, Sikhism or Islam. The story is not spoilt: Selvon is too good for that. But it cannot be the same.

A Brighter Sun's chapters begin with a news flash-style current affairs overview, hauling the unwritten country into being. This technique can make the reader thirst for the storyteller to tell everything there is to tell. Salick calls for an investigation of the place of "lived experience" in the novel (166) in the face of critics often taking for granted the historical homogeneity of its "Indian" community, and forgetting Selvon's levelling was an artistic device to cover his own remoteness from non-Christian, non-urban material. This piece answers Salick's call. It is not about politics, or dutiful "representative" art. It is about the unwritten who read actively, not in self-effacing wonder. Their personal reminiscences can be read alongside Selvon, as memoirs or unwritten stories impinging on and interacting with his universe, forming part of the paratext, adding to the context of understanding.

II.

Candid reactions from three women readers can throw light on the nature of this encounter. "Girija" and "Uma" were born in the 1930s, "Janaki" in the 1960s. All are university educated. Girija is from a moderate Hindu family in rural East Trinidad/Port of Spain, Uma from a creolized central Trinidad/Port of Spain background, Janaki from a traditional Hindu family, moving between urban and rural. Girija's introduction sets the background for the non-Christianized families who, in *A Brighter Sun*, remain somewhat opaque and levelled:

> My father was born in 1898. He used to talk to me a lot when I was a child [...] The Canadian Mission (Presbyterian) had gone up to Sangre Chiquito to convert the Indians. My father went to their elementary school, leaving at the normal age of ten or twelve. There was no school for him to go to after that unless he went to Port-of-Spain. If he had converted to Presbyterianism, he could have become a pupil-teacher at twelve and gone on to teach and get a job. My father wasn't very Hindu. He just didn't want to change. He was himself. He had different jobs in different places: tailoring; dancing, cocoa [...] He became a store clerk and eventually ran his own store.

Uma is concerned to establish that Selvon worked at the *Trinidad Guardian* with Seepersad Naipaul, who would have discussed his own stories, becoming a source of information. Girija notes that Seepersad is a better comparison than V.S. Naipaul, who was urbanized and does not deal with the same communities as the older writers. Interestingly, Janaki notes that her parents, who belonged to the place and "the time Selvon wrote about", were not a target audience because they were "literary in Hindi but non-literary in English."

Whether and how arranged marriages like Tiger's were "in vogue" at all in the 1950s causes heated discussion. These readers provide a rich context, throwing light on the aesthetic motivations of much criticism of the wedding scene in the novel. Girija recalls,

> [a]t the time of *A Brighter Sun*, arranged marriages were very common, but arranged in a different way from the generation before. It wasn't that they didn't see each other. The boy would be taken to see the girl. She might go into the kitchen to get something. He would seize his chance to look at the cupboard, measuring her height to see if he was taller. And there were love matches. Two young people might notice each other and request a family introduction. The prospective groom would pay the bride's family social visits and talk to the bride-to-be.

She remembers Rookmin's wedding in 1944. The twenty-one-year-old Kshatriya bridegroom and his entourage arrive at the Brahmin bride's house by car. He wears a crown with torchlight bulbs going on and off, a pink robe and gold necklace. The women have dressed nineteen-year-old Rookmin in yellow. Two accompany her; her mother holds her arm, leading her to sit in the tent. The bride's mother is just thirty-six and draws the most compliments. Pink groom and yellow bride sit opposite, then next to each other, without looking at each other. Traditional male dancers perform the story of a king and his blue-sequined queen.

A generation younger, Janaki nonetheless agrees that "the sense of colour" is what, for her, is absent from Tiger's wedding:

> The first thing you have to understand about a wedding like that is the colour, the crowd, the chaos, the music…and it is beautiful. The fundamentals have to be there in any description. Poorer families sometimes have bigger weddings because they are less selective about the guest list. People traditionally would help out by dropping off 100 pounds of potatoes, flour, and so on. The bride dresses three times in three different colours, characteristically red, yellow and one other colour.

Selvon's women characters' sari-wearing astounds everyone. Uma exclaims: "Nobody wore saris! When my sister came back from university in India and wore saris, in Trinidad she was a phenomenon". Girija qualified this: "We came from a part of India where they wore a gangri (long skirt), jhulla (blouse) and an orhni (veil) tied at the waist, over one shoulder and the head, like how the upper part of a sari looks. The first Indian movie shown here, in the 40s, made people start wanting to dress up in saris for special events.

Attention kept circling back to the wedding, showing how the novel's fictionality explodes and turns informed readers into realist critics (not to say let-down "subjects"). Janaki, traditionally educated, explains in detail:

> The ceremonial bath isn't captured right. It should be given by several adults and the whole outfit the girl wears must be discarded. And you would only have done the rub down with hardi (turmeric) and chandan (sandalwood paste) on the Friday and Saturday, not for days. I'd still give the story the

benefit of the doubt, but the goats and sheep are a severe mistake. The wedding is tantamount to a puja. Even nowadays you can see in a car park people liming round cars with their drinks, but they won't carry alcohol in the consecrated area. It doesn't make sense to talk about portraying a generalized 'Indian'. That's not proper social commentary at all. It's like a Muslim eating pork.

Uma and Girija, from the older, outspoken generation of Trinidad and Tobago, are brought up short by the "ridiculous" and "very offensive" wedding. The novelistic levelling strategy is noted and rejected: "You can't make a unified portrayal of 'Indians' as the 'whatever' vs. Christian/creolized. Hindu and Christian are as different as Muslim and Hindu. But this was clearly meant to be a Hindu wedding: the red powder, the white sheet". Janaki and Girija note further that the sheet would have been "coloured or fancy"; in the 1940s, and to some extent today, white was the Hindu mourning colour, worn by widows. "It is kind of fundamental with the metaphors," Janaki sighs.

Education and creolization as the way out for Selvon's characters also provoked discussion and recreation of context. While Girija remarks on the lack of opportunity: "The Presbyterian Mission had not converted deep into the countryside, and the colonial government never put schools in those areas", Uma recalls an unrecorded diversity:

> Something you would see a lot in the country areas would be somebody sitting down reading the newspapers in English and translating them into Hindi for a whole circle of people. People spoke a lot of different languages: Hindi, Bhojpuri and other varieties and the translator would be able to translate into these. There were people who could have read if they had had the papers in Hindi script, particularly the Brahmins; though my father didn't read or write any Hindi.

There are further reminiscences about bilingualism and informal or organized attempts to teach both boys and girls Hindi and Sanskrit.

The idea of as yet unwritten stories from this community kept resurfacing, sometimes as extended reveries. How many potential novelists simply were sidetracked by circumstance? Could "writing back" now counterbalance the canonical accounts by Selvon, the Naipauls, et al.? Girija dreams of setting another scene:

> If I wrote a story with a hero from the canefield, he would get up early. The family would make food on the chulha (cowdung and earth oven), tie it up in a bundle and take it to the canefield, where the wife and husband usually worked together. The wife would stay home a bit to look after the child – then they would take the child out with them to keep an eye. The wife would mind the house only if the couple was better off. Big children would look after younger ones, cook and take food to their parents in the field. There would be no school to go to. In 1956 I taught the first set of children to go for education in a school the Sanaatan Dharma Maha Sabha had started in 1952. The children

did housework before and after school, once they were eight or nine and could
sweep and cook. They were very clean, neat, hair well combed. Hence this
revulsion towards going back and working the land. It represents the hardest
time in the life of the Indian. Today the attitude persists that agriculture is
backward.

Tiger's wife, Urmilla, also attracts these women's interest. Girija questions the
premise:

> The whole idea in that kind of family is: bring the bride to live in the house and
> help the mother. My mother-in-law ended up with one family in each room
> and one family in the pantry and one in the servant's room. And in areas like
> Pasea, families lived in long wooden barracks. No way was it the custom for
> the married couple to go back to the bride's house as part of the ceremony. The
> bride would be taken back home.

Uma, of the same generation, agrees: "A hut in Barataria! They had to go and
live in their own house? That was hardly likely. They wouldn't be going off to her
house or to a house of his own. And at that age Tiger would not have been able to
or expected to leave to make his own living."

Janaki, more modern yet with a more traditional upbringing, is moved at
this point not to critical commentary about the past, but to her own speculative
rewriting and her desire for another kind of story:

> Not sufficient attention is paid to the woman's journey. Hindu women's
> personalities are composite: very powerful in terms of sexuality, but that aspect
> is not explored in literature, more the stereotypes of the beaten wife, the
> alcoholic's wife, the woman deprived of education who ties herself up for her
> children. Has any writer truly captured the heart of the Indian parent? It's as if
> novelists want to scold them for being self-sacrificing. They are depicted as just
> pitted against the younger generation. Hindu parents dote. That doting can be
> confused with stupidity. It is not necessarily so. The community is progressing
> on the foundation, however ill-defined, put there by their parents.

Girija continues to ponder aspects of gender and class in relation to Urmilla's
situation, measuring the novel's depiction against what she knows from her own
experience in East Trinidad:

> It is a sign of oppression that Urmilla was called a whore for putting on makeup
> when most non-Indian women did. The Indian women of that generation I
> knew were mostly overpowdered, but hardly wore lipstick. Some wore lots of
> home-made kajal on their eyes. No Western eye makeup. But it varied: my
> mother wore powder, foundation, Tangee lipstick, perfume, high heels and
> stockings, and put some perfume on Pa, when they were going out. And it
> changed over time. I remember Hindu girls wearing dresses just under the
> knee. No cleavage. A little sleeve, not arm holes. My eldest sister didn't wear
> trousers. When I was 14, in 1952, I asked Pa to make me a pair of jeans. He
> said OK, but he was a little surprised because blue dock – it wasn't called denim
> then – was what prisoners wore. He asked me if I was sure, and made them.

Again diversity is notable; levelled horizons featuring aspirant Tiger-individuals open kaleidoscopically, showing modernization or creolization naturally developing, not necessarily with reference to Port of Spain, education or Christianity. Girija's commentary on the situation of women demonstrates this:

> Urmilla might have been of the level where you didn't address your husband directly; but there was very much variation, according to money, education, community status (your job, your caste). Typically women preferred talking to other women. But husband and wife would discuss important decisions. I knew families where the children didn't talk to the father, and the mother didn't talk in front of the children to the father. The father would come in, eat his food, and go to his room. The children would disappear. The wife would go in after him. She would never let herself be heard raising her voice to her husband. But every family I knew was different. Mine all sat down, sang songs, played games [...] My parents talked normally. At night I heard them talking until late, discussing things in quiet serious voices. The "typical Indian woman" was made up by people who mistook the absence of challenge in public for general docility.

All three readers are preoccupied by the degree and type of mutual everyday knowledge of Presbyterians and Hindus; these Hindu respondents report on misperceptions, and their Presbyterian cousins', colleagues' and neighbours' confidence in their insight. This material is extensive and provocative, requiring more space to analyze and different criteria from those in this chapter.

Finally, these women, close to the life and times in which *A Brighter Sun* is rooted, do not seek their reflection: they are a new generation of readers excited to venture into fiction. The fiction's own contradictory impingement on their reality turns them critical. This testimony has anthropological and paratextual value. These readers need to be reconceived as writers of both past and future.

Uma sums up:

> It does matter to get the things right. Books record the times you live in, as films and photographs do. For historical reasons it should be correct. The facts are wrong. The author is not free, in a multiethnic, multicultural society. If I see a book, I want to get information that is true and relevant to the time. Anyone can tell a story, in a way. For it to have meaning, it must be based on something that can make people think, make people aware.

Girija voices the curiosity that is the life of fiction:

> The narrator speaks with so much authority. But the wedding scene makes me see he was making up things about a community he didn't know about. He put what would pass. I feel angry because he has misrepresented a very important Vivah Samskar [sacrament] [...] The anger makes me curious to read the book to see what he has done with other things. It'll make me look out for the mistakes in Hindu things but also to see what he says about everything else. I'm willing to trust everything he says about Port-of-Spain, the legislative

community, the U.S. base, the prostitutes in town, the children playing in Dry River and so on. I trust these things because I'm checking them against my own experience, not because of the book's tone. And I still want to see how the story unfolds.

NOTE

1.   Special thanks to the Byragie Marajh family and to Savi Naipaul Akal.

CHAPTER THREE

A Man Who Knows His Capabilities and His Limitations is Benign to Papa Bois: On Omniscience, Autonomy and Paternal Authority in *Turn Again Tiger* and *Those Who Eat the Cascadura*

Lewis MacLeod

> My son, do not despise the Lord's discipline and do not resent his rebuke.
> — Proverbs 3:11–12

> The eyes of the Lord are everywhere, keeping watch on the wicked and the good.
> — Proverbs 15:3

*M*ore than fifteen years ago, Wayne Brown's essay "A Greatness and a Vastness: The Search for God in the Fiction of Sam Selvon", rightly and insightfully objected to the "distorting" effects that "staunch sociological moulds" of criticism had on Sam Selvon's fiction (35). Instead of reducing Selvon to "elaborations of simple racial distress" (35), Brown argued that "the essential impulse propelling [Selvon's] fiction was the search for God" (39). About ten years ago, I made a similar objection, claiming that self-consciously "progressive" strains in postcolonial discourse have worked "to kidnap certain sections of [Selvon's] work and force them into ill-fitting analytical frameworks aligned with particular political projects" (157). I argued that "discourses of masculinity [might] provide a critical apparatus that approaches (and [...] reaches) Selvon" in new and productive ways (158).

Here, I'd like to look at Selvon's under-addressed novels *Turn Again Tiger* and *Those Who Eat the Cascadura* to suggest that the search for God and the quest for masculine legitimacy might run together through notions of God the Father, or, alternately, the Father as God in his fiction. I don't mean this in any rigorously theological sense, but I do think that Selvon's sense of divinity was closely linked to matters to do with origin (as opposed to derivation), authority (as opposed to subordination), "presence" (as opposed to absence) and overarching knowledge (as opposed to finitude and ignorance). In every case, the Patriarch occupies the dominant pole.

Although family life has virtually no presence in Selvon's London novels, his Trinidad novels repeatedly involve almost mythic scenarios in which "the rule of the father" is enacted upon and/or contested by subordinates who are variously feminized or infantilized. To "be a man," is to escape the situating and subordinating function of some larger, more powerful, paternalistic force. In Selvon's fiction, the religious impulse toward "something higher" is registered in terms of an endlessly deferred and inconclusive movement into unambiguously masculine certitude and authority. Crudely, the "greatness" and "vastness" Brown sees in theistic terms might well be rearticulated in terms of the magnitude (greatness) and scope (vastness) of a patriarchal authority presented in specifically paternal and paternalistic terms. Thomas Pavel has argued that:

> the universe of societies that believe in myths unfolds at two different levels: the profane reality, characterized by ontological paucity and precariousness, contrasts with a mythical level, ontologically self-sufficient, containing a privileged space and a cyclical time. Gods and heroes inhabit the sacred space. (77)

With Brown, I regard Selvon's world as one deeply invested in the mythic, preoccupied with the distinction between ontological self-sufficiency and ontological paucity, and inclined to devalue a profane reality in order to (vainly) pursue a privileged and secure position in space and time. Paternal authority and power are seen as a means of entering the omniscient and omnipotent world of "Gods and heroes"; the absence of such powers signals an abject and impotent position.

As the title suggests, R.W. Connell's *The Men and the Boys* sees masculine legitimacy in precisely these kinds of "relations of hierarchy" (10), relations by which divergently articulated and enacted masculinities are legitimized, de-legitimized or rendered unintelligible. "Hegemonic masculinity is [...] defined negatively," she claims, "as the opposite of femininity [and] [s]ubordinated masculinities are symbolically assimilated to femininity (e.g. abuse of 'sissies', 'nancy-boys')" (31). Selvon's staging of these problems borders on the obsessive, as manhood constantly threatens to devolve into some kind of subordinated femininity. His first novel, *A Brighter Sun*, opens when his protagonist, Tiger, forcibly "comes-of-age" when he is compelled to marry as the result of an arrangement orchestrated by his father, Babolal: "Tiger didn't know anything about [his] wedding until his father told him. He didn't even know the girl" (4). From the outset, Tiger regards his apparent emancipation into manhood and masculine authority in terms of his situatedness and subordination: "The whole affair had been arranged for him; he didn't have anything to do with it" (5). His transition into manhood is a study in powerlessness, and he constantly wishes "he knew more about what was going to happen to him" (5). Tiger's emergence into manhood, then, is a straightforward function of his boyhood, insofar as he becomes a man according to his father's wishes; he becomes a man by being a good and docile (and consequently feminized) son.

In her generally persuasive essay on the novel, Janice Cools suggests that *A Brighter Sun* depicts masculinity in the following binary fashion: "If he is not a 'man' he is a 'boy' and if he is not a 'boy' he is a 'man'" (131). Originally, however, the opposite seems to be true. Tiger becomes a man because he is being a "good boy," and the apparent collapse of the man/boy binary is at the root of his manifold anxieties. He seeks absolute authority over his newly established household, yet both his authority and his household are structured by and contained within a larger notion of subordinating filial duty. He thinks that being "a big man" involves learning "to do things without the assistance of other people" (13), but the marriage which initiates and constitutes his manhood is itself an act of assistance to the ostensibly autonomous patriarch he both resents and seeks to emulate. In *A Brighter Sun*, then, much of the tension centres on divergent articulations of "belonging." Tiger is deprived of the comforts of boyhood and "belonging *together*" in his family. He is forced into "being a man" *even though* his independent manhood is a function of a different and more belligerent sense of his "belonging *to*" Babolal, of being his father's manipulable object. Even Tiger's paternity can be read as a function of Babolal's originary scheme. Throughout the novel, Tiger's confused and claustrophobic meditations indicate there is no greatness and no vastness in either the manhood or the paternity he feels are thrust upon him.

In *Turn Again Tiger*, things open in decidedly different terms. Tiger has "settled in" to married life and he begins the narrative as a knowledgeable and authoritative head of household. Almost immediately, however, he is compelled into an anxious re-negotiation of his filial duty when Babolal asks for his help in pursuing a business opportunity in Five Rivers. Babolal makes his case to Tiger in the following terms:

> "The thing is, you was the only boy-child I ever had, and I ain't have nobody to help me out with this new plan. What you think about going to Five Rivers with me and helping me with the cane? [...] All of we could live together [...] I not asking you to leave Urmilla and the child. All of we is family". (3)

Tiger's immediate response is telling: "I don't know why you say 'we'" (3). Tiger's relationship with his father precludes the mutualism of "we". Babolal strategically proposes a kind of "belonging together" sense of family unity, which Tiger perceives only in terms dominance and subordination, or, perhaps better, origin and derivation, as "belonging to" his father. Intuitively, Babolal figures himself as the maker of a "plan," his son as helper, duplicating the earlier arrangement by which the father provides structure and the son provides aid. "Don't think I want your advice, boy," Babolal says, "I just telling you" (3).

Tiger responds to this threat of subordination and containment with an exaggerated emphasis on his own weightedness and potency. When his father suggests that Tiger ought, again, to be situated inside his grand designs, Tiger foregrounds instead the degree to which his father *is currently* contained within a context of Tiger's own construction: "That chair you sitting in […] I work hard to buy it. The paint on the wall was expensive" (3). Tiger sees his walls and his furniture as existential as well as literal structures, as frameworks that make his own identity intelligible, as portals to ontological self-sufficiency; they provide the conditions by which an autonomous "I" becomes coherent. The prospect of abandoning his "house and garden [to] go back to work in canefield!" (5) is frightening to him and he tells his father, "I am not going to give up all I have to go and work with you" (4).

I do not wish to oversell this point, but the phrasing is significant. He figures working *with* his father (he would never admit to anything framed as working "for" him) as a move both backwards ("back to the canefield") and down (he must give everything "up"), as counter to his empire-building, self-authenticating project. He repeats the words of his neighbor, Joe, that "living with family does cause trouble" (5), but he means this only in the intergenerational sense proposed by Babolal. "Living with family" is masculine credential insofar as Tiger's house, wife and child are visible demonstrations of *his* proficiency as progenitor and breadwinner. "Living with Dad" has the reverse effect, as the re-introduction of *his* father precludes Tiger's own primacy and subordinates his masculinity into his father's, a fact made clear when Tiger anxiously points out that, if they all live together, his wife "Urmilla go have to do everything for him, too" (5).

This need to preserve his own sense of primacy is the consistency which underlies Tiger's manifold inconsistencies. Repeatedly, Tiger seeks conclusive signifiers which confirm his masculine legitimacy, the greatness of his power and the vastness of his scope. Early on, he marvels at the fact that, "it was easy to grow up, to become a man […] You worried about it and you wondered what it was going to be like, then one day you were a man, you were right into manhood, and nothing much had happened" (6–7). For Tiger, of course, "ease" isn't very easy. The apparent easiness of the transition into manhood is a source of anxiety because its very naturalness entails inconclusiveness and suggests incompleteness. Masculine legitimacy is simultaneously venerated as a matter of utmost importance and reduced to the commonplace of "nothing much had happened."

In *Manhood in the Making*, David Gilmore recognizes the anxiety inherent in an inconclusive and unverifiable masculinity. For Gilmore, hegemonic masculinity is a matter of "visible, concrete accomplishments" (36), a demonstrable achievement rather than an "easy" or default transition. For this reason, Tiger constantly seeks to make his manhood "happen" like an event, and he repeatedly seeks occasions and structures which will make his legitimacy visible and concrete. In his behaviour toward Babolal, Tiger demonstrates his strength and agency through his refusal of his father's plan, yet this urge toward demonstration and differentiation means that only opposition can register as an assertion of identity. Any form of agreement registers as capitulation, capitulation registers as containment, containment as feminized or filial subordination. Agreement is the stuff of boys and women; contestation is the stuff of real men.

After loudly decrying his father's proposal to Joe, Tiger comes home and asks Urmilla what she thinks about "the nonsense [Babolal] was talking" (6). Urmilla says, "I too glad you deciding not to go" (6). In his anxiety, Tiger registers Urmilla's affirmation as foreclosure. He doesn't feel as if she's agreeing with him so much as forcing him into a corner, reducing his options; his reaction is swift: "Who tell you I decide not to go? [...] Come to think of it, [...] is not such a bad idea, after all" (6). Anxious to avoid what he regards as a feminizing and infantilizing reduction of his scope, Tiger (here and elsewhere) reverts to the role of "wife beater and domestic tyrant" in an effort to strengthen his fragile sense of his own potency. Domestic bullying is derived from a larger "struggle against nonentity and nothingness" (Ramchand, "Calling All Dragons" 314). As a result, Tiger's self-definition as patriarch entails both isolation and perpetual opposition; it is negatively defined against both his father and his wife *even when* father and wife occupy categorically opposite positions. In Jonathan Rutherford's terms, Tiger is among many men who are determined to evade "those spaces which threaten fusion and the loss of self." The result is predictable: "invariably male heroism can only ever be a solitary pursuit" (129). To be an ontologically self-sufficient God or hero, is, it seems, to be antagonistic and alone.

Tiger needs to demonstrate to everybody that he can make his mind up for himself, but this means that "his mind" becomes reflexive and reactionary, devoid of any stable content. After his strenuous and high-volume demonstrations of his own pervasive authority, Tiger seems fickle and irresolute rather than stern and decisive. "Tiger boy," Joe says, "one thing with you, your mind not hard to change" (12). Perversely, then, Tiger's exaggerated performance of masculinized scope and authority (his greatness and vastness), figures him in terms which seem to come straight from feminist theory. "It is useless," Luce Irigaray famously claimed, "to trap women in the exact definition of what they mean, to make them repeat (themselves) so that it will be clear; they are already elsewhere [...] And if you ask them insistently what they are thinking about, they can only reply: Nothing. Everything" (*This Sex* 29).

This anxious linkage between the inconclusive "nothing" and "everything" of a subordinated feminized subjectivity and the de-situated "greatness and vastness" of its Godlike masculinized counterpart is particularly significant in Selvon's fiction, populated as it is with sensitive and physically unimposing, "force-ripe" men (Selvon, *Turn Again* 38) who feel trapped in a culture which regards "artistic expression and the tender emotions as womanish and likely to undermine manliness" (Ramchand, "Calling All Dragons" 323). The œdipal conflict between Babolal and Tiger is simultaneously a conflict between Babolal's "elemental" and physical masculinity (defined by "the developed muscle, the hardened bone" [Selvon, *Turn Again* 35]) and a less visible, more abstract masculinity rooted in literacy and linguistic dexterity, which favours Tiger. As tensions between the two escalate, the outraged and incredulous Babolal hisses: "Boy [...] who learn you to disrespect your father? Is all them books you reading?" (35–36). Babolal regards Tiger's burgeoning authority as part of "all that knowledge business" (36) that baffles and frustrates him and he seeks to make his own mastery and primacy visible through a concrete and conclusive physical confrontation. For Tiger, to be "caught in his father's powerful arms" is to be "done for" (36), to have his hard-won autonomy suspended or destroyed. For Babolal, physical supremacy is necessary to redress the marginality his illiteracy entails and to assuage the shame he feels because he has "had to seek his young son's counsel" (2); he needs physical mastery to compensate for discursive inferiority. As ever, the struggle is for primacy and control, a test to see who belongs to whom, if the son belongs to the father or the father now belongs to the son. Babolal must "tame his son [...] or else suffer the indignity of being beholden to Tiger" (36). Tiger must evade "the grip of steel" (35) his father's authority encodes and enforces.

Given the above conditions, it is hardly surprising that issues of oversight, control and containment dominate the novel. Babolal originally explains the nature of the job in Five Rivers in terms of infinite oversight and unimpeded jurisdiction. "[T]hey offering me a job, to supervise everything" (3), he says, and as the novel progresses the legitimacy of this claim of Godlike omniscience becomes a matter of enormous significance. The roles of foreman, overseer, and supervisor are minutely distinguished, each delineating a specific level of potency and establishing hierarchical relations between overarching patriarchs and their variously defined subordinates. As Tiger gradually becomes aware that "sooner or later a white man would turn up to whom he would have to give account" (43), his fantasies of agency and scope crumble.

And, given the apparent impossibility of fraternity or mutualism (the hardwired nature of paternal and filial hierarchies), any lack of oversight entails some corresponding degree of being overseen. If "the job [isn't] a supervising one after all" (43), then it necessarily entails being supervised, and Tiger feels himself reverting to "the picture printed in on his memory [of] when he was a little boy working in Chaguanas with his father" (47). In "The Situation of the Looker-On", Beth Newman persuasively argues that "the role of onlooker [is] the conventional position of the masculine spectator with respect to the feminine spectacle". Such a scenario establishes "the narrator as [a] voyeur defending himself against the threat of the feminine by objectifying a woman, by telling her story, writing it down [...] and seeking in his oblique way to make it—and her—his own" (1034). For Newman, the links between oversight and ownership are clear: "looking [is] telling" and uninterrupted observation "works in the service of regulating the family [...] to preserve order for the male head of the house" (1035). And, as Tiger's original anxieties about his father's plan make clear, there can only be one head of household. His decision to leave Barataria, then, is almost instantaneously felt as a catastrophic error. He leaves a scenario of unambiguous and originary authority and oversight to enter into a world of manifold contestation and subordination.

This telescopic sense of multiple subordinations is played out in terms of a double process by which the roles of hegemonic masculinity and subordinated femininity are reversed. In *Turn Again Tiger* the role of the white overseer, Robinson, is ultimately minor relative to the role of his wife, Doreen, who becomes the greatest challenge to Tiger's sense of masculine legitimacy. Doreen enters the narrative in what ought to be a straightforward scenario of feminized sexual spectacle processed and contained by an authoritative masculine voyeur/narrator. Unaware that she is being watched, Doreen is swimming naked with her back turned to Tiger such that "it [is] as if the water and the sun made her skin glow" (48). Instead of erotic interest, however, Tiger feels a blank and paralyzing fear. To a degree, this fear is motivated both by a general anxiety about trespassing on "the white man's land" and by more specific internalized injunctions not to "go near the overseer's house [and to] turn your head away if you see the white man's wife" (49).

This is fairly straightforward stuff, but it is wrong to imagine the scene as one in which Tiger is primarily fearful of the overseer's proxy power over an object he values. Instead, Tiger is explicitly afraid of Doreen's subjectivity. When she gazes at and calls out to Tiger, he feels "embarrassed that she was looking at him, as if he were the naked one in the water" (50). This specular reversal is prophetic and telling. He fears not so much her husband's power but the female appropriation of the situating function: female oversight. As Newman puts it: "[i]n assuming the role of spectator, [woman] seeks a 'masculine' position that because she is a woman, redefines her as a 'monster' or 'witch'" (1032). This triggers an anxiety about the uncanny ability of the female to titillate (when passive) and terrify (when active). "We have not far to travel," Newman writes, from "'fascinating creature' to Freud's 'Medusa Head,' the direct sight of which evokes the terror of castration in the male spectator" (1030–31). As an object, Doreen is a potential site for authoritative masculine oversight and sexual performance/contemplation.

As a subject, she compromises Tiger's sense of oversight, mastery and control. Although she enters the narrative naked, the clothes she has discarded by the water look "like a man's clothing" (48) to Tiger, and her apparently superior specular and structural positions threaten Tiger with emasculation and subordination. From the outset, then, Doreen is an uneasy blend of erotic enticement (insofar as she is a naked female and Tiger is male) and disciplinary power (insofar as she structures and situates both his desire and—by proxy—his financial well-being).

Once he flees Doreen's presence, Tiger finds himself "slashing at [a] bush" (52) which he mentally transforms into an image of her. Shielded from her direct presence, Tiger symbolically disciplines a satisfactorily inanimate vision of Doreen, *then* engages in the erotic reverie her terrifying presence forestalls. When he imaginatively summons up a vision of her "white and magnificent under the fall of water" (52) he feels "a belated desire as the picture floated in his mind" (52). The distinction between a contained pornographic "picture" that "floats" in the mind and a substantive and active woman is a significant one; the picture soothes away the anxiety an actual woman produces.

It is Doreen, not her husband, who ultimately functions as literal and figurative overseer of Tiger. As he feels himself being subordinated by her disciplinary gaze, he begins an anxious itemization of his masculine credentials: "He, Tiger, who had his own house, who had a wife and a child, who worked with the Americans during the war, who drank rum with men and discussed big things like Life and Death, who could read and write" (51). Almost helplessly, however, he volunteers to be her yardboy, to put himself directly under her supervision, and she functions as an unseen but constant presence in his life, as the ontologically self-sufficient authority that confirms his ontological paucity. His muttering of "Doreen, Doreen, Doreen" (63) as involuntary incantation makes this clear. Acutely aware of his own subordination, Tiger rejects the sources of his own authority, burning his books and reverting to a self-anaesthetizing alcoholism. If literacy once made Tiger a "top man in the village" (38), his growing sense of masculine inadequacy leads him to reject books and their claims toward mastery and control. When he burns his books, Tiger claims that "Plato, Aristotle, Shakespeare [...] ain't help me to solve nothing" (112).

Of course, it is precisely the "solving" impulse that Tiger must learn to avoid. Tiger originally sees books as a way of bringing the world under his control and oversight, of entering into the greatness and vastness, of expanding his jurisdiction and authority. He has always regarded knowledge as a way of locking down and *solving* the world rather than opening it up. When Doreen looks at Tiger, he feels himself contained within her larger design and feels the futility of his own strategies of containment. When he sees her "looking at him through the window" (145) of her house, he sees himself as feminized spectacle rather than patriarchal force. In many ways the abrupt and violent sexual encounter between Doreen and Tiger duplicates and serves the same function as the earlier fistfight between Babolal and Tiger. He needs a physical and literal confrontation to free himself from the feminizing/infantilizing situating forces he despises. It is significant, then, that the chapter following his sexual encounter with Doreen opens with a meditation on Urmilla's pregnancy. The implication seems clear: when Tiger frees himself from infantilized subordination through confrontation with Doreen, he enters (or, perhaps, re-enters) the world of paternal authority, and the new child confirms his regulatory power and biological primacy. As a visible, concrete accomplishment, progeneration seems to re-establish Tiger as a real man; the "results" prove his potency.

This is partly true, yet there is a crucial revision here. Asked by some undefined interrogator if he wants "a boy-child," Tiger expresses for the first time his comfort with his own limitations. "Whatever come, come. What is to is, must is" (149). Asked how a man "who could read and write" could have allowed "a white lady [...] to have you like a little boy" (150), Tiger refigures masculine legitimacy in terms of what can be endured more than what can be surveyed, known and controlled: "[a] man could stand anything" (150). At the end of the novel, Tiger's various exercises in humility make it possible for him to conceive of greatness and vastness in terms that aren't explicitly self-aggrandizing. As he returns from working in the canefield, he is grateful to be reunited with his daughter and his wife, happy to accept the forces of fusion he previously rejected. Reminded that a new life, "perhaps the greatest thing of all" (181), is on the way, he is at peace with a greatness that isn't vast and doesn't directly belong to him.

In *Those Who Eat the Cascadura*, concerns about oversight and authority are revisited in ways both distinct from and similar to those in *Turn Again Tiger*. The novel again foregrounds the function of literacy and storytelling relative to other discourses of mastery and control, this time through the characters of Prekash, a young Indian, and Garry, a somewhat disreputable visitor from England. Like Tiger, Prekash uses "book knowledge" (29), to establish himself in "a sort of overseeing position" (29), but, as with Tiger, he routinely discovers that this sort of oversight never escapes its subordination within the larger discourses from which its parasitic authority is derived. When Garry turns an ambivalently defined vacation in Trinidad into the occasion for writing a book about obeah, he seems to do so not out of an anthropological interest in self-authenticating cultural practices so much as a condescending practice of containment and knowledge, as a way of domesticating mystery and making it subject to his narrative processes.

By now, we recognize these constructions and the authoritative and disciplinary patriarchal positions to which they aspire. Even more than *Turn Again Tiger*, however, *Cascadura* involves pronounced meditation on the nature of patriarchal pretences toward omniscience. This is partly a straightforward matter of position. *Turn Again Tiger* is preoccupied with subordinated masculinities and the circuitous routes through which they seek power, while *Cascadura* is directly concerned with dominant discourses. The novel is replete with failed or absent patriarchs, and with gross miscalculations as regards the appropriate jurisdiction(s) of hegemonic masculine authority.

The novel opens with Roger, a white plantation owner, regarding his wife's death as a positive thing. Her death registers as an escape from the social and sexual containment of marriage. "He had only married her because he thought she was pregnant, and when that proved false he came to Trinidad to get away from the dreary burden of living with someone he didn't love" (13). From the outset, then, a discourse juxtaposing desire and containment is made clear. Rather than regard the idea of his wife's pregnancy as validation of his potency, Roger feels *eros* dissolve into *thanatos*, expansive sexual energy reduced to a "dreary burden." This is what Barbara Ehrenreich calls the "flight from responsibility" (171), yet "flight" is here regarded as positive self-direction more than fearful retreat. Despite the emphasis on both breadwinning and progeneration as masculine credentials, David Morgan has argued that "family relationships have often [...] been 'feminised'" (223) because any integration into the family unit threatens to undermine masculine autonomy. "[M]en who run away from family involvements," Arthur Brittan argues, "are not signalling their general abdication of power; all they are doing is redefining the arena in which that power is exercised" (52). This is made most clear in Roger's callous handling of the girl he imagines to be his illegitimate lovechild, Sarojini.

"The arena in which power is exercised" is, of course, at the root of Selvon's thinking about paternity and paternal authority, and throughout the novel Roger delineates between "fathering" and "parenting" as well as between "households" and "families" in illuminating ways. Larry May has rightly noted that we tend to use the phrase "fathering a child" in such a way that "[p]aternity is [...] used as a synonym for procreation" (33). "[T]o father," he recognizes, often means simply "to beget" (33), while "English has no corresponding term to 'mothering' for identifying the role of nurturing and education performed by a male parent" (33). The unintelligibility of a care-giving articulation of "fathering" is what troubles Tiger for most of both *A Brighter Sun* and *Turn Again Tiger*, and informs Roger's behaviour throughout *Cascadura*. To beget is to be regarded as source and origin. To mother is to be supplemental, to come second to both the vitalizing impulse of the father and the pervasive needs of the child. From the point of view of patriarchal authority, "to mother," then, is simultaneously and perversely to become filial, to assume a subordinate position. Similarly, the movement from "family" to "household" enacts a move out of obligation and into autonomous authority. To be *part* of a family, even as head of household, is to be less than whole. It suggests *lack* and enters into a network of potentially unsettling subjectivities. To *own* an estate reinforces a satisfying set of subject-object relations that confirms masculine agency and forestalls the threat of alien and alternate authorities. It allows "belonging *to*" to trump "belonging *together*."

In *Cascadura*, anything remotely signifying boundedness is rejected by Roger, as he seeks a detached and omnipotent authority, not a "committed" or situated one. He wants (and often has) a "voice [with] so much authority that questioning [is] unnecessary" (122). Although he believes he has "fathered" Sarojini, he refuses to parent her because he rejects both the localization of his authority (he desires jurisdiction over his entire estate, not just his biological offspring) and the implication of softness caring for children seems to entail. Instead, he quietly and anonymously bankrolls her "other" father, subordinating Ramdeen's (admittedly poor) social performance of fatherhood to the primacy of both biology and finance. He simultaneously installs himself as the gatekeeper of Sarojini's transition into womanhood, a transition that, even at the novel's opening, "should have taken place years ago" (17). Through these processes, Roger installs himself in the panoptic position of the unseen seer, the invisible first principle from which all other movements are derived. He seeks a level of surveillance that would mean each of his disciplinary objects are "totally seen without ever seeing", while he can "see everything without being seen"' (Foucault qtd. in Dandeker 25). In short, he refuses to be a dad and instead attempts to function as God the Father. This desire for omniscient authority without the threat of imposition is sustained. When Sarojini belatedly and circuitously takes up residence in his home, Roger first chafes at the prospect of curtailment, then narcissistically seeks affirmation of his own primacy and agency. Although he feels "nettled" "that his movements [are] impeded in his own house" (170), he also takes the opportunity for more pronounced and still unrevealed surveillance, seeking any "little idiosyncrasy that might indicate his blood in her veins" (170).

In *Surveillance Society*, David Lyon tellingly differentiates between observation-as-attentiveness and observation-as-discipline, and does so in ways which speak directly to paternal function:

> I may ask you to "watch over" my child to ensure that she does not stray into the street and risk being hit by a car. In this case, I have protection primarily in mind so that the child is shown care in a context where she can flourish. Or I may ask you to "watch over" the same child to ensure that she does not get up to mischief. Now I am appealing to moral criteria [...] to do with direction, proscription, perhaps even control. The same process, surveillance – watching over – both enables and constrains, involves care and control. (3)

Very clearly, Roger is preoccupied with control more than care, a fact made manifest in the novel's catastrophic climax, when cosmological forces mass to mock all pretensions toward overweening power and authority. As a major storm threatens, Roger's housekeeper, (who regards him as a kind of god) wonders "Why Mr Roger don't stop it?" (140), yet Roger's powerlessness against the storm is matched by his obliviousness to the vulnerability of his subordinates. When the storm is over, the neighbouring estate owner, Devertie, is baffled by Roger's ignorance and/or indifference to those who are "his" as regards control, but apparently free agents as regards care. In the terms I've been using, they "belong to" Roger but he doesn't want them around; they don't belong together.

> "You didn't keep [your workers] on the estate?"
>
> "No?"
>
> "You should of kept them in the big house, they would of been better off. I had my men here and their families too."
>
> It hadn't occurred to Roger to do that. He remembered now that he had gotten the impression that the villagers had expected something of that sort. (152)

When a difficult situation arises, Devertie is paternalistic in the caregiving, not the law-making sense. He's also endearingly *fraternalistic* to Roger, offering to "lend [Roger] some men" (171) to help with the clean up after the storm. Roger's imperious and defensive reply, "On what terms?", stems from his inability to comprehend a mutualistic discourse of care. The exasperated Devertie reminds Roger that "We talking as friends", but even when Roger believes that the offer is "genuine, and without strings," he hesitates because he does not "want to be obliged" (171). Again, this all stems from an intense discomfort with "those spaces which threaten fusion and the loss of self" (Rutherford 129), an inability to grasp relations that aren't structured in the omniscient paternalistic terms of domination/subordination or primacy/derivation.

This anxiety about fusion is most pronounced in Roger's sexual behaviour, first in his clandestine affair with Sarojini's mother, and more dramatically in his nocturnal sexual encounters with Kamalla, a local woman with whom he has no public interactions. Their wordless sexual encounters take place in "total darkness" (121) and depend on Roger's godlike power to surprise: Kamalla is never "sure exactly what hour he would be coming" (121). More significantly, these encounters depend on strict delineations of agency. "[H]e did not mind if she slept: in fact, she had a feeling he preferred it that way [...] sometimes she pretended sleep to give him greater kicks" (121). These rape fantasies, which take the complete objectification of the female to be a straightforward erotic good, simply exaggerate his general tendencies. In one sense, Kamalla's objectification works to "bracket" Roger's less ennobling bodily behaviours (his "clawing" and "panting" "like a hungry dog" (121)) and allows him to seamlessly resume a position of detached, almost disembodied authority and oversight. In another sense, it works to contain the very fertility it enacts. In flight from commitment, aligned with household/estate and against family, Roger needs a mode of sexual behaviour that precludes future complications. An inanimate object is incapable of change and, as such, is by definition infertile. The rape fantasy converts woman to object and in so doing forestalls the futurity and instability entailed in fertility. Everything reverts to containment.

It is fitting, then, that Roger discovers the details of Sarojini's sexual relationship with Garry in the context of his own sexual relationship with Kamalla. When Kamalla tells him that "they been doing it" (122), he reacts with characteristic hubris. He asks, "How could such things happen in Sans Souci without him knowing?" before concluding that he hasn't found out, *Because he didn't want to know*" (122, original emphasis). Here, troubling suggestions of evasion and alternate agency (people doing things that he can't see or understand) are refigured in terms of what he wants to see, brought into the orbit of his desire, and reframed in terms not of what *they* did, but rather what *he* wants. The scene ends with a more emphatic demonstration of the same impulse. Kamalla, fearful Roger might be "getting fed-up of [her] quiescent lump of flesh," explores the possibility he might prefer a more active partner. She puts out "a tentative hand to explore his [...] genitals" and gets "slapped [...] so hard her ears [are] still ringing" (123) when Roger leaves.

When Kamalla rejects her fixed status as object and threatens to reveal the nature of their relationship to the community, Roger's effort to suppress the revelation speaks to his desire not to have the abstract and consequently limitless arena of his authority situated and compromised. When Kamalla comes to his house and taunts him, he slaps her once more with "a forceful blow which he instantly regretted" (176). The regret here is procedural more than ethical. Roger doesn't regret slapping her, but he's uncomfortable with any remotely public suggestion that she has the power to provoke him. As ever, his exaggerated emphasis on his own dignity and autonomy precludes the possibility of any reciprocal or contestatory agency. After the initial slap, the third person narrator intervenes with the following startling commentary: "had Roger augmented the blow with a few clouts and kicks as any sensible Trinidadian would have done [perhaps] he would have driven ambitious ideas from her head" (176). This may be true, but the larger, stranger, point is clear. Roger is not, and has no desire to be, "a sensible Trinidadian" because he refuses membership in any community and abides by no community protocols. An unobserved nocturnal slap is acceptable for disciplinary purposes, but a public fight necessarily legitimizes the adversary, entails an admission of the formidability of the other person. For Roger, such an admission is unthinkable. A fight, even a beating, amounts to a sustained *engagement* with another person and works to undermine the position of detached, disengaged authority he desires. "A sensible Trinidadian" can deliver a beating because he is willing to admit he *knows* (and even, in some perverse way, *cares about*) the person with whom he is engaged. Domestic abuse is ethically abhorrent, but it takes place between figures on the same plain of existence and entails a threat of integration and fusion that Roger could never admit or allow.

Roger obviously fears a public scandal, but, because he is oblivious (or indifferent) to the values of the community, he fails to recognize that the revelation of his embodiedness would work to increase his status in the village. It would amount to a type of incarnation, godlike authority taking human form. In the eyes of the community, the revelation of Roger's sexuality, even his apparently *deviant* sexuality, would not harm his "prestige and standing;" instead, "the men would approve and appreciate that white man or no white man, he had to dip his wick now and then," while "[s]ome of the women might [...] wish they were the lucky one" (176–77). To Roger, sexuality is always a matter of monologic containment rather than heteroglossic rupture. Under cover of darkness, Roger is prepared to bite and scratch but, in the worlds of daylight and discourse, he refuses to acknowledge any "lower" self, any self that would reveal him as a "regular guy" rather than an omnipotent force. Unable to navigate any kind of productive synthesis of embodied presence and abstract power, his remoteness produces his repression and Kamalla acts as receptacle for his inarticulable desires. He seeks to approach sex in panoptic, disciplinary terms while the members of the community would happily regard it in less regimented, boundary-defying, Bakhtinian terms, as "unruly biological and social exchange" (Freer 56).

Cascadura's most unruly figures of all, of course, and the greatest challenge to human claims to "greatness and vastness," are the various superhuman presences that lurk just beyond the novel's directly signified world. Soucouyants, lagahoos and douens are creatures whose origins are unclear and whose jurisdiction defies bounds. They mock both panoptic oversight and patriarchal primacy. Early on, Manko (an obeahman of marginal power) describes an old woman who "used to turn into a *soucouyant* in the night and go to suck human blood. Especially babies" (47, original emphasis). The lagahoo manifests as both bull and cow (48), and the douens are "children who never been christened [...who] have their feet turned backwards, so when you think from the footprint that they going one way, they really going the opposite" (90). The preoccupation with gender and fertility is impossible to overlook here, as is the challenge they present to the neat dualism of Christianity and the all-encompassing paternity at its head.

Yet, these superhuman forces never challenge panopticism in any direct way. Instead, they challenge the assumptions upon which the doctrine of omniscient authority is based. These are emphatically *embodied* cosmic forces: blood suckers, shape shifters, children with misaligned bodies. They are always situated, with clearly articulated strengths and weaknesses. As such, they don't participate in the desire for overarching panoptic containment. While Roger seeks both to disappear and to control *everything*, the novel's other supernatural forces are both manifest (hence situated) and *limited* insofar as they have specific salient powers or qualities (they only have power at night; you have to look at them, etc.). Seduced by his own self-aggrandizing vision, Roger wonders why he doesn't know and see everything. Manko, in contrast, lives most of his life in servitude and is content with occasional "uncanny *glimpses* into the past and future" (51, emphasis added). Manko's vision is partial and fragmentary, heteroglossic, and (most of the time) he recognizes that his authority and jurisdiction are limited. Unlike most of Selvon's male characters, Manko (an unmarried and childless laborer) recognizes a distinction between looking and telling. His glimpses do not situate or contain.

In the single instance when Manko seeks to control what he can only tangentially observe, he regards his punishment as just:

> He himself was under penance because he thought he could challenge what had been decreed [...]. [A] man had been marked for doom and he, little Manko, had shaken his fist at the sky and tried to turn the will of the gods. (157)

As with Tiger at the end of *Turn Again*, Manko's strength is derived from his acceptance of his littleness; he accepts that "what is to is, must is." The storm at the end of *Cascadura* is a kind of cosmic punishment for overarching ambitions, and those who acknowledge their "littleness" before it fare best. In his role as latter-day Crusoe, master of all he surveys, Roger attempts to control a circumstance that extends far beyond "the arena in which his power is exercised," before succumbing to his own oft-denied finitude. In the face of the storm's unambiguous power, his pretensions at containment and control become ludicrous and his behaviour becomes scrambled and erratic as he confronts the limits of his own authority. Ultimately, then, he is reduced to the abject position under which the villagers live most of their lives: "[I]t was like spitting in the ocean to take precautions [...] the best thing was to kneel and pray, and [to] stay kneeling until it was over" (138).

Kneeling, then, works better than shaking a tiny fist at the sky, and it is precisely this acceptance of his own subordination and inadequacy that protects the visiting English writer, Garry, on his irrational journey to save his lover Sarojini, who is lost outside in the storm:

> A man who knows his capabilities and his limitations is benign to Papa Bois and the spirits of the forest. That night if Garry had gone out raging and waving his sword, with hopes of victory and conquest, he might have met quick, ignoble death. As it was, he was almost humble in his hopeless inadequacy. (146)

"Papa Bois", the mythical master of the forest, is the only truly all-encompassing patriarch and those who seek to usurp his vision and power must be punished. Hopeless inadequacy is a survival strategy.

Indeed, Garry's position throughout the novel ultimately serves as a critique of Roger's determined and entrenched detachment. While Garry's book on obeah might be conceived as an imperialistic exercise in containment, and while he sometimes shares his friend's smug sense that there is no special "compulsion to involve himself in the day" (68), he is also consistently prepared to entertain possibilities beyond what he can "coherently grasp" (47). Early on, Garry intuits "a connection between [...] incidents [that he] could not understand" (46). Later, he allows embedded and intimate experience to overrule rational determination: "He did not want to stop and say: Well now, how did this start, and why, and if. There was a sensational jumble of time and place and incident in his mind" (80). Just as Tiger's epiphanic revelation ("What is to is, must is.") involves a suspension of the desire for omniscient, situating oversight, Garry recognizes the value in situations he can neither control nor understand. In so doing, he opens himself up to experiences Roger has no possibility of accessing.

In "Andrea del Sarto," Robert Browning famously observed that "a man's reach should exceed his grasp/Or what's a heaven for?" (117). What he was pointing to, I think, is the need to differentiate between our powers of reception (what we can reach) and our powers of understanding (what we can grasp). Outside of an overarching godlike perspective (the view from heaven), the ambition to grasp everything we touch is misguided and unproductive. Just as Tiger is happiest when he ceases to see reading as a way of solving the world, Garry's "sensational jumble" occurs because he is willing to feel things he can't "grip" or subordinate. As such, the jumble is "sensational" in both an evaluative (in which sensation is synonymous with "excellent") and a phenomenological sense (insofar as the jumble is about experiencing "sensations"). It is impossible to imagine Roger regarding a jumble as sensational, because it would necessarily threaten both his overarching designs and his desire to hold himself aloof from shared feelings and experiences. Roger's desire to grasp everything makes it impossible for him to "touch upon" things that refuse to be situated and subdued. When he wonders if it is appropriate for his daughter to be mixed up with "someone *like* Garry" (170, emphasis added), for example, he turns his individuated friend into an abstract Platonic type and strives to create some kind of overarching, omniscient resolution to the problem: "in his own way and time he would resolve things" (170).

Harold Barratt has argued that, in the Tiger novels

> Tiger learns that manhood does not mean possessing a wife and fathering a child; nor does it mean smoking and drinking rum. Manhood means awareness

of one's identity as a unique individual; it also means satisfying one's hunger for
knowledge. ("Sam Selvon's Tiger" 29)

He's right about the first part, wrong about the second. Here, I have tried
to suggest that, as regards paternity at least, the quest for a singular position
of enlightened masculine oversight and control is at the root of most of the
problems in *Turn Again Tiger* and *Those Who Eat the Cascadura*. In Selvon,
"hunger for knowledge" bleeds directly into "desire for omniscience", and "desire
for omniscience" is a function of untenable godlike, paternalistic aspirations.
To valorize the uniquely constituted and enlightened perspective of the single
masculine individual is to re-encode patriarchal desires for oversight and control.
In Jonathan Rutherford's terms, assertions of singularity and vision (uniqueness
and knowledge) seek "to evade fusion with the maternal object through a
compulsion to sustain control and mastery over the signifier" (129).

Fusion, I'd like to suggest, is what makes friendship and connection possible.
As with Alison Donnell's argument in the next chapter, I think merger is a matter
of, "belonging together" rather than "belonging to" and it offers a way out of
masculine supervisory and disciplinary impulses. Most of the successful moments
in these two novels involve a suspension of otherwise pervasive impulses to situate
and regulate, moments when the hard divisions between imperious paternal
subject and subordinated, feminized object start to break down, moments when
some kind of cooperative mutualism establishes itself. Their variously defined
ambitions notwithstanding, Selvon's patriarchs are not always happiest when the
omniscient I/eye commands the abject "they," but rather when otherwise isolated
masculine strivers accept the comforts of connectedness, "belonging together,"
and peace. For Selvon, success isn't finally a matter of "you" belonging to "me";
instead, it comes in rare moments of fraternal merger, in friendship and in love,
when "[y]ou is one of we" (*Turn Again Tiger* 62).

CHAPTER FOUR

The Island and the World:
Kinship, Friendship and Living Together in
Selected Writings of Sam Selvon

Alison Donnell

[G]lobalisation is bringing peoples closer apart and places further together.

– John Rennie Short, *Global Dimensions*

While the insights of postcolonial and diasporic criticism within the fields of Caribbean literary criticism have been intellectually exciting in many ways, in my own critical work I have tried to argue that one of the unintended legacies of scholarly attention to Caribbean diasporic writers and writings has been to generate an assumption that interesting thinking to do with living in a globalized world takes its cues from migrant, mobile, unhoused subjectivities.[1] What is eclipsed in this modelling of the Caribbean is the region's equally privileged perspective on another major challenge and reward of occupying a glocal world – that of living together in difference. This is a challenge that operates for Caribbean subjects at the multiple and intersecting levels of community, nation-state, the region and the diaspora. It is also a challenge to which Caribbean writers respond through writings that represent and imaginatively coordinate communities and nations within, as well as across, geographical space that seek to challenge the historical marginalization of one group by another – a core ideology and legacy of colonialism.

Reading through this lens, we might see the contemporary value of Selvon's writings to lie in his rendering of a world that is both pleasurably globalized and stubbornly unequal, a rendering that remains alert to how things are and yet is imaginatively responsive to the possibilities for a different organization of social and cultural life. Taken collectively, Selvon's works capture the tensions and asymmetries of acts of settlement and community, whether these are the rivalries between Jamaicans and Trinidadians, the often prominent contests between men in pursuit of women, or the more fundamental and structurally managed separation of the middle classes from the working poor. Beckoning towards global justice agendas with comic, tender and serious intent, his poetic rendering of black workers taking over London on the night shift in *Moses Ascending* brilliantly reinvests the value of hidden black labour in a 1950s twist on the "Occupy" movement (5–9).

Significantly, alongside all the unruly and competitive encounters that Selvon's works document, there is a sense of people living together that is stronger still. We might now read this sensibility as being akin to what Paul Gilroy in his 2005 work, *Postcolonial Melancholia*, frames according to the concept of "conviviality": "the processes of cohabitation and interaction that have made multiculture an ordinary feature of social life in Britain's urban areas and in postcolonial cities elsewhere" (xv). For Gilroy, these location are places "in which cultures, histories, and structures of feeling previously separated by enormous distances could be found in the same place, the same time: school, bus, café, cell, waiting room, or traffic jam" (70). The lively, textured and boisterous collectivities of basements, bars and buses in Selvon's works present a nascent conviviality where the dramas around difference are always located, and often diffused, within the everydayness of shared spaces, entangled lives and dynamic communities.

In developing this argument, I am going to venture a very broad generalization about Selvon's work. The ethical force of Selvon's writings comes from the particular configuration of living together that he is interested in. This is the living together alongside and in difference that he explores in terms of his focus on the relations between neighbours, friends and lovers, rather than the kinship relations of family. I see his works as mapping horizontal zones of attachment and possible solidarities across groupings that reconfigure vertically inscribed genealogical paradigms of belonging to place and each other based on models of historical continuity and inheritance.

I conjecture further that this modelling of elected rather than actual families may be a particular trait of Trinidadian writing from the early yard fictions of C.L.R. James and Alfred Mendes through the work of Merle Hodge, to contemporary writings by Elizabeth Nunez, Lawrence Scott and Shani Mootoo. In the work of all of these writers, the idea of interaction and kinship across difference is a recurring trope and there is a shared investment in writing scenes of conviviality rather than consanguinity, as well as scenes of friendship and neighbourliness rather than of hereditary family. Perhaps more than any other Caribbean space, Trinidad's history and geography have provoked a multiplicity of cultural encounters and exchanges that have made imaginable the delicate and yet worthwhile warp and weft of an alternative social fabric woven by these scenes. This different model of human connectedness is important because of the concentric loyalties and affiliations that it promotes. The reason that I suggest that Selvon's writings have ethical force in this regard is that while the model of the family can be expanded outwards towards the idea of a nation (inasmuch as both are traditionally modelled on loyalty and belonging on account of sameness and shared origins), the idea of a nation which we reach towards when we stretch out friendship or neighbourliness is rather different and, significantly, more inherently pluralistic and inclusive, as well as less dependent on heteronormative relations.

Although Selvon travelled to London in 1950, the rise of West Indian Federation in the 1950s and its collapse in 1962 arguably casts a long shadow over his work. The limit points of cross-island solidarity are often rehearsed at the level of friendship and neighbourhood groupings when national or ethnic identities are brought to the fore. As Andrews declares in Selvon's 1955 novel, *An Island Is a World*: "Ah, with all the differences in these islands it will be one hell of a job to unify and have a common loyalty" (212). All the same, it is this possibility of unifying at a level of human interaction and mutual recognition that I believe Selvon insistently writes towards. One of the most immediate and yet striking aspects of his works is his alertness to the variety of human population. There is no sense in any of his works that the world is made up of people who are all the same. Indeed, while it is the exaggerated, often humorous differences and distinguishing features of each character that feed the structure of Selvon's ballad style this alertness has a less *kiff-kiff* remit too.

In an article for *The Geographical Magazine*, also published in 1955, entitled "The West Indian Patchwork", Selvon gives a photographic and textual tour around the islands.[2] The foreword to the piece states:

> Princess Margaret's visit to the West Indies this month will draw attention to a group of islands which, seen from afar, look much the same. Their great variety when closely viewed is emphasized by the author, a West Indian of East Indian descent. (516)

The visual account offered by this piece does map different geographical features of the islands: from the colonial architecture and plantation sugar estates of Codrington College, Barbados, through the fluid French, English and Scottish cultural imprints in Grenada, to the newly erected blocks of flats in Port of Spain, Trinidad, "a result of the report of a Royal Commission" and its findings of urban-overcrowding. However, it is most concerned to represent the diverse human geography of the West Indies.

The caption for an image of smiling Afro-Caribbean young boys reads, "Descendants of Negroes imported to work on the sugar plantation form the majority population in the West Indian islands. The hopelessness of slavery tended to reinforce the indolence of the Tropics" (Figure 2). Here Selvon consciously ruptures any idea of determinist racialized identities in his strong referencing of social environment and forced exploitation. This line of argument continues with Selvon's caption for the group photograph of so-called "poor whites" – a term about which he indicates his own suspicion through his use of scare quotes:

Palatial by comparison with the flimsy structures that they replaced, these blocks of flats were erected in Port of Spain, Trinidad, as a result of the report of a Royal Commission to examine social conditions in the West Indies, among the worst of which was urban over-crowding. Such buildings exemplify not only the new standards of life that West Indians are setting them-selves but also the many new skills, involved in their construction, that are being acquired by local craftsmen

Figure 1

*Descendants of Negroes imported to work on the sugar planta-
tions form the majority of the population in the West Indian
islands. The hopelessness of slavery tended to reinforce the
indolence of the Tropics ; and, as a result, they have not in
the past been very earnest seekers for material advancement*

Figure 2

"It would be a mistake, however, to attribute this characteristic to racial causes. In
Barbados and Grenada there are communities of 'poor Whites' who have lived the
same humble, rustic life for 300 years, since their forefathers were deported from
Ireland after Drogheda or from England after Sedgemoor" (Figure 3).

It would be a mistake, however, to attribute this character-istic to racial causes. In Barbados and Grenada there are com-munities of 'poor Whites' who have lived the same humble, rustic life for 300 years, since their forefathers were deported from Ireland after Drogheda or from England after Sedgemoor

Figure 3

The two images of Indo-Trinidadians again reference their cultural distinctiveness and contribution. The first caption explains how this group came to the island after abolition to labour in the plantations, while the second comments on their additions to the cultural geography of the region: "the Indians brought with them their religion, Hindu or Moslem, adding temples and mosques to the landscape of Trinidad" (Figure 4).

Besides the clean mud-and-thatch of their villages, the Indians brought with them their religion, Hindu or Moslem, adding temples and mosques to the landscape of Trinidad. These links with their ancestral way of life, and the holy men who practise it, are still deeply cherished by some of the Indians

Figure 4

Selvon does not write an idealized portrait of the West Indies. As the chosen images show, and his title "patchwork" implies, there are seams and divides that run between places and population groups. In sketching a history of the region, he refers to the strike in Trinidad in 1951 (517), to the sadly fated home migration of Indians who had been indentured and wanted to exercise their right to return passage after the Independence of India (518), as well as to the geographical segregation of the poor whites or "Redlegs" who are shunned and stereotyped as, Selvon notes "'He come from behind the cliff'" (Hackleton's Cliff in Barbados), but who still do not intermarry with black people (517).

When the Negroes were freed in 1834 many of them deserted the plantations and the dearth of labour led the planters to seek workers elsewhere. They were found in India and brought to the West Indies under 'indentures', binding for a term of years. A third of Trinidad's inhabitants are now East Indians

Figure 5

As these historical markers suggest, common cause and identity between different ethnic groups was not always evident or easy to witness. Yet, while Selvon acknowledges the distinctions and tensions among different peoples, the composition of his article and the vision he summons of a creole culture in fractions, but also in the making and in his imagination (the very fact that he talks about marriage summons it as a possibility), suggests a whole that is more than the sum of its parts. Interestingly, Selvon's one moment of unbridled optimism comes when he talks about the founding of the University of the West Indies (UWI) in Jamaica in 1948, although again we hear the echo of parallel, horizontal communities, as well as of the promise of togetherness: "Here the opportunity exists for West Indians of all races and colours to acquire the knowledge and experience necessary for responsible leadership in their several communities" (519).

What Selvon documents in this 1955 piece is what we now see as a commonplace of Caribbean or West Indian realities. The differently marked arrivals of Africans, Indians, Chinese, Irish, Syrians and other Europeans who were brought to the region as part of forced, misled and opportunist migrations, alongside the decimation of the majority of the indwelling populations by disease or violence, meant that in this region, in a way that is more pronounced and extreme than almost anywhere else, the relation between people and place is discontinuous, layered and precarious. As has been repeatedly noted, this fabric of fragments towards a whole occasions both loss and gain, problem and potential. Much has been written theoretically about the liquidity of Caribbean identity and yet the failure of lateral solidarities is an enduring and vexing issue in many West Indian societies. Splinters were felt most keenly in Trinidad and Guyana between those of African and Indian descent where they have led to ethnic strife and communal violence. As part of his own vision for a horizontal mode of engagement and an ethical paradigm of cross-cultural imaginings and relations, Homi Bhabha asks a fundamental question:

> How do strategies of representation or empowerment come to be formulated in the competing claims of communities where, despite shared histories of deprivation and discrimination, the exchange of values, meanings and priorities may not always be collaborative and dialogical, but may be profoundly antagonistic, conflictual and even incommensurable? (2)

A complicated entanglement of mutual hostilities and shared hopes for substantial freedoms across different ethnic, class and sexual groupings can be traced to the distinctive history of the Caribbean region. It is in the context of colonialism and the labour demands of the plantation economy that we might best understand why the relations between peoples and their claims to belonging have come to assume a conflictual rather than supportive character. Yet, it is also in this context – of imagined, crafted and invented relations to others – that we may find the (literary) resolution to such lateral hostilities. Although Selvon never wishes away the hold of the historically embedded rivalries that fostered an unhelpful model of identity politics based on, "the inhabitants [...] thinking of themselves not as Trinidadians or Barbadians or Jamaicans, but as East Indian or African" (Selvon, "Three into One" 11), he writes these claims into fictional worlds that can also host other possibilities.

For me, Selvon's writing is aware of both of these dimensions of the region's constitutive experience at once and the energetics of his works and their formal structures often teeter at the fulcrum between the opposing states of consciousness which West Indianness provokes: loneliness, introspection and a retreat into identarianism on the one hand and community, relationality as well as an expansion of conviviality and of possible identifications on the other. In his extended interview with Kevin Roberts and Andra Thakur, "Christened with Snow," Selvon says,

> I consider myself [...] first and foremost a person from the Caribbean [...] I'm a citizen of the world. I don't belong to any particular part, but I could fit into any culture, and things like that. So for me the Caribbean person has this – mark you, in a way, he loses a kind of national identity that people like to feel, and a pride in being what they are, and to me this is one of the reasons that has kept the whole, all the Caribbean nations, slightly apart from one another, that they haven't had this feeling of oneness. (97)

Selvon is not alone in expressing this sensibility. George Lamming, in his classic 1960 analysis of colonial relations, *The Pleasures of Exile*, also highlights the exceptional cosmopolitanism of West Indian subjects:

> We in the West Indies can meet the twentieth century without fear; for we begin with colossal advantages. The West Indian, though provincial, is perhaps the most cosmopolitan man in the world. No Indian from India, no European, no African can adjust with greater ease and naturalness to new situations than the West Indian. (37)

This idea of West Indians as environmentally privileged in forming an identity that has the potential to be anti-identitarian and cosmopolitan in its multiple affiliations, shines out in Selvon's writings set in Trinidad.

This same Caribbean sensibility and a continued fascination with friendship and neighbourliness continue to inform the moral and political integrity of his London novels. Whereas the extended family may serve as a microcosm of the conservative self-interested nation, the elected family of friends and neighbours that we find in Selvon's metropolitan writings offers a different model of kinship in which concentric affiliation and solidarity is based on goodwill, care and kinship that can, and must, accommodate diversity, strangeness and even rivalry. Most notably, we witness this in the heroic Moses who leads the tribe in *The Lonely Londoners* and *Moses Ascending* but for whom the rewards of creating elected families are often less present than the responsibilities.

In *Londoners*, Moses is not blind to how the demands of hustling a living can come to override the capacity for neighbourliness:

> It had a Jamaican fellar who living in Brixton, that come to the station to see what tenants he could pick up for the houses that he have in Brixton [... he] let out rooms to the boys, hitting them anything like three or four guineas for a double. When it come to making money, it ain't have anything like "ease me up" or "both of we is countrymen together" in the old London. Sometimes he put bed and chair in two or three big room and tell the fellars they could live in there together, but each would have to pay a pound...five-six fellars in one room and the test coining money for so. And whenever a boat-train come in, he hustling down to Waterloo to pick up them fellars who new to London. (27–28)

However, while the model of landlord exploitation may seem all the more ruthless by a fellow West Indian, for the men who live in such conditions as his exploitation allows, the compression of living together still affords real solace and has a value beyond the financial rewards reaped by the landlord. Selvon never eulogizes his characters; he shows their flaws and failings as much as their hopes and achievements. All the same, in the strained conditions of immigrant life, the moments of intimacy and companionship, rather than simple proximity, do add up to a mode of living together that his works endow with value. As Moses reflects towards the end of the novel, the secular communion is what sustains:

> Looking at things in general life really hard for the boys in London. This is a lonely miserable city, if it was not that we didn't get together now and then to talk about things back home, we would suffer like hell. Here is not like home where you have friends all about. (130)

The Housing Lark, Selvon's sixth novel, originally published in 1965, is a work that shares some of the tropes and traits of the Moses trilogy and yet is significant in its more amplified and self-conscious register of attempts to settle in the mother country and differently inclusive in its gendered friendships and acts of living together. *The Housing Lark* narrates the lives of a group of West Indians, with Battersby as their Moses figure, who share the hope of buying their own property. In this book, there is a collective hope and anticipation of a shared future that is explicitly stated as a way of living together in which individual fortune or failure has the possibility of being buffered by community:

> Is so life was, you had to take chances, and one day your luck might turn. And if you yourself ain't have anything to offer, it good to stick with fellars like Harry, and Alfy and Syl and the rest of the boys. All of we can't be blight, Bat think, out of six seven fellars, one bound to be lucky, something good bound

> to happen to one of we. Bat ain't care who it happen to, as long as he around to share in the good fortune. (46)

The sense of an inclusive neighbourhood where sameness and difference can be entertained is also voiced clearly in the episode when Gallows inadvertently stows away in Port of Spain and

> find himself adrift in Londontown. He make his way down to Brixton with the last two and six he had. Somehow he figure out that that was the safest district to go to, that he bound to meet some fellow countryman who would ease up the situation, give him some shelter and a meal.
>
> And as luck would have it, a Jamaican fellar what had a club give him work to clean it out, and say he could sleep in the club for a couple of nights until he get a place. (48–49)

However, the episode that yields most productively to my reading of Selvon's representation of what Gilroy calls "convivial culture" is the group excursion to "Hamdon Court" for which each person pays one pound, with the funds directed at the collective housing project.

> Battersby was standing up near the door with the driver, ticking off the members of the party and collecting money as they get in. It look as if the whole of Brixton was going on this excursion to Hamdon Court. Friend invite friend, cousin invite aunt, uncle invite nephew, niece invite godfather, and so this Sunday morning bright and early all of them congregate in this side street behind the railway station. (104)

Although Poor and his char-a-banc which arrive to compete for passengers again hint at the competitive culture within the community, the narrative's familiar turn to a passive construction (as in the earlier "Is so life was") seems to suggest that the socially cohesive forces of the collective group are larger than individual splinter missions. Indeed, this rivalry winds up as unintended cooperation: "As things turn out, it has more people than the coach could hold, and Bat couldn't stop them from going with Poor" (107).

The centripetal force of this gathering in difference and with tension is also indicated by the presence of Charlie, one of "a lot of them fellars in town who go about as if they don't want to have anything to do with West Indians" (109) who tells Bat, "I heard about your efforts to raise money to buy a house and I must say it is commendable. In fact I thought of patronizing the excursion and helping the cause" (111). Again self-interest in the day excursion and altruism are represented as mutually enriching. Moreover, as Charlie's yearnings for solidarity overtake his sense of his detached singular self, he starts drinking from the communal rum bottle.

Selvon's focus in this long episode is to catch the vibrant, jostling encounters that make the event worthwhile rather than the excursion itself. As the narrator observes, "In point of fact, if all of them did get together and went in the park, or if to say the coach did really break down and they couldn't reach, it won't of made any difference" (112). Yet, while the book invests in the bonding and braiding of lives that this excursion makes visible, it also recognizes that social power cannot be dissolved by conviviality alone. In a strongly inter-textual reference to the earlier work, *The Lonely Londoners,* which has a highly poetic, uninterrupted description of the particular (bachelor) joys and freedoms of summer at its heart, *The Housing Lark* signals the end of that era through the involvement of women:

> Summer can't last forever. All of them tulips and daffodils and blue skies have their day of bloom and depart. And though you might think that the singsong life the boys lead will go on and on, after one time is another. Is true with them fellars you could never tell what would be the outcome of any conversation.
>
> They might say they moving east, and you see them heading west, they might say they coming when they going.
>
> But when women get together, is a different story altogether. (133–34)

The realist narrative of accounting, both financial and personal, that the women insist upon does tell a different story and structures a different model of friendship and neighbourliness.

It is under the pragmatic female gaze that the male community's investment in Harry – the budding calypsonian – is held up for scrutiny. Not only do the women point out that Harry has effectively been abandoned by the "boys" since he was sent to jail, but they also call time on the deferral of the housing plan until Harry is released from jail and the fund boosted by the anticipated earnings from his calypso recordings: "'Let me tell you something', Teena says, "that recording ain't going any place but the dustbin'" (141). The assertiveness of the women and their insistence on a feasible plan that can be translated into productive action offers a bold rewriting of male-female relationships from the Moses novels, where fantasies of male sexual conquest stream through as an imaginative buffer to the vulnerabilities of migrant masculinity.

Here, the women literally assert their own teleological narrative onto the shape of the story – collapsing the space of an imaginative, speculative "lark" in their blunt interrogation of action: "Chapter Two is this: What you actually do about this house? You been to see any agents? You been to see any places?" (141). All the same, the evident tension between these gendered communities and narratives is also one that can be productively accommodated. While the women may mock the "lark" approach, they do not mock the housing scheme. Indeed, their rewriting is an act of translation that marks the historical transition from the early phase of migration when mainly male migrants arrived with a mottled consciousness of adventure and ambition that was rewarded by the equally uneven blending of unencumbered and unaccommodated lives, to the later phase when relationships established and the questions of raising families and building neighbourhoods provoked a more direct engagement with the prospect of how to live together in Britain (announced as "Chapter Two" by Teena). What the women bring to the discussions in the book is the sense of struggle and context of a racist society in which the housing lark is truly no longer a joke. Teena's speech against everything being a "skylark" points out: "You know the distresses we have to go through, you know the arse black people see to get a roof over their heads in this country" (145).

While the conservative solution to living together that the women articulate is for the boys to "think of marrieding and settling down [...] A good woman will soon straighten out the set of you" (145–46), it is not their story alone that the novel tells. Indeed, while the women's plan begins to take shape and the housing scheme takes on a more real footing, in a final twist, an agent appears who wants to sign Harry as the next calypso star. Having conceived of living together as a dream grounded in material realities and one fraught with everyday challenges, the narrative also delights in the exaggerated story of Harry's success and his extraordinary act of friendship towards Poor:

> The last rose of summer was fading when Harry Banjo come out of jail, but the rosiness of the future help him to forget the past. The agent went to town on the story, big photo in the papers, and his ballad about the loyalty and bonds of friendship that exist among the coloured members of the community. Poor turned out to be destitute with a large family to support and that's why Harry Banjo, being single and of chivalrous mettle rarely seen in modern times, decide to take the rap. The story went on that he would be cutting his first disc soon, with some numbers that he compose while awaiting Her Majesty's pleasure in the Brixton jail.
>
> Down in Brixton OUR PEOPLE rise in support. One or two reporters who went sniffing around get some tall tales about how Harry do good in the neighbourhood, giving money to the needy, giving away his clothes to the naked, visiting the sick, succouring the sorrowful. And as for talent, his ancestors were kings of calypso in the islands. (152–53)

While the story of conviviality and solidarity fed by agents and to reporters may be consciously inflated and ironized in the way the capitalized "OUR PEOPLE" indicates, these staged and performed acts of friendship are nevertheless underpinned by real acts of living together that are no less valuable for being imperfect and highly-charged.

For the Trinidadian writer and intellectual Earl Lovelace, calypso catches the distinctive cultural energies of the creole space of shared living with its attendant tensions, and is a form that speaks over the ethnic, racialized or national space of competitive belonging: "the voice of the Creole world in which the ordinary people lived, in which they celebrated themselves, their heroes, recalled important events, and expressed attitudes to life and the world" ("Calypso and the Bacchanal"). While Lovelace's may be an idealistic version of a democratic aesthetic, it is difficult not to be persuaded that Selvon's novels of migration deployed this concept of the calypso form, imaginatively structuring companionable spaces in the often inhospitable mother country and allowing the multiple registers of dream, of struggle, of community and of performed success to be heard in a chorus of living that, although not always harmonious, unforgettably creolized the sound of London.

NOTES

1. For more on this argument see Donnell, *Twentieth-Century Caribbean Literature* (77–129).
2. I am grateful to Nalini Mohabir for first sharing a copy of this article with me.

CHAPTER FIVE

Three into One *Can* Go?
Creolizing Narrations of "East Indian Trinidadian West Indians" in Selvon, Lovelace and Motoo

Denise deCaires Narain

> By the time I was in my teens I was a product of my environment, as Trinidadian as anyone could claim to be, quite at ease with a cosmopolitan attitude, and I had no desire to isolate myself from the mixture of races that comprised the community.
>
> – Samuel Selvon, "Three into One Can't Go"

While popular, Sam Selvon's first novel, *A Brighter Sun*, has received relatively little critical attention in comparison to his third novel, *The Lonely Londoners*. As Kenneth Ramchand argues in chapter one, *Londoners* effectively secured Selvon's literary reputation, in particular, his renown as a maestro of a stylized Trinidadian literary voice. As well as its calypso-style narration, many critics have drawn attention to the way "the boys" in the text gather in a loose, convivial community to protect themselves from the racism of the city of London. They may live in diminished circumstances but liming together, they adopt an irreverent black urban attitude that exudes style and confidence, their redeployment of the "jungle" stereotype wryly alert to its performative power.

Selvon's lonely Londoners have come to embody a stylishly subversive black metropolitan identity. In his discussion of the text, Stefano Harney argues that the "muscle" (107) of Caribbean style is not produced exclusively via the encounter with Britain but is a cultural force, powered by "centuries of Caribbean popular culture" (105) that Moses et al. bring *with* them to the city. The "predatory creolization" that the boys enact as they transform London in their wanderings is "powered by the inevitable creolization of Trinidad" and informed by Selvon's "base in the street culture of Port of Spain" (114–15). Harney concludes, "[t]his idea of a predatory creolization as national culture is Sam Selvon's contribution to the national community of Trinidad" (115). In Harney, the *inevitable* creolization of Trinidad is contrasted with an actively "predatory" creolization in London; where one "naturally" unfolds, the other involves a more self-conscious and rebellious agency. Harney's use of "predatory" is strongly affirmative, aligning creolization with an agentive resistance that, to me, too neatly positions black Caribbean men as archetypally subversive figures. This view of creolization as irreverently performative coheres around the figure of the "rude bwaii", its enduring appeal driven by the demands of cultural nationalism.

Re-reading *A Brighter Sun* now, in light of the above, it is easy to see why its uneven, anxious treatment of creolization might seem far less subversive than that of *The Lonely Londoners*. Certainly, Tiger is no rude bwaii: he does not exude the stylish cool of a figure like Moses, the linguistic verve of Cap or the bravado of Galahad. I argue here, however, that *A Brighter Sun* offers a more complicated and contradictory idea of creolization, one less easily reconciled with creolization-as-resistance. Indeed, it invites us to question how "resistance" might be figured textually and whether it is, in any case, what we should continually read *for*. If creolization, as it unfolds in *A Brighter Sun*, is anxious, incomplete and altogether less boldly "predatory" than it appears in *Londoners*, its *inevitability* in Trinidad is also more troubled than Harney implies. Where, in London, the logic of white racism casts all the boys as "black" (refusing recognition of the difference that "*Indian* West Indian" might signify), in the Trinidad of *A Brighter Sun*, everyone is hailed by precise racial epithets. Attending to Selvon's first novel foregrounds the place of Indo-Trinidadians in creolization that the later novel elides. It also disturbs the easy alignment between "Trinidadian" and "cosmopolitan" that many associate with *Londoners* and that Selvon implies in the epigraph above.

Following discussion of *A Brighter Sun*, I offer readings of two more recently published novels by Trinidadian authors, Shani Mootoo's *He Drown She in the Sea* (2005) and Earl Lovelace's *Is Just a Movie* (2011), which share some of the concerns identified in Selvon's novel. In focusing on the way these three texts stage Indo-Trinidadian involvement in Creole culture, my readings are less oriented towards identifying the specificity of *Indian* contributions to the national or regional "callaloo" than in mobilizing a creoli*zing* reading practice that responds more openly to the contradictions and possibilities that the texts suggest. There are intriguing continuities and discontinuities in the texts which, when read together, invite a more fluid calibration of the creolization model. Rather than thinking of creolization as a process that can be completed or a destination that can be arrived at, I place emphasis on a reading practice that embraces the piecemeal, partial and contingent.

From Creolization to Creoli*zing*

Creolization as a concept has a vexed history across several disciplines and contexts. When deployed *within* Caribbean studies, it is critiqued for its exclusive anchorage in the binary European/African race politics of the plantation; when it travels widely *without* the Caribbean, to become a description of a contemporary globalized culture, it often appears glib, devoid of the specific power struggles that generated the term in the first place. My readings of Selvon, Mootoo and Lovelace suggest more fluidity than these contestations about *within* and *without* imply. Elsewhere, I have argued that the "primary binary" of African/European, which Kamau Brathwaite presents as the central constituents of Creole society, generates a combative cultural nationalist politics and an exaggeratedly, "hyper-hetero" performance of black male resistance ("Naming Same-Sex Desire" 198). Privileging the plantation as origin limits the interpretive parameters of creolization and dooms each group of Caribbean arrivants (Indians, Chinese, Portuguese, etc.) to identify their particular cultural contribution to creolization by establishing their place with reference to numbers and dates of arrival in a cultural politics of adding up and adding on. Not only does the plantation paradigm *structurally* exclude Amerindians and assign post-plantation arrivals to *belatedness* (with its whiff of inauthenticity) but it also locks interpretive frameworks into the chronology of recorded History. So Brathwaite's argument (that Tia and Antoinette's friendship in *Wide Sargasso Sea* is *historically* impossible (*Contradictory Omens* 38)) implies a directly mimetic relationship between life and literature at odds with the spirit of many Caribbean literary texts (including those discussed here) that manifestly refuse to be constrained by strictly realist bounds.

Wilson Harris has contested this very *literal* idea of literacy, persistently pushing against the limits of realism towards an intuitive mode of writing that might release more creatively creolizing human potentialities. Although recognizing that classic realist writers (Dickens, Austen, Hardy) were "excellent in their way", he points to the limits of this mode for the Caribbean writer:

> Literacy then functioned to achieve an order that offered little chance for sensitive persons to weigh the dangers and the cross-cultural possibilities in a community of different ethnicities: Indian, African Chinese, Portuguese and others. (qtd. in deCaires Narain, "Wilson Harris" 13)

This resonates clearly with Edouard Glissant's ideas of cultural entanglement and "the complicity of relation" (*Poetics of Relation* 147), which he sees as a crucial feature of creolization's transformative potential:

> We are not prompted solely by the defining of our identities but by their relation to everything possible as well—the mutual mutations generated by this interplay of relations. Creolizations bring into Relation but not to universalize. (89)

More recently, Michaeline Crichlow asks if creolization "is a prisoner of the Middle Passage?" (xi). She argues for creolization to be loosened from its moorings in the plantation, as a "one-time event", so that it can function more fluidly "as a *creative cultural evolutionary process*" (21, emphasis original) that mutates according to the contingencies of the particular instances in which it is produced. For Crichlow, widening the conceptual parameters of creolization does not imply a glib idea of global hybridity, "the world in creolization", but is an argument for recognizing "creolization-in-the-world" (21) that involves:

> grappling with several more *présences* than those offered either by the specifically island-Caribbean context or, I should add, also by the binds of ethnic originaries. It requires, too, that we flee the historical and intellectual constraints of the plantation's centrality to *creolization*'s processes. (219, original emphasis)

A more imaginative and promiscuously creoli*zing* concept of creolization recognizes the local and global (and the particular and universal) as *always already entangled* in the shifting, historically contingent contexts and spaces in which creolized cultural practices emerge.

Harris, Glissant and Crichlow prompt us to engage with creolization without succumbing to a narrative of belatedness or inclusion. This is tricky given a context where, as David Dabydeen argues, "[s]cholarly research has been focused overwhelmingly on the African dimension, and in the resulting Afro-centric view of the Caribbean, the Indo-Caribbean is relegated to a footnote" (Dabydeen 10). When Indian cultural practices *are* addressed, as Viranjini Munasinghe argues, they tend to be discussed as evidence of *acculturation* to the dominant Afro-Creole paradigm, rather than as dynamic *agentive* processes within the creolization matrix:

> From this perspective, the choice open to East Indians in the New World is either as retainers of traditional "pure" culture or as imitators of "impure" Afro-Caribbean culture because "creole" remains the dominant analytic for interpreting cultural change in the Caribbean. (557)

To return to Selvon, it is worth noting that in 1958, six years after *A Brighter Sun* was published, Eric Williams famously referred to Indians as "a hostile and recalcitrant minority", a clumsy and politically costly error of judgment.[1] In this context, it is tempting to read Selvon's embrace of a more widely creolized cultural landscape as evidence of his willingness to "throw in his lot" with the nationalist creolization project (unlike, say, V.S. Naipaul). But this reading, I will argue, elides some productive tensions and entanglements and perhaps is not attentive enough to Selvon's probing of the unevenness of creolization and of its relationship to an idea of the cosmopolitan.

"I do not know if I am East Indian, Trinidadian, or West Indian"[2]

In "Three into One Can't Go", Selvon reflects wryly on the impossible equation of his identity as an *East Indian Trinidadian West Indian*. Although his father was "pure Madrassi" and his mother of mixed Scottish and Indian parentage, Selvon insisted elsewhere:

> I was never Indianized. As a child I grew up *completely Creolized*, which is a term we use in Trinidad, meaning that *you live among the people*, whatever races they are, and you are a real born Trinidadian, *you can't get away from it.* And, of course, with a great deal of western influence – I grew up on American films and music. (Nazareth 426, emphasis added)

A life lived "among the people" makes creolization and West Indianness *inescapable* and though a rigid racial hierarchy was firmly in place, it was constantly eroded by the daily rough-and-tumble of living side-by-side that characterized Selvon's boyhood. Selvon argues that the modernizing dynamic that energized creolization for his generation produced unease about both "a Hindu wedding" and "a Shango ceremony":

> one even felt a certain embarrassment and uneasiness on visiting a friend in whose household Indian habits and customs were maintained, as if it were a social stigma not to be westernised. The roti and goat-curry was welcome, but why did they have to play Indian music instead of putting on a calypso or one of the American tunes from the hit parade? ("Three into One" 9)

Creolization here involves discrimination about "traditional" culture (Indian music – but not roti and goat curry) while the embrace of modern forms seems unequivocal (calypso and American pop, both arguably *already* creolized forms via Africa and African-American cultures). The matrix that constitutes creolization, then, involves a complicated set of negotiations between the cosmopolitan and the creole that perhaps undermines the ease of Selvon's assertion that he was "completely Creolized". *A Brighter Sun* also implies a much less complete idea of creolization.

Shani Mootoo, writing over two decades later than Selvon, also has cause to reflect on the co-ordinates of her identity as someone born in Ireland to Indo-Trinidadian parents, raised in Trinidad and living in Canada. Her experience as an Indo-Trinidadian *girl*-child was not one of easy passage into "complete creolization" but of being *prohibited*, as "a good Indian girl" from involvement in it:

> A town-Indian girl, burning with the town's current fever of Trinidad nationalism, wanted to assert her Trinidadianness, to take up space on a stage and gyrate her hips like the young black girls in the new national dance troupes. She wanted to dress in a costume and jump in the streets to the rhythm of calypso music on carnival Tuesday. She wanted to play, not the piano, but pan. ("On Becoming" 87)

Debarred from Afro-Trinidadian culture and uneasy with prescribed Indian femininity, Mootoo's "On Becoming an Indian Starboy" offers a wry account of the way she models her young self on the starboys of Bollywood movies and then later, on the less macho but flamboyant style of rickshaw drivers in Delhi. In her novel, *He Drown She in the Sea*, Mootoo extends *and* creolizes her interest in the Indian starboy in the figure of Harry who I argue is both spectacularly and quietly creolized.

Earl Lovelace, unlike Mootoo and Selvon, has never migrated and has not, as far as I know, been prompted to reflect similarly self-consciously on his West Indianness. Most of his novels and short stories are firmly located in a recognizably Trinidadian landscape, to the extent that Jennifer Rahim is prompted to urge that this commitment to the local not be read as retrogressive nationalism but as exemplifying Lovelace's argument that, "[n]obody is born into the world. Every one of us is born into a place in the world, in a culture, and it is from that standpoint of the culture that we contribute to the world" (qtd. in Rahim 152). If Lovelace's work contributes from its firm grounding in the creolized world of Trinidad, he does not take the terms of that creolization for granted but persistently expands the matrix of its co-ordinates. This is amply demonstrated in *Is Just a Movie* where one strand in that narrative offers nuanced reflections on the concerns that Mootoo and Selvon explore about their own position as East Indian West Indians.

"It was a big thing if you were one of the boys, creolized", but "what sort of man was that?"[3]

A Brighter Sun is often heralded as a text that stages Indo-Caribbean involvement in creolization in exemplary ways. Sandra Pouchet Paquet argues that, "The novel concerns itself with Tiger's quest for manhood and with the process of creolization which Tiger and his young bride, Urmilla, undergo in multi-racial Barataria away from the influence of their parents" ("Introduction" vii). In choosing to propel the couple *abruptly* out of their childhood in an Indian village and into the racially and culturally diverse village of Barataria, Selvon heightens this sense that the couple *undergo* creolization, rather than already being *in it*, in some form, in their home village. They are given a cow, two hundred dollars and a hut and dispatched into the equally foreign terrain of adulthood and a creolized habitat. We are told at the outset, "[t]he village was almost as cosmopolitan as the city. Indians and Negroes were in the majority" (9), two sentences that establish a very cagey sense of "the cosmopolitan" in that it is configured in terms of *percentage*, rather than in terms of an easy accommodation of cultures. The precariousness of Barataria's cosmopolitanism is consolidated by the description of a racially spatialized demographic: "[i]n the back streets the Indians lived simply, observing their customs and tending their fields", while the "Negroes were never farmers, and most of them did odd jobs in the village or the city" (9–10). Selvon's use of the term "cosmopolitan" rather than "creolized" adds to the sense that Urmilla and Tiger are entering a much "wider world" than the one they have left. The cosmopolitan appears to frame creolization here. This framing is most obvious in the prefaces to many chapters which list apparently random events, including developments in the build-up to WWII, economic activity in Trinidad, and ordinary and out-of-the-ordinary local happenings (a mad East Indian dips a key in the sea; a burly Negro called Mussolini chases a small boy). The impact of these conjunctions is to suggest an imbrication of the global, local, political and personal in the unfolding of everyday life in Trinidad that the narrative is unable to deal with fully in all its complexity. This "worldly" framing of Tiger's life adds piquancy to his own erratic, jumbled apprehension of "the wider world", as something he yearns vaguely to have access to.

Tiger and Urmilla are welcomed into Barataria by their neighbours who unhesitatingly offer support and friendship. Joe and Rita are Afro-Trinidadian and fully grounded in Trinidadian life, positioned in the text as supremely well qualified to guide Urmilla and Tiger into a more creolized, modern way of living. Joe is pivotal to Tiger's creolization and functions as the archetypal Creole: he plays pan, limes in Port-of-Spain, drinks rum, loves women, quarrels noisily with Rita, and lives his life fully in the present tense, as is conveyed in his wry comment to Tiger that "[w]at is to is, must is" (38). When pressed by Tiger into conversations about the future and the wider world, he is dismissive, saying "I cud live without writing" (42) and "[i]s experience dat go teach yuh, not books" (110). Despite regular beatings from his grandmother, Joe recounts a boyhood of truanting and play and declares his philosophical contentment with his present life as follows, "Ah don't want to be no millionaire, Ah have enough money. But *Ah still living good*, and Ah does have some happy times wid my friends. So wat happen now?" (111, emphasis added). Tiger respects Joe's greater experience of the city and of creolized Trinidadian culture, but finds his satisfaction with the status quo and his lack of curiosity about the world baffling. Reflecting on Joe's values, Tiger muses:

> It didn't prove you were a man. Nor drinking rum, nor swearing, nor screwing a woman. The way Joe talked, you would think these things counted. But look at Joe, man! He still young and yet he have no ambition! *What sort of man is that?* (112–13, emphasis added)

Tiger, then, is emphatically not persuaded by the rough-and-tumble liming culture that Joe represents and inducts him into; the conviviality of creole liming culture is not enough.

Soul and Soil

Two other (Indian) men, Sookdeo and Boysie, also function as crucial reference points for Tiger as he strains towards manhood and a more secure place within a Trinidad that is itself straining towards independence from colonial rule. Sookdeo is a prolific drinker but also a productive gardener and one of the few literate villagers. He offers Tiger fatherly advice and teaches him to read and write. Sookdeo, who "lived on rum and memories" (65), represents the Indian rooted in the land and still tied by fragile bonds to Indian customs. As such, he represents a connection to the land that both contrasts with Joe's easy mobility and resonates with Tiger's desire to anchor himself in Barataria. Although Tiger is resolute about never again working in the canefield, he labours in his garden with care and tenderness. The garden provides material sustenance but is also a space in which he reflects on his place in the world at several key moments in his life. Roydon Salick speculates that Selvon's original title for the novel was *Soul and Soil* (*The Novels* 16), a title that certainly resonates well with the centrality of land in relation to cultural belonging in *A Brighter Sun*, where the land is presented as the least complicated foundation of Indian Trinidadian belonging. It is a space of creolization in that on it, in it and through it Indians adapt to and anchor themselves in Trinidad. Sookdeo dies shortly after his desperate scrabble to retrieve money he has buried on his land as the Americans hover with their bulldozers, ready to clear his garden to make way for the road. Tiger is deeply moved by his death and the loss of the remnants of an Indian way of life that he is associated with. Although he recognizes that this old way of life is no longer tenable in modern Trinidad, Tiger senses the vacuum its absence signifies. If Joe signifies the oral culture of the current moment (calypso and pan), Sookdeo is tenuously associated with the vestiges of an older, scribal culture.

Tiger's shifting attitudes to the land in *A Brighter Sun* suggest a trajectory that rejects the grim labour regime of the cane plantation but does not give up on the land as source of sustenance and pleasure. There are parallels here in the way the market garden provided the enslaved with alternative possibilities for rooting in the land as well as a space of sustenance, creativity and economic independence. This may not signify a far-enough flight from the plantation (in Crichlow's terms) but it does suggest how, in fleeing the plantation, we might take more note of indentureship as a process in which bodies *and* land are marked by Indian labor. One strand of my argument, then, is to suggest that Tiger's relationship to the land represents an Indo-Creole investment in it that can be read as a creolizing force.

"[W]hy everybody can't live good together?"[4]

Like Sookdeo, Boysie also works hard on his garden, but he spends his evenings drinking and liming in town and has a Creole girlfriend. Young and handsome, his cavalier lifestyle echoes Joe's, as does his "live-in-the-moment" attitude:

He used to say that all this business about colour and nationality was balls, that as long as a man was happy that was all that mattered. He got a delight out of seeing the stares of deep-rooted Indians when he walked around the Queen's Park Savannah with Stella holding on to his arm. "Look at dem," he used to say, "dey so stupid, is as if Ah committing ah crime. Girl, yuh happy?" and when Stella nodded —"Well, I happy too. Is why everybody can't live good together?" (79)

Boysie introduces Tiger to the excitements of Port-of-Spain and provides him with tantalizing glimpses of the world of politics with his account of the Governor's arrival at Red House ("Dat is house fadder, boy!" [80]) and the excitements of Woodford Square. Boysie's plans to migrate to America suggest a world beyond Trinidad that fuels Tiger's frustrations with Barataria, though the men do not share a similar kind of curiosity about the wider world, as is evident in this exchange:

"So tell me something, Boysie, when I used to work in the canefield, and help make sugar, it went to England too?"

"Yes, man."

"You think the people who eating sugar over there does think about we who making it here?"

"You does tink bout who make de shoes yuh wearing?" (88)

Tiger replies that he *does* think in detail about the process and labour involved in the production of a commodity like shoes, signalling an awareness of the way labour operates as a *worlding* configuration. Boysie is baffled, "I for one don't want to know which part it come from, as long as Ah cud get it" and concludes that, "[y]uh shoulda been ah scholar instead of planting tomatoes!" (88). As with Joe, Tiger is attracted to Boysie's creolized lifestyle and the cultural vitality associated with it, but the very vitality of its living-for-the-moment ethos implies a suspension in the present tense and an eschewal of reflection that Tiger finds inadequate. In short, creolization here appears not worldly enough for Tiger's "cosmopolitan" ambitions.

Joe is presented as unquestionably "Creole" and Boysie is shown to be as fully committed to a creolized cultural world. But neither they nor the other men who lime, smoke, drink and talk the nights away at Tall Boy's rumshop provide adequate role models for the kind of man Tiger aspires to be. Midway through *A Brighter Sun*, Tiger muses, "[n]ow he was — what? A man? Maybe, but not a man like Joe Martin or Boysie or any of the others. *They were content, he was not*" (113, emphasis added). Tiger's inability to find intellectual companionship in the village presents an impasse to creolization; a life of liming risks segueing into unreflective complacency. So while Tiger is buoyed up by the camaraderie of "the boys" of *A Brighter Sun*, the novel does not suggest that he embraces the lifestyle they embody. Instead he remains poised between several possibilities: the rum shop and liming culture, migration (like Boysie), the garden (as indicated in the novel's final sentence, "Now is a good time to plant corn" [214–15]) and writing (having submitted a short piece to the *Trinidad Guardian*). As I read it, in constructing Tiger as a man yearning for a sense of *intellectual* as well as cultural and social community, Selvon aims to critique *and* extend the possibilities signified by creolized figures such as Joe and Boysie.

Curdella Forbes, in a perceptive discussion of *Turn Again Tiger*, argues that Tiger's concentrated self-making in that novel, "is fuelled also by the repeated frustration of his efforts to find a community of mind – what may be termed an intimacy of thought – among other men" (123). The "community of mind" that Tiger yearns for is also missing in the liming and "living good" that characterizes his friendship with Joe and Boysie in *A Brighter Sun*. Forbes argues that Tiger is failed by all the models of manhood he encounters because they rely on Caribbean gender norms that limit selfhood for both men and women. I agree and would add that Selvon targets a particular aspect of *creolized* manhood in particular in his Tiger books. Further, if we look at Selvon's representation of intimate friendships between *women*, we may find an alternative vocabulary of intimacy and camaraderie and of "living good together" that might usefully be calibrated against that between men. Away from the picong and laughter of the rum shop, quieter registers of creolizing intimacy *are* possible, even if the text does not place them centrally.

"But when women get together, is a different story altogether."[5]

Urmilla and Rita's relationship develops from shy exchanges over the fence into an intimate friendship. The closeness they establish, despite cultural differences, is presented as unfolding easily, in contrast to the deliberated workings of Tiger's creolization. Rita is the archetypal strong Afro-Caribbean woman: feisty, independent and outspoken; Urmilla is the archetypal submissive, hard-working and wily Indian woman. What (just about) redeems these (and other) cultural shortcuts is that they are often addressed directly in the novel, as when Rita is complaining about Joe's temper and asks, "Why Creole can't quiet like Indian, quiet and nice?" (31).[6] Some of these articulations are clumsy, the working-out of the cultural and historical background to the arguments too deliberated. Nonetheless there are several moments where Selvon is suggestive in his depiction of these intimately creolizing cultural encounters.

When Urmilla is pregnant with her first child, it is Rita who guides her in what to expect and eventually delivers the child. Such is her concern about Urmilla's comfort, that she insists on lending her her own bed, which she painstakingly takes apart, carries over piece by piece, and assembles in Urmilla's hut. Later in the novel when Tiger, emboldened by finding favour with the Americans, invites them to his home for an Indian meal, Rita lends cutlery, linen and glasses and trails the electricity cord from her own into her neighbours' house so that they don't have to rely on lamps. These transfers of household items are partly comedically relayed, as might be expected, given Selvon's keen eye for the way tussles over everyday objects, especially for those who own little, can generate humour. But to my mind, the intimate nature of these transfers are profoundly significant to the novel's focus on cultural encounter: Tiger and Urmilla's baby is delivered on Joe and Rita's bed; the electric light strung like an umbilical cord between the two houses allows the current to be shared. Interestingly, Joe and Rita do not have children but raise Henry, a relative's child, as their own. This underscores the symbolic significance of Selvon's representation of an Indian child delivered by and into a Creole space. The intimacies that animate the everyday domestic arrangements of "living close" strike me as crucial dimensions of the creolization process. The sheer labour (of love) that Rita's offering of the bed entails, is significant and Urmilla, too, shares the fruits of *her* labours by giving Rita tomatoes she grows and milk from her cow. It may be that Selvon relies too readily on a lazy assumption that all women are bound by a shared experience of domesticity, but, nonetheless, the quiet, steady consolidation of Rita and Urmilla's friendship can be calibrated in the novel against the declamatory swagger of Tiger's relationships with men. Selvon understands that gendered constructions of masculinity are limited, as Forbes argues, even if the argument about the need for the transformation of female roles remains latent. So even if Selvon doesn't tell the "different story" that emerges when "women get together", he does provide glimpses of alternative spaces in which more intimate creolizing possibilities flourish.

By way of concluding this discussion I want to turn to a moment when "the wider world" intrudes forcefully into the domestic space. The establishment of an American military base at Chaguaramas (historically, 1941–43) allows Tiger to get involved in building the Churchill-Roosevelt Highway, first clearing the land by hand and then operating a bulldozer. After his promotion, Tiger invites the Americans to have an Indian meal in his home, a move that might be read as an attempt at extending convivial creolization across *very* rigid boundaries of race and class. The Americans declare their desire to "go native"– "[w]e'd like everything to be as it always is" (167) – by which they mean squatting on the floor, eating with their hands and so on. But they also insist that Urmilla leave the kitchen and join them, despite Tiger's protestations that this is not part of Indian custom. Larry waves a knife in Tiger's face, admonishing him to make *choices* and not simply obey custom: "You mustn't let things rule you, John, you must rule things" (172). Selvon presents the Americans as boorish and cavalier;

not only do they persist in hailing Tiger by the generic "John" but they behave as if their power can be temporarily disavowed to facilitate a temporary, convenient conviviality. They can allow things not to rule them because they rule things in Trinidad in a way that Tiger does not. The force of their bullish intrusion into his home is exacerbated by the fact that his wife and his hut have been beautified with Rita's help. Urmilla is wearing make-up and the table is set with unfamiliar dishes that gleam in the borrowed light. Tiger is unmoored by these changes and after the Americans leave, beats Urmilla so severely that he causes her to miscarry their second child.

This scene brings together several strands in Selvon's treatment of creolization; it is an obvious critique of American complacency but it also foregrounds the gendered limitations of Tiger's stumbling engagement with creolization. If the Americans represent a wider, cosmopolitan world and Rita, a creolized culture, then Tiger perceives *both* their interventions as particularly threatening – or, indeed, *unmanning* – when they are focused on *his* wife within the walls of *his* home. Selvon implies that Tiger's "creolizability" is confused and precarious: he admires the worldliness of the Americans (their technological skills, their knowledge, their music) and the Martins' generosity and ability to embrace modernity (their embrace of fusion-cultures such as calypso and pan, and their modern domestic arrangements). But when these intrude into his domestic space, they are perceived as emasculating. In a sense then, the cosmopolitan and the creolized collide here to create another impasse in Tiger's thinking – *and* in the narrative. Writing in 1952, Selvon must navigate the choppy waters of creolization with little by way of relevant textual examples to guide him. Writing after Selvon (and self-consciously so), Lovelace and Mootoo share a similar interest in and anxiety about "creolization-as-national culture" but their texts seem less burdened by uncertainty about *how* that might be represented.

"We had gone forward to right back where we had begun"[7]

Like *A Brighter Sun*, *Is Just a Movie* is finely attuned to the contingencies of quotidian life in all its messy complexity, though the later novel is more encyclopaedic in reach and considerably longer, with several stories and lives densely entangled within it. The framing narrative is a lament for the failure of the Black Power Movement in 1970s Trinidad and the subsequent cultural fall-out and drift towards identity-based politics in which "everybody was finding his own ethnic harbour" (186). Lovelace's retrospective view assesses the cultural, political and literary ambitions that were part of this cultural moment, including by implication his own exploration of carnival as resistance in *The Dragon Can't Dance* (1979). Lovelace continues probing creolization-as-resistance and the possibilities for expressing a righteous refusal of injustice that in *Is Just a Movie* is voiced as

"I not fucking taking that" (54). In the essay "Reclaiming Rebellion", Lovelace argues that we refuse the historical association of rebellion with "delinquency" and instead recognize the persistence of rebellion as a crucial "starting point [...] to a vision of another world" (69). His novel attempts to guide the reader towards seeing the human potential that rebellion – even unsuccessful or "accidental" ones – can release. Sonnyboy, a central character in the novel, drifts into his status as a Black Power radical because, although not involved in the group's activities, he is imprisoned with them for the simple reason that, on a whim, he raises his fist in a Black Power salute. There are many other such "accidental acts of agency" when performance becomes performative but here I want to turn to a figure whose journey into creolization most directly relates to that of Tiger.

In Lovelace's novels, Indo-Trinidadians are invariably part of the creole fabric. Manick, though not central in the same way as Sonnyboy, performs a significant role in *Is Just a Movie*. His father, a reclusive Indian, arrives on a steamroller at the Settlement and stays "doing nothing to change his status of stranger beyond his mumbled good evening" (151). His gradual engagement with the community is facilitated when he, like everyone else, is enthralled by watching Franklyn bat on the savannah. Franklyn's style of batting is a spectacle of skill and beauty that conjures obvious parallels with Brian Lara. Manick's father (as he is always known) recognizes the talent, application and discipline of Franklyn's batting and that, "to accept Franklyn was to remove any impediment to accepting the community that Franklyn represented and from which he (Manick father) had held himself aloof" (155). Lovelace extends this silent moment of recognition by suggesting that once Franklyn's innings is over, Manick's father's own energies are infused by the batsman's style and purpose so that he goes about his farming duties with renewed vitality. It is a wonderfully resonant image of cultural transfer, akin perhaps to the transfer of the bed in the Selvon text, but where the signifying potential is latent in *A Brighter Sun*, Lovelace is self-consciously attuned to its significance, as can be seen in the way he pursues this idea of cross-cultural transfer across generations in Manick.

After small forays fielding the ball while minding cows, Manick becomes "one of the boys" who play cricket on the savannah, eventually becoming a respected batsman himself, though with a patient style more akin to that of Shivnarine Chanderpaul than Lara. With the arrival of Black Power in the village, the boys meet to organize their participation in a demonstration. While the other two Indians in the group, Soogrim and Romesh, opt out, Manick stays and, unsatisfied when given the "Africans and Indians Unite" placard for the tokenism it might imply, asks to carry the red flag. The green flag is for peace, the black for the land and the red for the bloodshed as part of the black struggle. No one speaks but the atmosphere is tense with suspicion *and* possibility, and the narrator silently reflects:

he is the only Indian here, how could we allow him to carry the red flag, the principal symbol of the Black struggle. And how could he, knowing the situation, *want* to carry the red flag? (161–62).

The affective turbulence is left unresolved and Manick leaves.

"Show them the man you is"[8]

Manick's perceived "neutrality" allows him to continue to "straddle two worlds" (321) until, in the carnival with which the novel ends, he appears wearing, "with an exultant sobriety" (343), the glittering costume his father has been quietly making over several years. When pressed about why he hasn't shown the costume before, Manick's father explains that he "couldn't go with a half piece of a thing" (320), prompting the narrator to wonder whether "what kept us from moving out of our different ethnic harbours was that we were perfecting our offering to the world we had to enter" (322). This implies a much greater degree of volition and self-conscious reflection for a significantly creolizing involvement in culture to be effected – not the ponderous "big thoughts" of Tiger but a more everyday, organic reflexivity. The care with which Manick displays his costume, rather like his batting, endorses another, more laboured register of style than the flamboyance of Sonnyboy's refusal to "die quickly" when he is an extra in an American movie. But it is *style* nonetheless. As well as Manick's direct involvement in carnival, Lovelace also stitches this performance tightly into the fabric of Caribbean writing via resonances with Aldrick's dragon and in the echoes we hear of Walcott's "Mass Man": "Hector Mannix, water works clerk, San Juan, has entered a lion" (99). Lovelace's Manick is also a Public Works clerk. *Is Just a Movie* is thickly punctuated by literary allusion and references to writers and writing, so the enfolding of Manick's performance into this creolized matrix is important. Lovelace does not present Manick as a figure who has acculturated or *undergone* creolization successfully. Rather, he invites the reader to see Manick in the fullness of his creoliz*ability and* creoliz*ing* potential.

It is not just Indian Trinidadians whose creolizable/creolizing potential is revisited in the novel. Lovelace also revisits and revises the figure of the "bad john", a crucial figure in his configuration of creolization-as-resistance. In *Is Just a Movie*, we see Afro-Trinidadian men, "badjohns" like KingKala and Sonnyboy, negotiating ideas of selfhood in a wider range of contexts and registers of intimacy than in *The Dragon Can't Dance*, so that distinctions between private/domestic and public/political are more fluidly "raced" and gendered. Lovelace's approach here implies a creolization that is always ongoing and in flux as he attends to a greater range of components and registers of a creolizing potential. Manick's appearance as mas man at the end of the novel "with his red flag waving" (342) does not signify that he has arrived *at* creolization – finally able to carry the flag signifying "the principal symbol of the Black struggle" (162); rather, it contributes to the wider recognition of a more complex and shifting creolizing potential.

"Everybody same-same. Ent so?"[9]

Mootoo's *He Drown She in the Sea*, like *A Brighter Sun*, is set during World War II, but on the fictional island of Guanagaspar, a loosely disguised Trinidad. Focused around a love story between a servant's son, Harry St George, and her employer's daughter, Rose Bihar, the novel ends with the couple's elopement in a boat. The success of this is left uncertain, as it is immediately followed by a lyrical description of a tsunami that they miraculously appear to survive. The key players in this novel are all "Indians and Indians alike" (123) but class disrupts any easy assumption of a shared "Indianness". This is most forcefully demonstrated when Mr Sangha ("Boss") returns late one night to find Rose and Harry, then very young children, in bed together asleep. Harry is violently expelled and thereafter the two children are kept apart and Dolly (Harry's mother) eventually leaves the Sangha's employ. Mootoo's first novel, *Cereus Blooms at Night*, boldly flouted conventional gendered identities as well as exploring same-sex desire. A good deal of that narrative focused on the character Chandin Ramchandin's abortive attempts to mimic white masculinity in his quest to marry a white missionary's daughter. When that effort fails, he implodes violently, exerting control over his daughter in a series of brutal rapes. Incest is presented as the violent but violently logical outcome of a colonial regime that is vicious in its enforcement of white cultural authority to the abjection of all else. If *Cereus Blooms at Night* refuses cultural endogamy via bold representations of hybrid, creolized and queer subjects, *He Drown She in the Sea* offers a more tangential approach to such concerns.

Harry is an Indian who has a powerful Afro-Creole "back-story": his father Seudath was abandoned as a boy in the seaside village of Raleigh and taken in there to be looked after by an old African couple, Uncle Mako and Tantie Eugenie: "They say leave the child with them, that is God who send this little boy for them to keep as their own. A Indian child they bring up, like if he is one of we. And you know, in time he come true-true like one of we!" (105–06). Dolly falls in love with Seudath, whose physique and style she admires as he cycles round selling fish, and who "could not have been more unlike the Indian men of Central" (91). Dolly tells Harry with delight that his father "didn't possess the pious calm or dignity of her father. He was brazen more like black people [...] he was brazen, for so" (90). Seudath is lost at sea and Dolly eventually marries and leaves Raleigh but Harry always remains in touch with his father's adoptive parents.

Although Harry's connection to African culture is not placed centre stage, it is symbolically important and pivotal to the narrative's denouement. Mootoo boldly transplants an Indo-Trinidadian boy into an Afro-Creole household to explore possibilities for other creolizing routes. The intimacy of "living close" generates affective ties across the generations so that Seudath's son is permanently shaped by them, even if his wife chooses otherwise. Uncle Mako, in turn, is also affiliatively bound to the boy he raises and to his son. He makes the ultimate sacrifice at the end of the novel by offering Harry and Rose the boat he has been carefully preparing for his longed-for trip back to Africa. Rose, a strong swimmer, has timed her disappearance in the sea (the only way she can conceive to escape her marriage) so that the currents will take her safely to Uncle Mako. Lovelace's "ethnic harbours" resonate here as a more malleably comforting concept perhaps. The "back-to-Africa" strand in Caribbean culture might be considered sacrosanct but Mootoo hijacks it audaciously in instructive ways. *He Drown She in the Sea* is narrated in a largely realist mode but I would read the extravagant conceit of Harry and Rose's elopement in Uncle Mako's back-to-Africa boat as a willingness to deploy the realist mode in ways that defy realistic expectations. This resonates with Harris's call for a less literal literacy, and Lovelace's insistence that Manick *can* play mas. Mootoo also insists on the necessity of bold cultural transfers and on the narrative conceits and transgressions that facilitate them.

It is notable too that Harry's embrace of his Afro-Creole heritage does not include him modelling himself in the brazen and bold (rude bwaii) manner of his father. Instead, he grows up to be a cautious and thoughtful man. On migrating to Canada, he works as a taxi driver before patiently working his way up to running his own landscaping business. With his taxi-driver friends, he enjoys wine-tasting events and is generally at ease in Canada. Mootoo contructs Harry as a gentle man, not to be confused with Ramchandin's aspirations to be a "gentleman". And unlike Tiger who is unable to really *hear* Urmilla, Harry listens to Rose and takes women seriously as equals. Lovelace's calypsonian narrator, KingKala is also a reflexive, gentle man. The careful inscription of Harry and his friends as connoisseurs of fine wine might also be read as Mootoo's playful and self-conscious commentary on the rum-drinking "boys" that populate Selvon's texts. In relation to Mootoo's concerns in her first novel, it is tempting to read Harry as a playful queering of the heteronormative. But, in the context of my discussion here, I want to emphasize instead the *creolizing* possibilities he represents and suggest that Harry, rather like Manick, figures the kind of reflexivity, cultural hybridity and patience that a figure such as Tiger appears to struggle for.

These three novels shift the emphasis in Caribbean culture away from the muscular "jungle" style of the rude bwaii and towards a self-consciously reflexive idea of (male) self-making in which *creolizing* impulses animate narrative trajectories in less certain but more varied ways than *creolization* has thus far suggested. Writing after Selvon and into a fuller and more complex web of representations of Caribbean life, Mootoo and Lovelace are able to forge (or, indeed *force*) more intimately imbricated narrative possibilities than were perhaps available to him. Nonetheless, read together, these three texts suggest fruitfully creolizing narrative possibilities that provisionally "solve" Selvon's conundrum; as the readings above have aimed to show: three into one *can* go.

NOTES

1. See Colin A. Palmer, *Eric Williams & the Making of the Modern Caribbean*, chapter 8, "The Economics and Politics of Race" (255–303) for a full discussion.
2. Selvon "Three into One" (11).
3. Selvon, qtd. in Birbalsingh (*Passion and Exile* 151), and Selvon *A Brighter Sun* (113).
4. Selvon *A Brighter Sun*, (79).
5. Selvon *The Housing Lark* (133–34). I am indebted to Alison Donnell for highlighting this quote in the preceding chapter and note that her astute discussion of conviviality resonates productively with aspects of my discussion here.
6. See chapter six for a complete discussion of Selvon's use and complication of stereotypical representations of Caribbean women in his other Trinidad-set texts.
7. Lovelace *Is Just a Movie* (183).
8. Lovelace *Is Just a Movie* (149).
9. Mootoo *He Drown She* (147).

CHAPTER SIX

Symptoms of a Malaise:
Diagnosing Post-War Caribbean Identity in
An Island is a World and *I Hear Thunder*

Lorna Burns

D etailing the despondency of Trinidad's middle class, *An Island Is a World* (1955) and *I Hear Thunder* (1963) explore a territory distinct from much else in Selvon's oeuvre. Like *A Brighter Sun* (1952), both novels speak to what Harold Barratt refers to as a particular Trinidadian "angst" specific to the frustrations of "identity, self-awareness, and wholeness in a colonial, pluralistic society crippled by self-contempt and the psychic scars of slavery, and the equally dehumanizing Indian indenture system" ("An Island" 26). But it is only *An Island Is a World* and *I Hear Thunder* that survey this world through characters who speak from a position of social and economic privilege. Selvon's fiction rarely gives centrality to such a world-view, making the comparison of what Roydon Salick refers to in *The Novels of Samuel Selvon* as Selvon's "two middle-class novels" (5) a salient if little-observed point of entry into these works. As Salick's study demonstrates, both *An Island Is a World's* Foster and Adrian of *I Hear Thunder* represent a restless, uncertain and anxious generation of the Trinidadian bourgeoisie.[1] However, what has been less well-observed in criticism is the way in which the two novels mark a shift in Selvon's own attitudes toward his contemporary political climate. Written during the period immediately preceding the short-lived political union of Anglophone Caribbean nations, the West Indian Federation (1958–62), *An Island Is a World* reflects the hope and stresses of unity in its portrayal of the complex political climate of late 1940s Trinidad. National unity and identity, creole culture and the coherence of intra-Caribbean relations all fall under the spotlight as Selvon's characters seek to escape the confines of their small island. The later *I Hear Thunder*, on the other hand, was published in the immediate aftermath of the failed Federation and, as such, can be seen to offer a more cynical appraisal of the tensions between individual and society.

An approach that reads these novels in light of Selvon's disenchantment with Federation might follow in the footsteps of Michael Niblett's *The Caribbean Novel since 1945* and find in Selvon's work a Jamesonian form of national allegory, as indeed Niblett finds in *A Brighter Sun* (48–56). This essay, however, addresses the issue of historical context in *An Island Is a World* and *I Hear Thunder* from a different theoretical perspective, one informed by the philosophy of Gilles

Deleuze and related debates concerning the relationship between the specific or particular on the one hand and the singular or universal on the other.[2] In the work of Deleuze this distinction informs the conviction that literature can be read as a "symptomatology" of the world. The critical and clinical task of Deleuzian literary criticism involves a reading of a novel that explores both the novelist's critique of a particular social situation and their imagining of a future freed from conditions of oppression. This essay applies such a perspective to Selvon's "middle class novels" and in doing so plays upon V.S. Naipaul's claim that *An Island Is a World* and, most notably, the novel's protagonist, Foster, could be read as "a *symptom* of the intellectual malaise that is eating away at Trinidad and the rest of the West Indies" ("Caribbean Voices" 111, emphasis added).

Naipaul's contention that Selvon's earlier novel offers us a symptomatology of his Trinidad holds equally true for *I Hear Thunder*. Where Foster spends much of *An Island Is a World* contemplating his own existential crisis and, from the outset of the novel, appears almost incapable of action due to his feelings of insignificance, Adrian's solipsistic soul-searching leads him to moralize against the values of the island, only to fail in his attempt to remain celibate for one year. In these existential concerns such characters are indeed symptoms of a post-war "malaise" as Naipaul suggests. However, this claim is more telling than might first appear. By reflecting on the social, political and cultural climate of post-war Trinidad from either side of the Federation, these novels, I argue, do indeed offer readers a "symptomatology" of Selvon's Trinidad and, more generally, the post-war Caribbean. In making a connection between the work of literature and that of symptomatology, this essay emphasizes Deleuze's conceptualization of literature as "health". Creating symptomatologies of the world, Selvon's novels allow us to elaborate the scope of Deleuzian literary criticism beyond the select few writers that he chose to focus on. At the same time, the symptoms of malaise that Naipaul finds in the two novels may be read not as a sign of an endemic situation of Caribbean dependency, but as a literary diagnosis of Selvon's world and the potential for imagining new ways of living.

The note of despondency that Naipaul identifies in *An Island Is a World* is one that takes on greater significance with the publication of *I Hear Thunder*, a novel dismissed by Derek Walcott as "erratic", "ceremonious" and concerned with "middle class [sic] disenchantment, middle-class frustration, middle-class adultery, etc., in Trinidad" ("The Action is Panicky" 125–26). Both novels are concerned with the interior lives of their protagonists, rooting around, as Isabel Quigly noted in her 1955 *Spectator* review, "in that dangerous dustbin the soul, and com[ing] up smeared and surprised (I speak technically; his book is in no way improper) at the garbage" (109). However, the symptomatology that Selvon offers is closely related to the political and social climate of his contemporary Trinidad.

In *An Island Is a World*, for example, the novel's protagonist, Foster, encapsulates a sense of unease with his place in the world:

> Foster imagined Trinidad as it was, a mere dot on the globe. But he saw himself in the dot.

> He saw himself in the dot, and he transmitted thoughts into the universe. He was lying down on the dot and thoughts radiated from him like how RKO introduce their films with a radio station broadcasting into space. (1)

This image offers a sense of relationality in which the "dot" forms a ground from which the individual can relate to the whole. However, what potential there is in that global-local relation is immediately lost as the image is inverted and we are told that at other times "Foster was big and the globe was small, spinning off there in space" (1). This frustration, tied to a sense of ambitions too big for the possibilities offered by the context in which one lives, persists throughout the novel and accounts, in part, for the "intellectual malaise" that Naipaul identifies. In many respects, Foster can be seen to represent the contemporary position of Trinidad, a small island trying to find its place in the emerging world order. This is captured in an overwhelming sense, as with Selvon's first novel *A Brighter Sun*, of limitation: a parochialism that he perceives to be endemic within Trinidad and which prevents the novel's characters from fulfilling their ambitions and potential. For Foster, however, parochialism is a condition that he encounters time and again in his travels: "No one thinks of the world. I am an Englishman. I am an American. I am a white man. I am a black man. No one thinks: 'I am a human being, and you are another'" (155).

In moments such as these, Selvon appears to be anticipating a kind of cosmopolitanism: a universalistic vision that encourages every one of us to look beyond our own closed world and to acknowledge a shared human existence. Yet this move is thwarted in other respects. For example, during his time in London, Foster's first-hand experience of prejudice, isolation and loneliness (foreshadowing that of Moses and the "fellars" in *The Lonely Londoners*) leads him to question the sufficiency of cosmopolitanism. In his letters to his friend Andrews back home in Trinidad, he writes:

> sometimes a man feels as if he hasn't got a country, and it's a lonely feeling, as if you don't really belong nowhere. I used to think that this had merit, that we'd be able to fit in anywhere, with anybody […]. I used to think we belonged to the world, that a Trinidadian could go to Alaska and fit in, or eat with chopsticks in Hong Kong […]. I used to think of this philosophy as being the broadest, the most universal […], that we'd be able to see the way clearer, unbounded by any ties to a country or even a race or a creed. (106)

But, he continues, "[y]ou can't belong to the world, because the world won't have you. The world is made up of different nations, and you've got to belong to one of them" (107). The cosmopolitan freedom of a universal citizen, exempt from national ties and particularity, is lauded by Foster in the former extract even while, as Michael Niblett notes, the latter testifies to Selvon's persistent faith in the nation-state as a necessary mediator between the individual and the world (207). In presenting these two opposing readings of the Caribbean's global cosmopolitanism (one celebratory, the other sceptical), Selvon occupies a middle-ground between nationalism and universalism, and in doing so emphasizes the importance of both specific, located articulations of identity as well as relational, universal frames of reference. As in the opening image of the RKO transmitter, one's thoughts may be broadcast far into the universe but they always emanate from a particular ground or dot.

There is in Selvon a move between the particular and the universal, and, as a result, his exploration of the malaise experienced in his contemporary Trinidad is one that operates between these twin poles—a distinction that, as we shall see, is crucial to Deleuze's definition of a literary symptomatology or health. Moreover, this is a sense of the particular wholly freed from what Glissant would term "atavistic" modes of belonging (*Faulkner Mississippi* 114). Where the complete absence of "any ties to a country" or race is revealed to be insufficient to live in this actual world (characterized as it is by a global world order founded on nation-states), the novel nevertheless resists essentializing belonging. The immigration of Indo-Trinidadians to India in the wake of Indian independence is a prominent example of this:

> men who had forgotten their nationality in the cosmopolitan population became aware of themselves as Indian. A flame of nostalgia began to spread. Men who had forgotten who they were dusted their memories and began to talk about going back home. (*An Island* 161)

Expedience and nostalgia are suggested as the driving forces behind this return, but the fact that the Indian population feels so little attachment to "the country in which they had worked their lives away, to go to distant India purely for sentimental reasons" (210), is presented as a failure of Trinidadian society to be truly cosmopolitan in Appiah's sense of the term (xiii). It is this struggle that Foster's closest friend, Andrews, clearly highlights: "this is their country, and they should help to build it, and suffer with it, and go through all the struggle that we have to undergo before we find a place on the map" (181).

Selvon's concern with the problems of national identity persists in the later *I Hear Thunder*, where the potential unity expressed in Andrews' statement seems a distant promise indeed. That *An Island Is a World* holds out, as Alison Donnell argues in chapter four, the "possibility of unifying at a level of human interaction and mutual recognition" is borne out by the political ambitions of characters such as Andrews. However, her claim that this unifying vision is one which "Selvon insistently writes towards" is somewhat tested by *I Hear Thunder*, published in the immediate aftermath of the failed West Indian Federation. The nostalgia present in the Indo-Trinidadian community and in characters such as Seeta and Motilal is highlighted as a barrier to integration:

> Seeta [...] lived as though she were still on the banks of the Ganges, faithful to every sign and symbol that registered her nationality. Motilal, her husband, had absorbed some of the local atmosphere, but Adrian was sure that if pushed he would fall back even more vehemently on the tradition and custom of the Motherland. (13)

Nevertheless, while *An Island Is a World* holds up cross-cultural and creole interaction as a potential way beyond narrow nationalism, and what Glissant would term a nostalgic "reversion" (*Caribbean Discourse* 16), in *I Hear Thunder* the inter-racial relations that exist are revealed to be barren. Both texts portray the paucity of "reversion":

> The first impulse of a transplanted population which is not sure of maintaining the old order of values in the transplanted locale is that of reversion. Reversion is the obsession with a single origin: one must not alter the absolute state of being. (Glissant *Caribbean* 16)

Motilal's reaction on learning that his daughter, Polly, is pregnant with the child of a local white man, for example, highlights this obsession with purity and an absolute, unchanging state of being:

> She let the race down! I don't know about your family [to his wife], but none of mine ain't interbreed up with no nigger or chinee or white man, you hear! If was Indian, I wouldn't mind so much, it time she get married anyway. Indian got to stick together, we got to keep we own blood and don't mix up. (145)

He complains to his wife shortly before that "[y]ou didn't bring that girl up Indian, you know. She too creolised for my liking. If you did bring she up Indian, that never happen!" (145). However, in a parallel situation in which an Afro-Trinidadian family discover that their daughter is pregnant by the same white man, Randolph, Selvon appears to undermine the potential of creolization or at least *métissage* to address such "reversional" attitudes.[3] Knowing that Polly is pregnant with his child, Randolph nevertheless fixes his eye on a young black girl, Josephine, since, "[f]or him, each conquest was dead and gone the moment it was accomplished. [...] He was living in an island where the white colour of his skin was more desired than food and drink and opened a gateway which was like the legs of a woman spread apart" (153):

> He dispatched Josephine with a minimum of time and effort and leapt away with a practised alacrity to seek fresh fields. When Josephine confessed to her mother that there was no hope of a marriage, her mother said:

"It ain't him we want, girl, is the *colour*! Bastard, lanyard or mustard, is a
white child you going to have! The good Lord smile on you and you ain't
know it". (154)

There is a marked difference between the parental responses from the Indo- and
Afro-Trinidadian communities: if Motilal expresses a sentiment of reversion, then
the response of Josephine's mother is at best one of "diversion". As a mode of
concealment and of alienation, Glissant characterizes diversion as acts of mimicry
and camouflage that operate, always, "as if *the Other is listening*" (*Caribbean
Discourse* 22, original emphasis), as a reaction to the dominant, white presence.
The mother's happiness at the prospect of a white grandchild at the expense of
her daughter who is little but another "conquest" to Randolph, only prolongs the
existing colonial hierarchy which values the colour of white skin above all else.

In *I Hear Thunder*, *métissage* remains at the level of "diversion" and as such
"*leads nowhere*", offers no "real potential for development" or reconciliation
with the material conditions of the postcolonial Caribbean (Glissant, *Caribbean
Discourse* 23, original emphasis). Like Seeta's pestle and mortar crushing and
mixing individual spices into a single paste, *métissage* can only lead to a productive
creolization if it can move beyond the current status quo and produce "*something
else, another way*" (Glissant, "Creolization" 270, original emphasis):

Backwards and forwards Seeta's hands moved, her elbows like pistons, a mere
flick of the wrist lending pressure as the stones ground each tiny seed, each
variety combining with the other in a subtle affinity, until in the end there was
no one individual flavour or smell. (Selvon, *I Hear Thunder* 69–70)

Seeta's indistinct paste stands as a metaphor for a limited form of creolization: a
mixing and synthesis (*métissage*), but one that falls short of the production of a
new, alternative and distinct creolized form. Insofar as creolization "opens on a
radically new dimension of reality", it designates a moment of difference that "is
realized in going beyond" current possibilities (Glissant, "Creolization" 270 and
Poetics 82). As such, it cannot be defined as a generalization, as a combination of
parts that synthesize into a form in which "no one individual flavour or smell" can
be discerned. As Glissant clarifies, in the processes of Relation and creolization,
"elements don't blend just like that, don't lose themselves just like that. Each
element can keep its [...] essential qualities" (qtd. in Diawara 63). As I have
argued elsewhere (Burns 145–47), far from returning us to essentialism, here
Glissant stresses the singularity or what he calls the opacity of creolized elements
(the unique "thisness" of the individual). The creolized is not a "blend" of pre-
existing parts but something that emerges as a new, singular form: a distinction
that Selvon privileges in the contrast between Seeta's paste in which "no one
individual flavour or smell" is produced and the distinctive singularity sought
by Adrian at the novel's close when he searches for a "touch of individuality"

(192). The emphasis on "individuality" suggests that, while fixed and diversional/ reversional identities are criticized in the novel, Selvon, like Glissant, resists the notion that the alternative is a state of absolute indistinguishability. Viewed in this light, the chaotic carnival space of the novel, a site of fluid identities and indistinct genders, where class and race no longer matter – "Black, white, brown and yellow, rich and poor, doctors, lawyers, and Government officials, all were out on the streets jumping up in the bands" (189) – emerges as similarly limited as a means to overcome the characters' malaise. Carnival is presented as a "temporary barrier to the future" (191): a moment of escapism that must either be overcome, in the case of Mark who sees himself as a future member of the island elite, or, for Adrian, maintained through a hedonistic lifestyle. The infidelity of Polly and Mark's wife Joyce, as well as the seeming indifference expressed by Mark on discovering that his best friend Adrian has committed adultery with Joyce, reflect the moral paucity of the island lifestyle as it is depicted in the novel. The best hope offered in the end is not to be found in Mark, a man who is happy to overlook his wife's behaviour and break a promise made to his mother that she could come and live with him:

> Now he was civilised and sophisticated, past the stage of basic, primitive ideas which Adrian was still trying to overcome. He had to live like that – trusting and hoping, and putting up a front of worldliness to protect himself. And if this meant losing his mother and allowing his wife to go out with other men, he had to pay the price. (48–49)

In this light, Mark is far from the novel's "symbol of success" and his estrangement far exceeds that of his linguistic position in relation to local Trinidad, as Wyke argues (71). *I Hear Thunder* is a story of few successes; ultimately what hope there is lies with Adrian, who strives to maintain "just that little touch of individuality" that will enable him "to make a small distinction and keep him company as he limp[s] onwards" (192). A "touch of individuality", not Seeta's paste pounded until "there was no one individual flavour or smell" (69–70), is sought at the novel's close.

Recalling *An Island Is a World* and the uneasy exploration of Trinidad's position in a global context, here the need to retain a "touch of individuality" suggests something of the risk of integration—the threat of the erasure of difference in a homogenous whole. In "Three into One Can't Go", Selvon draws attention not only to the disidentification he felt as a child watching Indian religious ceremonies being performed in Trinidad, but to the creation of a community apathetic to and alienated from their cultural roots as a result of their assimilation of Western norms: "there were as many Blacks ignorant or indifferent to the Shango cult [...] as there were Indians to their own ritual" (9). The West Indian Federation offered an opportunity for Caribbean nations and peoples to interact, "observe and try to understand the differences and prejudices that exist from islander to islander" (something Selvon was able to experience only by coming to England, he suggests) (9). Significantly, while Selvon regarded the collapse of the West Indian Federation in 1962 as a sign of the region's inability to move beyond a narrow nationalist agenda, "the failure to organise a unified body that would be representative of the Caribbean as a whole" (9), he does not regard such union as the potential erasure of difference and particularity. In the face of a divisive politics that kept the region in a subordinate position of economic development and political influence, Selvon argues that it is time to revive "the Federation dream, and [...] to broaden our concepts to include the whole Caribbean area" (11). Writing in 1986, Selvon is able to revive the enthusiasm for inter-island cooperation and Caribbean unity that is an aspiration of *An Island Is a World*. However, *I Hear Thunder* is largely bereft of such hope, a sign of the novel's closeness to the collapse and Selvon's disappointment at the way in which "the dream of Federation had evaporated" (9).

These reflections on the failures and forms of alienation within Trinidadian society might indeed inform a reading of these novels as a national allegory and the disillusionment of various characters, their inability to look to the future and create a successful, cosmopolitan and creolized identity, as a troubling sign for the postcolonial Caribbean. When viewed from a Deleuzian perspective, however, reading literature simply as an allegory of national and nationalist sentiment is to underplay its potential to imagine new forms of identification; indeed, it is to underplay its potential for "health". Selvon's novel does offer a critical reflection on his contemporary world, but the remainder of this essay will be concerned to explore those aspects of his work which point beyond the status quo towards, to recall Glissant, "*something else, another way*".

Such is the key distinction that Deleuze draws between a major literature, which conforms to established conventions, and a minor one. The latter signals not a marginal status or "minority literature" but a literature involved in the processes of becoming and, since minor literature and subjectivities exceed fixed and standardized forms, they designate the revolutionary potential to become new. When viewed from a Deleuzian perspective, the fixity of the "major" is precisely the issue with the concept of nation: a nation is a majoritarian formation with the image of the father and the law at its core. In *Kafka: Towards a Minor Literature*, for example, it is the image of the father that territorializes, hierarchizes family relations and creates boundaries ("territories"), which extend into other socio-political formations: "The photo of the father, expanded beyond all bounds, will be projected onto the geographic, historical, and political *map* of the world [...] An Oedipalization of the universe" (10, original emphasis). Similarly in "Bartleby; or, The Formula" Deleuze finds in the works of Herman Melville a recurring identification that bypasses the oedipal hierarchy enforced by the image of the father:

> many of Melville's novels begin with images or portraits, and seem to tell the story of an upbringing under a paternal function [...]. But in each case, something strange happens, something that blurs the image, [...] but also undoes the subject, sets it adrift and abolishes any paternal function. (*Essays* 77)

What makes "Bartleby" and other works "minor literature", then, is precisely this undoing of fixed, hierarchical or majoritarian forms: an undoing described as a deterritorialization. Finally, it is because such forms are undone (deterritorialized) that the ground is prepared for the emergence of something new, a becoming which exceeds the status quo. That becoming is the revolutionary potential of literature and why literature is not simply a reflection of an extant state of affairs, but the creation of a *new* symptomatology of that circumstance and its future potential for "health".

Within the above analysis, Deleuze, like Selvon, recognizes the persistent tensions between the particular and the singular that underlie the liberating lines of becoming that characters like Bartleby engender. The challenge acknowledged by Selvon of how to foster a pan-Caribbean relationality and cooperation that both leaves behind atavistic modes of being and yet, nevertheless, retains "just that little touch of individuality", is precisely what Deleuze finds in Melville:

> Like Melville before it, pragmatism will fight ceaselessly on two fronts: against the particularities that pit man against man and nourish an irremediable mistrust; but also against the Universal or Whole, the fusion of souls in the name of great love or charity. Yet, what remains of souls once they are no longer attached to particularities, what keeps them from melting into a whole? What remains is precisely their "originality", that is, the sound that each one *produces*, like a ritornello at the limit of language. (*Essays* 87, original emphasis)

Bartleby's formula, "I would prefer not to" (Melville 11), is one such "ritornello", marking the "limit of language", pushing language beyond itself. In other words, what resists both reversional modes of affiliation or particularities that delimit communities and pit one group against another *and* complete fusion into a whole is an individual's singularity. The capacity of each particular life to resist the status quo, produce a sound or effect that goes beyond what is currently possible, is a sign of the virtual, singular life that unites all beyond any totalizing wholeness.

Part of the symptomatology offered in *An Island Is a World* and *I Hear Thunder* reflects the failure of a particular, historical political union of Caribbean nations. Nevertheless, Selvon also intuits, notably in *An Island Is a World*, something of that singular life which resists "melting into a whole" and which marks the productive capacity of literature itself. Such an awareness of life as both an actuality and a becoming is signalled in Foster's letters home, in which he observes that "[t]oo many people forget the actuality of life, the exact moments of existence. Each action is mechanical, habit charting a beaten, circular course" (128). With this heightened sense of the particular follows a realization in which Foster senses something of life as a singularity:

> To escape from this, dream dreams, write books, compose music, paint pictures, is not the way out. There is something false and hollow about each creation of the artist, something lifeless and useless, inapplicable to the common-place, every day actions [...].

> Life as it intrinsically is cannot be depicted. The artist steps over life to get at the person [...]. Any attempt to present life as it is either recounts events which have already happened, or speculates on what is to come. The present, in truth, is a farce. It does not exist. (128–29)

Foster's comments on art and literature here are striking in their pessimism, and seem at odds with other sections of the novel in which the narrative is used to defend different art forms such as popular music and modernist painting. Despite this negativity, however, they nevertheless hint at an approach to life and to literature that brings us close to Deleuze's own.

While Deleuze's literary-clinical project remained incomplete at his death, his interest in exploring the idea of literature as a symptomatology and as the potential for health can be traced back to his early work on Nietzsche and the writer Leopold von Sacher-Masoch in *Masochism: Coldness and Cruelty* (1989).[4] Masoch's work is, of course, an exemplary case regarding the relationship between literature and symptomatology: Krafft-Ebing's original categorization of masochism in his book *Psychopathia Sexualis* (1886) directly attributed the new term to Masoch's fictional rendering of this "perversion". However, for Deleuze, the value of Masoch's work lies less in the fact that the term "sadomasochism" was taken up by psychoanalysis in order to describe two opposed forms of sexual perversion than in his claim that Masoch's fiction gives us a new symptomatology of masochism. In identifying the contract as the primary sign of masochism, Masoch distinguished the symptoms of masochism from those of sadism, where previously they had been treated as a single neurosis.[5] This takes us far from psychoanalysis; indeed, Deleuze and Deleuze and Guattari go so far as to stress the precedence of the literary case: "[i]t seems, moreover, that an evaluation of symptoms might be achieved only through a *novel*" (Deleuze, *Logic of Sense* 273, original emphasis); "there is no longer even any need for applying psychoanalysis to the work of art, since the work itself constitutes a successful psychoanalysis" (Deleuze and Guattari qtd. in Tynan 4).

The distinction at work here reflects the anti-representationalist nature of Deleuzian thought. Literature, for Deleuze, should not be misunderstood as a direct reflection of a particular set of "real-world" affairs: the text is not a sign that signifies something other or prior to itself. As he famously argued:

> There are, you see, two ways of reading a book: you either see it as a box with something inside and start looking for what it signifies, and then if you are even more perverse or depraved you set off after signifiers. And you treat the next book like a box contained in the first or containing it. And you annotate and interpret and question [...]. Or there's the other way: you see the book as a little non-signifying machine, and the only question is "Does it work, and how does it work?" How does it work for you? [...] This second way of reading's intensive: something comes through or it doesn't. There's nothing to explain, nothing to understand, nothing to interpret. (Deleuze, *Negotiations* 7-8)

In other words, the act of reading and of literary criticism is not one that seeks to uncover what the text "really means" or what it tells us about the writer's psychological state of mind, treating the writer or their socio-historical context as if they were subject to the treatment of psychoanalysis. Rather,

> authors, if they are great, are more like doctors than patients. We mean that they are themselves astonishing diagnosticians or symptomatologists. There is always a great deal of art involved in the grouping of symptoms, in the organization of a *table* where a particular symptom is dissociated from another, juxtaposed to a third, and forms the new figure of a disorder or illness. (Deleuze, *Logic of Sense* 273, original emphasis)

The writer or the text is not a "patient" to be cured or a "box" to be unpacked; rather, in producing a work of literature the writer creates a new symptomatology that helps us to better understand the world. For Deleuze, "[s]igns imply ways of living, possibilities of existence, they're the symptoms of life gushing forth or draining away" (*Negotiations* 143). In stating this claim, Deleuze does not reduce literature to an account *of* an author's evaluation of the world, but establishes it as the organization, juxtaposition and dis/association of signs (symptoms of life) in such a way that a "new figure" of life, new "possibilities of existence" emerge: a productive, creative expression rather than a reflective, derivative one (a "box with something inside").

Returning to Foster's reflection on life and his pessimistic thought that "[l]ife as it intrinsically is cannot be depicted. The artist steps over life to get at the person" (129), there is, in *An Island*, an echo of Deleuze's own characterization of the relationship between signs, symptoms and new figures of "life". Consider the way in which Deleuze reads Charles Dickens's *Our Mutual Friend* in his late essay "Immanence: A Life":

> A disreputable man, a rogue, held in contempt by everyone, is found as he lies dying. Suddenly, those taking care of him manifest an eagerness, respect, even love, for the slightest sign of life. Everyone bustles about to save him, to the point where, in his deepest coma, this wicked man himself senses something soft and sweet penetrating him. But to the degree that he comes back to life,

> his saviors turn colder, and he becomes once again mean and crude. Between
> his life and his death, there is a moment that is only that of *a* life playing with
> death. The life of the individual gives way to an impersonal and yet singular
> life that releases a pure event freed from the accidents of internal and external
> life, that is, from the subjectivity and objectivity of what happens. (Deleuze,
> *Pure Immanence* 28)

It is this distinction between this particular life and *a* life that is of greatest
interest. *A* life, here, is understood as that which is beyond any particular instance
of being: a distinction that, when read in tandem with *An Island*, gives new sense
to Foster's claim that "[l]ife as it intrinsically is cannot be depicted" (129). *A*
life cannot be depicted directly, only, as in Dickens, intuited. As a result, signs
as the expression of "life" and possibilities of existence necessarily involve two
poles or planes of reality: the particular (this life) and the singular (a life). It is
this distinction, I suggest, that Selvon's novel makes explicit. At one level, the
artist must "step over life to get at the person" because pure, singular life "as it
intrinsically is cannot be depicted". At the same time, however, this is insufficient:
"There is something false and hollow about each creation of the artist, something
lifeless and useless" when it "either recounts events which have already happened,
or speculates on what is to come" (Selvon, *An Island* 129). In representing the
specific traits and trials of a character's particular life, the artist may find that they
are simply recounting events past or speculating on futures to come: in other
words, imagining a particular way of being. Dealing only with the specific, such
a vision fails to capture the potential of a future ("what is to come") that cannot
be predicted. Deleuze's point is that literature is at its most powerful when it hints
at the presence of a life behind the particular, as in the Dickens tale. A life means
the potential for life and for different ways of life in any context: life as becoming,
not being. However, if the example of *Our Mutual Friend* demonstrates the power
of a singular life as a plane of becoming beyond subjective reality, Selvon's novel
reminds us that an opposite but complementary move also remains necessary: we
can only ever experience this particular life, even if that life's potential to become-
new lies in its singular form.

Deleuze's reading of literature exposes the coexistence of the singular and the
specific, while maintaining that it is the power to become in unforeseen ways that
represents literature's (and life's) potential to break free from the strictures of daily
routine and mechanical existence. Foster's problem is that, rather than recognizing
the singular sense of "[l]ife as it intrinsically is", as the potential to become and
to escape essentialized ways of being, he too often falls into the trap of nihilism.
For example, while surveying his fellow passengers on a bus ride into town, he
thinks, "[e]veryone in this bus is more or less happy, thinking about small pasts
and presents and futures. It is the way of life (as if I didn't know). Alternatively,

oblivion" (4). While dialectical thought privileges becoming over being, unless – like Foster's counterpoint in the novel, the priest, Father Hope – one is able to accept the fundamental premise that the ultimate aim of the dialectic is the realization of the Ideal (God), then one is in the position of nihilism. Foster's fear of life therefore vacillates between nihilistic despair and an over-determined existence wherein he tries to "live in a state of acute consciousness of being" (129): a consciousness of everything at the same time. And in the meantime he forgets to actually live his particular life.

If there is something false in the representation of the artist, it is a necessary deception (and indeed Deleuze characterizes art as working through the power of the false). It is not possible for a particular life to be conscious of all things, but it is Foster's flaw to fall into nihilism. In the end, Naipaul's claim that Selvon's protagonist could be read as "a symptom of the intellectual malaise that is eating away at Trinidad and the rest of the West Indies", gets close to the heart of the matter. Foster is indeed a symptom of malaise, or more accurately the diagnosis of one: "On the journey, he diagnoses this sorrow: the result of too much aimlessness and hopelessness" (4), a diagnosis that is carried through to *I Hear Thunder* in the novel's vision of "the petty intrigues and affairs which made up the life-blood of the island's middle-class" (12). But this is precisely the role of literature as Deleuze presents it: "[m]ore a physician than a patient, the writer makes a diagnosis, but what he diagnoses is the world; he follows the illness step by step, but it is the generic illness of man; he assess the chances of health, but it is the possible birth of a new man" (*Essays* 53).

Following Nietzsche, in *Essays Critical and Clinical* Deleuze argues that literature is "an enterprise in health" (3) precisely because writers diagnose and create new symptomatologies. But in showing us how particular symptoms or forms of malaise come to be what they actually are, literature opens up alternative ways of becoming. Thus, although Foster is unable, in his "present" (the prologue to the novel), to escape his malaise – a nihilistic sense of aimlessness in life – Selvon's novel offers the reader a range of conflicting perspectives, playing characters and ideas off of one another, showing us how things came to be what they are, thus hinting at the possibilities of a future that might become very different. This is never utopian, but, as both Andrews and Adrian intuit, a struggle: always a tension between the particular hardships of this specific life and the singular sense of being (becoming) that is the potential for "that little touch of individuality [...] to make a small distinction and keep [us] company as [we limp] onwards". Political positions, literary diagnoses are produced not by rejecting the singular and focusing purely on the specific, but emerge from a relation between both.

NOTES

1. Commentary on *I Hear Thunder* can be found in Barratt's "An Island is Not a World", Salick's *The Novels of Samuel Selvon*, and Wyke. Ramchand's introduction to *An Island Is a World* provides an important critical context for a similarly overlooked novel.
2. The pairing of specific and singular in a postcolonial context is an obviously loaded association following Peter Hallward's *Absolutely Postcolonial* (2001), in which he identified the "singular" nature of postcolonial writing as both Deleuzian in its constitution and indicative of postcolonialism's apolitical nature. Hallward's reading of Deleuze and the singular is one that I have challenged elsewhere (Burns 12–18).
3. The distinction between creolization and *métissage* is one drawn by Glissant: "When we speak about creolization, we do not mean only 'métissage,' cross-breeding, because creolization adds something new to the components that participate in it"; "[c]reolization is unpredictable, whereas the immediate results of cross-breeding are more or less predictable. [...] creolization opens on a radically new dimension of reality [...] [it] does not produce direct synthesis, but 'résultantes,' results: something else, another way" ("Creolization" 269–70).
4. As Aidan Tynan notes, following the publication of *Coldness and Cruelty*, "Deleuze suggested that the concept of literary symptomatology had a potentially wide scope and that he wished to write a series of books in that vein on various literary authors, including Beckett, Robbe-Grillet and Pierre Klossowski" (3). Although the subject continued to appear in his work, these studies did not appear.
5. For further discussion of Deleuze on Masoch and/or health, see Bogue (11–22), Burns (156–61) and Tynan.

CHAPTER SEVEN

Racialized Femininities in Samuel Selvon's Trinidad Novels

Kate Houlden

*T*his chapter discusses the racialized representation of women in three of Samuel Selvon's Trinidadian novels, *Turn Again Tiger* (1959), *I Hear Thunder* (1963) and *The Plains of Caroni* (1970). Each of these texts focuses on an Indo-Caribbean man having sexual relations with a white woman: in the first, Tiger has a violent sexual encounter with Doreen before returning to his Indo-Caribbean wife, Urmilla; in *I Hear Thunder*, Adrian has passionate sex with his friend's English wife, Joyce, before repairing his relationship with Indo-Caribbean Polly; last of all, Romesh rejects the control of his overbearing mother in favour of a relationship with white Caribbean Petra.[1] In the final scene of each book, the protagonist is reunited with his partner as a reward for his trials, a consistency of narrative closure that shares much with the traditions of romance fiction and one that indicates the centrality of male-female relationships to Selvon's fictional world. As suggested by the novels' emphases on the experiences of Tiger, Adrian and Romesh, female sexual desire is consistently focalized through masculine need and women are primarily acted upon, rather than demonstrating their own individual sexual agency. Yet, at the same time, there is strong evidence for there being a trajectory across these works whereby stereotypes of white and Indian femininity are broken down in the service of a creolized regional (rather than ethnic) identity; it is this process which tempers the potential conservatism of the first two novels, in which the protagonists return to Indian women after an excursion through white flesh. With their focus on diverse forms of Indo-Caribbean selfhood – Tiger is the self-educated son of illiterate peasants who has an arranged marriage at a young age; Adrian is a middle class, educated and urban "fete-boy" (Walcott, "The Action is Panicky" 126); while university-educated Romesh is from cane stock but is now a member of the professional classes – these texts counter what Shalini Puri has described as "the erasure that has dogged Indo-Caribbeans since their arrival" (*The Caribbean Postcolonial* 66). However, their sexual politics engender another kind of erasure, as there is a curious absence when it comes to the possibility of black women partnering Indo-Caribbean men. If sexual relationships are one of the primary mechanisms by which their protagonists cast off the legacies of the past, then the endings of these books invoke a Caribbean future predicated on the heterosexual family and a troubling negation of black claims to citizenship.

When viewed in sequence, these texts could be interpreted as promulgating a move towards whiteness, as the protagonists' choices of long-term partner progress chronologically from submissive young Indian wife, to creolized Indian girlfriend to educated white Caribbean woman. It is more convincing, however, to view the books as being focused on expunging the fantasy of European superiority as symbolized by the white female body. It is as though Selvon compulsively replays the same encounter between Indo-Caribbean man and white woman to slightly different effect each time, with his final outing rejecting the racialized charge of the earlier two works and emphasizing the couple's parity instead. As well as undermining the stereotype of the imperious white mistress, these novels also complicate the trope of the submissive Indian wife. On the one hand, they offer a diverse range of Indo-Caribbean female characters, some of whom illustrate the psycho-sexual costs of this traditional role. Accordingly, they overturn the connection between Indian femininity, racial purity and domestic order, problematizing the mobilization of women's bodies in the service of ethnically-based nationalist claims. On the other hand, all of these women are punished (in one form or another) for transgressing the boundaries of hearth and home and all are eventually subordinated to a man. Selvon's Indo-Caribbean women therefore have a more conflictual relationship with racialized models of gendered behaviour than his fictional white women. Overall though, the novels bear out Sandra Pouchet Paquet's assertion that "[t]he use of stereotype [...] is at the core of Selvon's conception of character. [...] having established a stereotype, it is also characteristic of Selvon's method that he more often than not challenges it" ("Introduction" xxi). As an alternative to both these categories – imperious white mistress or submissive Indian wife – the books champion a creolized model of femininity grounded in racial expansiveness, sexual expression and the enjoyment of localized cultural forms like calypso and carnival. It is this alternative mode of femininity that goes some way to offsetting Selvon's tendency to use female characters as narrative foils for their menfolk.

If *Turn Again Tiger, I Hear Thunder* and *The Plains of Caroni* reveal Selvon's interest in overturning the gendered and sexual legacies of colonialism as experienced by those of both Indo- and white Caribbean heritage, then black women in particular appear to be excluded from this process. In *Turn Again Tiger*, women of African heritage are either sexualized or maternal figures, whereas in the latter two works, they have minimal presence. The novels therefore substantiate Alison Donnell's claim that "the issue of sexual encounters among Indians and Africans remains both the most sensitive and contentious zone of cross-cultural contact in Trinidad and a serious limit-point to the nation's imagined community" ("Caribbean Queer" 225). As Donnell's reference to national community suggests, idealized sexual formations are intimately linked to questions of citizenship. Mimi Sheller, for example, has argued that "normative scripts of sexual citizenship such as the good mother, the respectable woman, the worthy Christian, or the father of a family" have proven crucial to "taking up positions as free subjects" in the Caribbean (10). If the black characters – and specifically the black women – of these novels never inhabit such formations, then we might ask where the limits of subjecthood lie in Selvon's fictional world.

Across these books, the waning political (as opposed to personal) potential of the author's creolized vision is shown. *Turn Again Tiger* (1958) evokes early nationalist fervour as its protagonist tentatively enters the political domain on the encouragement of his Afro- and Chinese-Caribbean friends. In *I Hear Thunder* (1963), Selvon's disillusionment with both the Trinidadian bourgeoisie and the ethnic factionalism that followed independence is shown, as Afro-Caribbean Mark draws Adrian into his political ambitions mainly for his usefulness "among the Indian element" (191). By *Plains of Caroni* (1970), which offers a cynical perspective on the island's new freedoms, Selvon's disenchantment has reached its zenith. In this novel, political aspirations are solely an Indo-Caribbean preserve, as Romesh's mother attempts fraudulently to engineer his electoral success. Romesh only escapes these plans by leaving for England, a course of action making clear the extent to which the creolization Selvon favours has become politically untenable in an island increasingly riven by ethnic divisions. This failure of national unity is, I argue, anticipated in the novels' sexual relationships, which are almost solely concerned with the dynamic between those of Indian and European heritage. Both *Turn Again Tiger* and *I Hear Thunder*, for example, close similarly on a (re)unified Indo-Caribbean couple pregnant with child. Having worked through their issues of white superiority through sex with a white woman, the protagonists are ready to take on their roles as patriarchs and citizens, normative scripts that exclude any possibility for black women of participating in either family or national community. In his essay "Three into One Can't Go", Selvon talks movingly of how, as a child, he absorbed the sentiment that "the Indian was just a piece of cane trash and the white man was to be honoured and respected" (8). At the same time, he acknowledges the widespread belief amongst Indo-Caribbeans that "White people came first, then Indians, and then the Blacks" (8). Despite their wider advocacy of creolization and the inclusion of politically-engaged black male characters like Mark, the sexual relationships in these novels nevertheless show their Indo-Caribbean protagonists reordering the terms of this description by making Indo- and white Trinidadians equal but maintaining Afro-Caribbean subordination.

Three into One

In *Turn Again Tiger*, the idealized white mistress serves as sexual rite of passage, with the protagonist asking whether: "under all the old-talk, all I wanted to do was to screw a white woman?" (149). When he succeeds in doing so, Tiger frees himself psychologically from the racial indoctrination of colonialism and is able, finally, to meet both his private and public responsibilities. His young wife, Urmilla, shows some character development, becoming more creolized, forging links with other women and, finally, challenging her husband with the words: "[y]ou think you is the only one in the world growing up, that nothing happening to other people, only to you […]. The same way you getting older, I getting older too" (126). In the closing pages, however, Tiger's move into local politics and Urmilla's concurrent pregnancy suggest a gendered division of active (male) and generative (female) roles in the birth of the new nation, with Urmilla being confined to domestic space. *Turn Again Tiger* therefore conforms to Partha Chatterjee's description of how, in an Indian context, "it was the home that became the principal site of the struggle through which the hegemonic construct of the new nationalist patriarchy had to be normalized" (631). Tiger and Urmilla's relationship also comes close to Doris Sommer's discussion of the "national romance" as being ordered by a "romantic rhetoric" that builds towards "productive sexuality in the domestic sphere" (76).

In *I Hear Thunder*, sexual abstinence is marshalled as a tool by which the protagonist can distinguish himself from the complacent values of Trinidad's middle classes, as Adrian sets himself the challenge of a year's sexual prohibition in preparation for a longer-term commitment. Normative patriarchal relations are again upheld – as well as a particular view of "respectable" male citizenship – when the protagonist vows "if he was going to be married, it was to be as near perfection as he could make it" (11), words that accord with John Rothfork's claim that "discipline, exemplified by sexual continence" (9) is an ongoing theme of Selvon's fiction. Like Tiger, Adrian is also tested by a journey through white flesh before he returns to his Indo-Caribbean girlfriend, Polly. Yet this racial ghettoization is undermined not only by Polly and Adrian's creolized natures – natures indicated by their names alone – but also by the fact that Polly is pregnant with a white man's child by the time they are reunited. Polly herself is sexually free and dismissive of racial demarcations. The reader is told, for example, that she sees that "the future lay in forsaking" her parents' "memory of a distant country and a way of life that had no place in the West Indies" (13). The novel ends with Adrian and Polly participating in carnival together, an event where, according to Selvon, "Black, white, brown and yellow […] all were out on the streets" (189). As was the case with *Turn Again Tiger*, however, the end of the novel also shows order being restored through the bodies of a united, heterosexual Indo-Caribbean couple expecting a child. The fact that Polly is pregnant to white Randolph tempers the ethnic exclusivity of this vision, although it still lacks the presence of black characters.

In *The Plains of Caroni*, the wifely figure represented by Urmilla in earlier novels has been corrupted into the sinister presence of Romesh's domineering mother, Seeta, who is expressly linked to the damaging racial legacies of both colonialism and the canefield. Like "countless Indian women" before her, she is likely to "peter out her life in the village, growing old [...] sustained on memory and hope" (165). A youthful sexual indiscretion, it is revealed, has poisoned the life of both Seeta and her one-time lover, Balgobin, with the couple forced apart by Seeta's arranged marriage to Balgobin's brother. The book stages a confrontation between the values represented by Seeta and those of Romesh's creolized white Caribbean girlfriend, Petra. Although the relationship ends with some ambiguity – Romesh is about to travel to England without Petra – their tentative promises to each other again reinforce the necessity of heterosexual union, although this time it is an inter-racial partnership between an urbane, creolized pair. Whereas Doreen in the first novel is a mere cipher of white femininity, here we have gone full circle, the series of novels closing with the protagonist's choosing an individuated white woman over an almost grotesque stereotype of Indo-Caribbean traditional femininity. Across the books, then, it is Urmilla's tentative creolization and Polly and Petra's freer sexuality and racial allegiance that are celebrated. Unlike the two earlier novels, however, *Plains of Caroni* closes with neither pregnancy nor a clear commitment to the nation; the creolized values championed by Selvon, it is suggested, must be tested across the ocean.

From Object to Subject

The figure of the white mistress, representative of colonial power and domestic order, looms large across these books. As Daniel Coleman explains, the "white Lady, high up in the big house", often formed "a distant and beautiful ideal", symbol of the "master's success" and outward "sign of his manhood" (59–60). This characterization is directly applicable to *Turn Again Tiger* when the protagonist first stumbles across Doreen, the estate overseer's wife, as she bathes in the river. Tiger immediately categorizes her as "a woman. A white woman" (48), a qualification that sets her apart in his mind. His first reaction is "to get away before he was seen — not creep silently, but to run wildly, as in panic. There was danger here" (49), a response attributed to the childhood warnings he received to "keep off the white man's land, don't go near the overseer's house, turn your head away if you see the white man's wife" (49). In this, Doreen is clearly marked as property, a commodification continued with the repeated references to the "glow" of her skin and her "golden" hair (48–49) – words that also make her an angelic, unreachable figure. When she calls out to Tiger, he runs away "like a little boy" (51), an emasculating moment that forms "a scar on his mind nothing could efface" (50). The inherent violence of his desire for her is also made evident when Selvon writes: "suddenly he was slashing at the bush around him […] it wasn't a branch he was swinging at but it was her, her whiteness and her nakedness, her golden hair and her proud, pointed breast" (52). Doreen's "whiteness" is here at the forefront of Tiger's mind, revealing the extent to which he, as Pouchet Paquet puts it, "is still tied to the fears and inhibitions of a debilitating respect for a value system that makes the white woman different from any other" ("Introduction" xi).

Later, when Tiger works for Doreen, the mounting tension of their daily contact causes him to start drinking heavily and he curses "[t]he bitch […] is she who cause me to be like this, she who cause everything. If the chance only come, I know what I go do" (145), words that are borne out when the pair meet again at the river. This time, with "[h]atred, fear, lust" in his heart, Tiger falls upon Doreen, so that "[w]hat he did was done blindly and vengefully and he never knew how it was" (146). Once it is over, Tiger experiences "the fire and the rage and the fear and the lust all dead within him, and he felt a curious elation" (147) that now, "he [had] shed this thing from him and it would go away and leave him in peace for ever" (147). Echoing this use of "thing" – which refers to Tiger's torment but is equally applicable to Doreen's role in the scene – Tiger recognizes that "what had happened had nothing to do with her" (146–47). When she leaves wordlessly, he bathes, a reversal of their first meeting with obvious symbolic resonance as psychic rebirth. As Michel Fabre acknowledges, "Tiger's symbolical cleansing in the pool shows his expurgation of the weakness in himself that remained vulnerable to the white woman as representative of white power" ("Samuel Selvon" 157).

The white woman herself, however, serves only as bodily vessel and psychic container. The reader is told that she "never cried out or made a sound but her body was trying like water to quench the rage and fury of his", while she was also "murmuring to him, words he didn't hear or care about" (146). Tiger is uninterested in her perspective on events, merely hoping "that she wouldn't break the silence that had existed" between them (147). Rothfork is therefore right to assert that "beyond the easily exhausted pornographic stereotype", Tiger has "no use for the white woman, much less her world" (18).[2] Although Tiger himself wonders whether their meeting was intentional or accidental, this line of inquiry is never pursued. As a result, there is some ambiguity as to the extent of Doreen's consent in this violent encounter, with the fact that Tiger "held" her, "crushed" her and "ripped the white cotton shirt off her shoulders" (146) furthering this indeterminacy.[3] Whether their encounter serves as an actively sought racialized thrill on her part or an unwarranted assault by a man in whom she has a genuine interest, we can never be clear, although the references to her "caressing" him and "murmuring to him" indicate some tenderness. Taken as a whole, Selvon's portrayal of Doreen conforms to Martha Nussbaum's seven forms of objectification, particularly in terms of instrumentality "(treat[ing] the object as a tool of his or her purposes)"; fungibility "(treat[ing] the object as interchangeable)"; ownership "(treat[ing] the object as something that is owned by another)"; and denial of subjectivity "(treat[ing] the object as something whose experience and feelings (if any) need not be taken into account)" (257). More specifically to the Caribbean, the ambiguities surrounding Doreen's presentation in this scene also relate to what Evelyn O'Callaghan has described as the "apparent absence of white women's narrative voices from West Indian literary history" whereby we can only "proceed by questioning what such "silence" might in fact articulate" (1).[4]

I Hear Thunder demonstrates a number of parallels with this disturbing encounter between Indo-Caribbean man and white woman. When Adrian meets his friend Mark's wife, Joyce, she is also named in racial terms as the "white wife" (8). Adrian, meanwhile, immediately feels a "slight uneasiness" and a "quick physical attraction" (34), this despite her being married to his best friend. Although he has managed to resist Polly's charms for almost an entire year, one moment is all it takes for Joyce to have him flustered, revealing the exceptionalism of white femininity as Adrian perceives it. Just as Tiger felt that Doreen "was laughing at him" (58), so too, Joyce "couldn't help laughing" (40) when she is introduced to Adrian, providing a similar affront to his masculinity. When Adrian first sees Joyce in swimwear on the beach, comparable imagery is also used to that employed in the description of Doreen: "[t]he pale colour of her skin made her breasts look higher and firmer [...]. He saw the gold of her belly and the beautiful curve of her thighs: the trunks fitted so snugly it looked like they were painted on her" (45). Again, her whiteness, her firm breasts, golden colours and a certain painterly quality are all emphasized, creating an uneasy sense of Joyce as unobtainable yet, at one and the same time, a possession, with the crucial issue appearing to be *who* possesses her, rather than the legitimacy of such ownership. Just like Tiger, Adrian experiences "a kind of panic" (46), while later, aware of the tension between himself and Joyce, he also begins to feel "an unreasonable anger" (55).

Once he is finally alone with Joyce – again next to water – Adrian "fell on her" and, ignoring her entreaties "grasped the neck of the dress to rip it down" (64), with "fell" and "rip" almost exactly mirroring the language used in Tiger's conquest of Doreen. In contrast, here, Adrian is foiled by his own premature orgasm. Chastened, he approaches Joyce again, this time, as he puts it, without any of "that melodramatic crap" (63) – words that form an implicit critique of Tiger's behaviour. Now, we are told:

> They came together straining and heaving, in a kind of heartless, cruel passion.
> [...] Silently she yielded, clasping him with arms like bands of iron, their thighs
> locked and wrapped, his body jerking and twisting. Until they were both wild
> and rolling, biting and clawing, murmuring and groaning. He reined as long
> as he could [...] fighting to be aware of each precious second that was robbing
> him of the ideal he held so dear. (64)

Violence again suffuses this interaction, with "cruel passion", "biting" and "clawing" directly echoing the earlier description. However, greater reciprocity is shown between the couple with "came together" and "clasping". Although Joyce yields "silently" like Doreen, this silence is broken mutually as both she and Adrian eventually murmur and groan in tandem. The fact that this is Adrian's second attempt at sex with Joyce (and she has not taken the opportunity to leave) also gives a greater sense of her acquiescence. Although "the ideal he held so dear" most obviously refers to Adrian's personal vow of chastity, the reader cannot help but read this through the racialized inflections of their coupling. Arguably, it is the second loss – Adrian's prior idealization of white femininity – which holds far greater narrative import than the plot motor of his failed abstinence.

Joyce's earlier conversations with Polly also suggest greater intentionality on her part than was the case with Doreen. When told about Adrian's vow, she asks, "Do you think he has really been a good boy all this time?", teasing "maybe he hasn't been tempted enough" (41). Intrigued, she also wonders "how did he think? It would be interesting to find out" (41), a lingering phrase that suggests her curiosity. Joyce is suspected of having an affair with a white man from the island, Randolph, and we are told that, when Mark married her, he was fully aware that she was not a virgin (39). In addition, she desires "the romance of green islands" and the "quaint native" (23), words adding a new aspect to her curiosity. There is, then, a grain of truth to Roydon Salick's claim that, although both Tiger's and Adrian's encounters share a "perfunctory brutality", in *I Hear Thunder* it is "less a matter of Tiger attempting to exorcize the ghosts of a colonial sexual fantasy [...] than a matter of Adrian falling victim to the siren song of a woman who knows what she will and must do" ("Sam Selvon's *I Hear Thunder*" 123). Salick, however, does not acknowledge one further difference between the encounters: Adrian is much closer to being Joyce's socio-economic equal. Whereas a clear divide existed between cane labourer Tiger and overseer's wife Doreen, here Adrian and Joyce inhabit similar social worlds. Despite channelling evident racial currents, their transgression appears, in line with Lorna Burns's argument in the previous chapter, as much a symptom of that "complacent and easygoing" Trinidadian life elsewhere critiqued by Selvon (Nazareth 425). Joyce's skin colour, then, is not her sole defining characteristic and a more realistic sense of the network of identifications animating bourgeois Trinidadian life is given.

Joyce is also far from conveniently disappearing from the narrative, as is the case with Doreen. When Adrian eventually confesses to Mark, all is forgiven and the foursome begins socializing again. The first time Adrian sees Joyce since their encounter, he "swept through any possible strain with an aplomb" (168), while she confidently asks him, "What's this 'Hi' and rushing off like that? [...] Don't we get a big kiss after such a long absence?" (171). As Adrian later notes, what is striking about this reunion is the ease with which they pick up their friendship, "as if they all possessed some supreme power to level out differences and shades and clashes and force circumstances to conform with their desires" (175). Unlike Tiger's experience of rebirth, for Adrian "nothing had happened, nothing at all" (176). Some trace of psychic disturbance is shown, however, when the two women use Joyce's make-up to paint Adrian's face for carnival. After Polly exclaims "now you almost as white as Joyce!", Adrian "snatch[es] the lipstick and marked his face all over" like a "Red Indian" (172). Those "differences and shades" Adrian feels have been successfully glossed over, here resurface. Although Adrian may have exorcized his fascination with white womanhood, a residual anger nevertheless remains and he claims another kind of "Indian" identity over and above any affiliation with whiteness.[5] On balance, however, racial concerns are not the only element of Adrian's interaction with Joyce, and the novel offers a more fully-rounded rendering of inter-racial sex between an Indo-Caribbean man and white woman than *Turn Again Tiger*.

This pattern is continued in *Plains of Caroni*, where, instead of the protagonist, it is his mother Seeta who, as Michel Fabre puts it, sees white skin as "a token of success" ("Samuel Selvon" 158). When she first encourages her son to talk to Petra, Seeta "had no eye for anything physical but the white colour" (42), whereas Romesh sees her as more of an individual, countering Seeta's repeated labelling of "the white girl" with the retort "[h]er name is Petra" (47). Reflecting on their previous acquaintance, Romesh recalls Petra being "interesting and attractive" and that, when they spoke, they had "found a mutuality and accord, almost sensing one another's thoughts without need for many words" (36) – an emotional and intellectual correspondence rather than Tiger and Adrian's bodily responses. Greater reciprocity is also evident in this second meeting; when Petra first sees Romesh, "a look of pleasant surprise came to her face" while he feels "sudden elation" (41). In contrast to the threat of emasculation which ran through the previous encounters, Petra easily voices her concern that Romesh needs to assert his "manhood" (106) against Seeta – rather than against her as a figure of white authority – to which he calmly agrees.

When Romesh and Petra first go to the beach together, the reader might be forgiven for anticipating what comes next, given the pervasive association of sex and water in the three novels.[6] Yet this encounter plays out in starkly different terms. Romesh finds:

> The first thing that came to his mind was sex. Sprawled there, with one leg drawn up, her breasts taut against the bikini's top piece [...] she was like a breathing holiday advertisement. There was a little down on her thighs that glistened golden even in the shade, tiny hairs giving off an iridescent glow. But there was more to her than that. (51)

The repetition of "golden" and "glow" links to the earlier encounters, as does the emphasis on Petra's pert breasts. However, Romesh's crucial acknowledgement that "there was more to her than that" sets this scene apart, as does his recognition that "[t]his was why he was here with her now: because they had formed a mutuality" (53). Romesh appears to experience, yet immediately transcend, the reflex of commodification that ensnared both Tiger and Adrian in the previous works. Rather than the frenzied couplings of the earlier novels, we are told that Romesh "put his hand out and rested it on her palm. Her fingers interlocked with his, gently, with no urgency or demand" (53). Mirroring his thoughts, Petra confirms that they previously "made a lot of sense to one another", to the extent that they were perhaps "both frightened by the suddenness of getting to know one another so quickly" (53). The considered and leisurely nature of their conversation then carries over to their first sexual experience, for which we, notably, hear little detail. All Selvon tell us, with a more poetic turn of phrase, is that: "the westering sun threw warm rays under the galvanise and coconut branch, sculpturing their oneness in a long shadow on the sand" (54).

Tracking across the three books, there is an increasing sense of the interior life of these white women, and the one Selvon devotes most attention to, Petra, was actually born in the Caribbean (whereas Doreen and Joyce are both English). Her portrayal therefore reinforces his point, in "Three into One Can't Go", that there are white people "who were born and bred in these islands [...] who make an essential ingredient in the melting pot" (11). Creolized Petra appears to have easy relations with Trinidadians of various ethnicities. When Romesh first meets her, they are in a "group of mixed students" (36) and, when thinking about the problems caused by European tourists, he takes the view that "this girl beside him now was 'different', though she was white" (52). Petra is also shown to be sexually free. Although she recognizes that, "of all the men she knew, Romesh was the only one who sparked a feeling in her", she nevertheless "had met many men, and indeed she was still meeting them" (136). As he prepares to leave for England, meanwhile, she asserts "time and distance might change me too" (166) – words echoing Urmilla's assertion of her own development in *Turn Again Tiger*. The climax of the novel, where Romesh finds Seeta and Petra "holding him, one on either side", so that he feels "trapped between them" (157), can be seen as a battle between two models of femininity, one stereotypically Indian, one white and creolized. In the end, Romesh chooses Petra, the liberal, white Caribbean woman. This episode can, I suggest, be seen as the dissolution of Selvon's stereotyping of white femininity across these three novels: whereas the series began with the one-dimensional characterization of Doreen, it ends here with individuated white femininity. While Nussbaum allows that some forms of objectification are not "always morally objectionable" (290), she does find the "instrumental treatment of human beings, the treatment of human beings as tools of the purposes of another", to be "always morally problematic" (289). Significantly, it is this aspect of Selvon's treatment of white women – as tools through which to expunge the fantasy of European superiority – which is itself excised across the novels.

The Obedient and Servile Indian Wife

Whereas Selvon's white female characters move in a straightforward trajectory from objecthood to subjecthood, his Indo-Caribbean women instead form an eclectic collection of markedly different individuals, which in and of itself shows the fallacy of the limited stereotype of the submissive Indian wife. As such, they provide evidence to oppose Frank Birbalsingh's criticism of the endemic "submissiveness of heroines in the work of earlier male novelists" of Indo-Caribbean extraction ("Indian-Trinidadian Women" 16). Rather, Selvon makes clear the psycho-sexual costs of this traditional model of Indian womanhood, implicitly celebrating a creolized form of Indo-Caribbean femininity. Yet, at the same time, all of his Indo-Caribbean women are punished, in one form or another, for transgressing the boundaries of hearth and home, and all are eventually subordinated to a man. The novels therefore shore up, as well as undermine, this particular racialized model of femininity (whereas their portrayal of white women is more of an unequivocal counteraction). If Selvon's treatment of Doreen, Joyce and Petra humanizes the stereotype of the white mistress, then his writing of Indo-Caribbean women offers a more nuanced questioning of the terms of objectification itself, one more akin to Judith Butler's emphasis in *Gender Trouble* on practices of signification. It is through his Indo-Caribbean women's attempts to negotiate and perform – in successful, compromised and failed ways – the stereotype of submissive Indian femininity, that the instability of this construction is exposed.

By the early twentieth century, as Gabrielle Hosein and Lisa Outar outline, "the dominant notion of the Indo-Caribbean woman as Hindu, as passive, as heterosexual, as conservative, as submissive, as guardian of Indian culture via her body and her morality" was well entrenched (1). This model of Indian femininity features centrally in the novels through the repeated characters named "Seeta": the first an inhabitant of Five Rivers in *Turn Again Tiger*, the second mother to Polly in *I Hear Thunder* and the third mother to Romesh in *Plains of Caroni*.[7] The first Seeta serves as guardian of Indian culture and is dismissive of new arrival, Afro-Chinese Berta. She warms, however, to the temptations of creolized living, even daring to follow Berta's lead and bathe naked in a river (79–83). In *I Hear Thunder*, Seeta consciously embodies traditional Indian femininity and has a fierce resistance to creolized behaviour. She is an enigmatic character that "lived as though she were still on the banks of the Ganges" (13). To cook, she uses an ancient grinding stone, which has "originally come from India" (69) and on which she "had seen her mother grinding [...] and her mother had watched her mother" (69), words making clear the longevity of the wifely role that she herself now inhabits. Her life appears an endless round of food production, occasionally interspersed with her husband's criticisms of her failure to discipline Polly. Thanks to the repeated references to Seeta's blank demeanour, her sari and the grinding stone prove the central devices through which her character is expressed and little sense of individuation occurs.

This bleak portrayal of Indian motherhood is continued in *Plains of Caroni* with Romesh's mother, Seeta. Although she is conservative, heterosexual and, to some extent, representative of Indian culture, Seeta does not display the expected passivity. Instead, the novel begins by emphasizing her dominance over her husband: her role is apparently "so unlike the traditional image of the obedient and servile Indian wife that Harrilal did not dare to let anybody know the true state of affairs" (12). Far from being the antithesis of this traditional image, however, Seeta is, rather, a corrupted version of it, overly invested in the fate of her eldest son. So desperate is she to further Romesh's prospects, that she has "even considered and accepted having herself fucked" for him (83). This is contextualized when we hear that Romesh is in fact the product of the one night she spent with her true love, Balgobin, before acquiescing to an arranged marriage with his brother. It is this original act of submission which has determined the course of Seeta's life and against which, the reader might infer, she has been in rebellion ever since.

When looking back at these events, Balgobin recalls how "[i]t was in the dark she had given herself to him, so freely, with such utter abandon that had he not known better he might have wondered" (123). Here, a very different Seeta to the cold woman of the novel's present emerges. In contrast to the stereotype, this is an instinctively passionate young girl who experiences sex as "ecstasy and [...] exquisite joy" (123). Accordingly, when she meets Balgobin again later in life:

> it was as if she stood completely naked inside and out, shorn of every pretension
> [...] leaving a bewildered, panic-stricken girl. She could not live with this new

self, too long she had practised another face and manner and attitude to show
the world. (130–31)

Stunted in her emotional development by her loss, Seeta transfers her feelings
on to her son, so that: "[e]verything I done for you was like doing it for him"
(151). The reader is encouraged to sympathize with her plight, recognizing that
she has suffered her whole life because of this illicit passion. Yet at the same time,
the relish with which her fall is written – the references, for example, to her
appearing "older, and haggard", "shaking" and unable to "keep her hands still",
"as if, without make-up, she could no longer act" (138–39) – indicates a degree of
narrative punishment for her control of her son.

These three examples make clear the losses that attend the traditional image
of Indian femininity. Whereas the figure of the white mistress is gradually
humanized across the three books, here, the opposite trajectory occurs, as the
servile Indian wife is made monstrous. A counterbalance is offered, however, by
an alternative, creolized form of Indo-Caribbean womanhood that also comes to
the fore. *Turn Again Tiger* celebrates shy, young Urmilla's attempts to assert herself
and become more creolized. She, too, has experienced an arranged marriage and
Selvon does not shy away from illustrating the negatives of her position, not
least Tiger's occasional physical abuse. Yet the novel also reveals how Urmilla has
"grown up from a girl into a woman, moulding herself with each new experience"
(6). Whereas the first Seeta does not pursue the possibilities of creolization, the
second simply replays the lives of her female ancestors, and the third finds her life
formed by the ethnic practices of her youth, Urmilla instead offers what Pouchet
Paquet has described as "a sensitive, intelligent complement to Tiger's maturing
consciousness", whereby she is "finally committed to the creole world of Barataria"
("Introduction" xvii).

After they have moved away to Five Rivers, Urmilla's reservations about its
predominantly Indian culture are made clear as she rejects the company of "Teeka's
wife who was always complaining of illness, or Manko's wife who prattled all the
time in sing-song Hindi […] none could she find the pleasure she used to have
[…] in Barataria" (77–78). At the same time, Urmilla's relationship with Tiger
also develops. Although she recognizes that submissiveness is expected "when a
woman was a wife", she nevertheless asks her husband about his worries, a "sudden
boldness" that "made her cheeks red" (44). This courage finds further expression
when the women of the village band together to challenge their husbands' drinking.
During these events, Urmilla discovers "her inward shyness completely gone […]
so that she found herself with the strongest voice", causing the others to announce
"Urmilla, you lead we, and we follow you!" (81). Although they are ultimately
unsuccessful in their mission, she finds new confidence in her role as "ringleader"
(87), while Tiger, in turn, recognizes that Urmilla has "done a brave thing" (88). In

these passages, as Ramabai Espinet acknowledges, "the interior monologue of the woman is given full force [...]. Selvon is able to suggest processes of reasoning and action which are specific to the experiences of women" (Clarke et al 58). Patricia Mohammed has outlined how Indian women have often been "considered largely outside of the mainstream struggle for female equality and equity" ("Changing Symbols" 2) within the Caribbean. Here, however, Selvon shows Urmilla actively working for change, albeit within a relatively constrained domain. As such, the novel accords with Hosein and Outar's call for greater recognition of the "subtle, subversive acts of working from within their group norms" (3) employed by Indo-Caribbean women.[8]

Selvon continues to explore creolized Indo-Caribbean womanhood in his later text, *I Hear Thunder*, with the character of Polly. At first, she is unsympathetic to Adrian's sexual quest, having "made it clear to her friends that she was free and single" (41) – a casual attitude echoing that of Petra in *Plains of Caroni*. Although hurt when she first finds out about Adrian and Joyce, Polly later "laughed to remember how little heed she had paid to him and his memory" (104). Subsequently, she takes up with Randolph, a local white who "mixed freely in all societies" and boasted of being "a 'born Trinidadian', uninhibited, free of all racial feeling and snobbery" (14). When Randolph brews a tea made from a "rare fruit which stimulates and excites desire" (105), it is Polly who jokingly claims "[y]ou won't try it out on *me!*" (116), a statement that precipitates their coupling. She goes into the bedroom to change, "leaving the door open" (118), with the intentionality of these words made clear as we are told that when he followed, she was: "standing naked before the mirror, powdering between her legs. She simulated surprise and embarrassment when she saw him, clutching her hands over her breasts and locking her legs together in the traditional manner" (119). Polly's agency in this scene is evident, although crucially, she couches her desire in a "simulation" of the "traditional manner", with "traditional" holding both sexual and racial connotations. These are exacerbated as Randolph himself observes that "she was roused so quickly that she must have wanted it ever since they were up on the hill" and we are told that "[h]e had never had an Indian girl before because they were supposed to be passive and stodgy in the act. But Polly could hardly wait for him to take off his clothes" (119). Polly's simulation, then, is as much of the traditional Indian girl as the sexual ingénue. These racial currents are taken further when Randolph wakes and discovers Polly naked and expertly wrapping herself in a sari. This arouses him enough to pull her to him for a second time, ignoring her protests that "you going to crumple up my sari!"; in fact, it is the sari that has "sparked off his fresh outburst of energy" (121). Like Seeta in her passion for Balgobin, Polly here displays an instinctive sexuality at odds with the traditional stereotype of Indian femininity. This anticipates the kind of female sexual agency visible within the work of a later generation of female Indo-Caribbean authors such as Shani Mootoo and Ramabai Espinet. However, neither Seeta nor Polly remains with the men who have engendered such passion on their part and we get little sense of comparable feelings recurring in their later unions with Harrilal and Adrian respectively.

Following their encounter, Polly falls pregnant to Randolph, who conveniently departs the country, leaving the way clear for a chastened Adrian to return to her side during carnival. As they dance together, she "burie[s] her head in his chest [...] content that he [is] back again" while he reassures her, "[e]verything going to be all right", with a mixture of "tender compassion" but also a "little edge of superiority" (168). After they have danced all night long, the book closes with Polly asleep in Adrian's arms, as he reflects on the theme of "repentance", ready to become "the symbol of a steady, reliable, collected man" his earlier superiority portended (192). Crucial to this outcome, for Polly, is her association with what Selvon views as creolized values. Whereas her traditional mother, Seeta, "had no time for all this nonsense that went on at Carnival time" (185), we are instead told, "there was Polly, a child kicking in her belly, dancing without a care" (175). While her father may admonish, "You didn't bring that girl up Indian, you know. She too creolised" (145), it is this creolization that has granted Polly the security of returning to Adrian – and their bourgeois lifestyle – after her sexual misdemeanour. Yet, at the same time, their reunification does conform to the patriarchal edict from Polly's father that "Indian got to stick together, we got to keep we own blood and don't mix up" (145).[9] The final relegation of both Urmilla and Polly to a child-rearing role bears out Brinda Mehta's claim that Indo-Caribbean women have been "subjected to a double literary displacement that has minimized their capacity to effectively engage in crucial issues of nation building, race, difference and identity" (2). These episodes therefore reinforce the idea that a bonded heterosexual union is the ideal of Selvon's fictional world, despite the fact that the (sexual) losses of such unification are also made manifest within it. Selvon's portrayal of Urmilla's emerging feminist activism and the third Seeta's and Polly's sexual agency does counter what Mehta also describes as "the myth of the eternal feminine [...] that negates the possibility of more wholesome and plausible representations" (28). These women may ultimately conform, but insight is also given into to the alternative gendered or sexual futures they might have attained.

Women of African Descent

As the brevity of this final section suggests, black women barely feature as sexual partners to Indo-Caribbean men in these novels, although some positive relations between Indo- and Afro-Caribbean individuals more generally are shown. In *Turn*

Again Tiger, for example, Tiger and Urmilla's creolization is mainly expressed through their appreciation of their friendship with Afro-Caribbean Joe and Rita and the novel is infused with sentiments such as Tiger's assertion to Joe, that "I creolise just like you" (156). The most productive connections between those of Indian and African heritage, in fact, are the friendships experienced by Urmilla, who recognises that: "it was strange that she couldn't find a good companion among her own people. In Barataria it had been Rita, and now it looked as if Berta would be her closest friend" (78).[10] Both Rita and Berta encourage Urmilla's developing sense of selfhood and their connections provide a tantalizing glimpse of a female cross-racial solidarity that counters what Mehta has described as the way that "Indian and African women have been pitted against each other as rivals in the fight for legitimacy and subjective autonomy" (64). Yet Rita and Joe are also framed as "surrogate parents" (Pouchet Paquet, "Introduction" viii) to the younger couple and Rita is primarily a maternal figure, even taking on midwife duties at the birth of Tiger and Urmilla's first child in *A Brighter Sun*. Afro-Chinese Berta, meanwhile, is mainly portrayed in bodily terms and as sexually available, imagery consistent with characterizations of black femininity emanating from the plantation. When she is first married to shop owner Otto, it is Berta's "beautiful body" (72) that is emphasized, while she "made eyes at the fieldhands" (71) and she is eventually rumoured to have cuckolded her husband with cane worker Singh (in the only hint across all three books of sexual relations between Indo- and Afro-Caribbean characters). Such characterizations clearly perpetuate a Madonna/whore dichotomy, limiting the ability of these figures to appear as fully-rounded individuals.

Aside from Rita and Berta in *Turn Again Tiger*, only two more minor references to women of (potential) African heritage are made. In *I Hear Thunder*, Randolph follows his seduction of Polly by having "a brown-skin lined up for the kill", a "sweet little thing", whose "parents had drummed it into her not to make friends with people who were darker than she was" and whom "he had already fingered during a preliminary bout" (152–53) – words that continue the crude association of black women with sexuality and which gesture towards those ethnic divisions unsettling the creolized vision of the texts. Finally, *Plains of Caroni* sees mention of "a pretty French Creole girl" in a taxi (25), whose specific racial heritage is left indeterminate. She "moved as near in as she possibly could to the driver, and clasped her handbag tightly, looking straight ahead" in response to the "vulgar conversation" of the male passengers and the fear of being raped (25), sentiments removing her entirely from sexual purview. These limited references give barely any sense of Afro-Caribbean femininity (much less subjectivity), while even the novels' more positive characterizations of Rita and Berta appear fairly stereotypical. Whereas Selvon carefully breaks down tropes of Indian and white femininity, no such process occurs with women of African heritage.

If sexual relationships are one of the primary ways to chart the author's shifting responses to the failures and possibilities of post-war Trinidadian society, then this exclusion of black women forms a troubling lacuna in his regional novels. It also mirrors the gradual eclipse of black families that occurs more generally across Selvon's Trinidadian texts, visible when comparing *A Brighter Sun* to these later works. Of course, no writer can be expected to give all perspectives equal consideration all of the time, and the majority of the action in *Plains of Caroni*, for example, occurs on an Indo-Caribbean-run plantation in a predominantly Indo-Caribbean area of Trinidad, thereby limiting the scope for including Afro-Caribbean individuals. However, if sex forms as big a part of Selvon's oeuvre as I claim, then these texts' failure to conceive of sexual relations between Indo-Caribbean men and black women suggests a broader negation of the place of black women in both family and polity. If they can be neither the "good mother" nor the "respectable woman" in partnership with "the father of the family" (Sheller 10), then their fictional subjecthood is restricted across these novels. Selvon's writing of sex therefore anticipates his works' growing "disenchantment over the failure of community" in the Caribbean (Pouchet Paquet, "Samuel Dickson Selvon" 443). In a 1971 *Guardian* interview, Selvon attributes this failure, in part, to "certain Negro elements in the black power movement who mean 'power for me and me alone'" and, in discussing this "souring" of relations between "Negroes and Indians", he recognizes that "now there are a lot of things to be threshed out between those two races" (qtd. in Knox). Whereas the sexual relations depicted in these novels do much to "thresh out" issues between white and Indo-Caribbean populations, they fail to do the same for Indo- and Afro-Caribbeans. With Kenneth Ramchand in this volume and Stuart Hall ("Lamming, Selvon and Some Trends"), among others, emphasizing Selvon's nationalist credentials, then, provocatively, we might ask whether the sexual relationships discussed here in fact constitute what Salick has called "a moral and emotional fortification against what many consider to be a rampant, insistent Afro-centrism" responsible for "marginalizing the Indo-Caribbean presence" (*The Novels* 96). At the same time, however, these novels do much more to undermine stereotypes of both Indian and white womanhood than has previously been credited.

NOTES

1. *An Island Is a World* (1955) also features Indo-Caribbean men having sex with white women. However, as these interactions take place *outside* of the Caribbean – in England and America respectively – that novel will not be discussed here.
2. As Lewis MacLeod argues in chapter three, we can take this apparent lack of interest in Doreen as an expression of Tiger's fear of her subjectivity and the disciplining gaze it may carry.

3. In this, I disagree with Ramabai Espinet that "Doreen is given agency; she is a fully developed sexual agent; and her desire for Tiger is as urgent and as inexplicable as Tiger's desire is for her" (Clarke et al. 58).

4. Tiger's interaction with Doreen is not the only reference to Indo-Trinidadian men and white women in this book. Local character More Lazy claims to have had a dream about a giant coming to raze the village, clutching a white woman in his arms. After More Lazy has vanquished the giant, he explains "the girl was too nice bad! She and me lay down right here afterwards. I treat she rough, man. I treat she rough" (105). As Pouchet Paquet summarizes, "in More Lazy's crucial alteration of the King Kong myth, the challenger is not a giant black ape, but a giant white American male" so that he "reverses the phallic image of superior fire power, and takes the white woman as his prize" (xiv). Similarly, we hear of Boysie, who has returned from abroad with a white wife, at whom "everybody staring [...] as if they never see a white woman before" (157). As Tiger recognizes when discussing Boysie's fate, "[o]ver here some of we still feel white people is God, and that is a hard thing to kill" (158), terms echoing his psychical "killing" of Doreen. Tiger's own personal crisis therefore becomes "representative of the chronic social and psychic illnesses which plague the wider island community as a vexing legacy of its colonial history" (Pouchet Paquet "Introduction" xiv).

5. This resistance on Adrian's part can be contextualized against Afro-Caribbean Mark's engagement with white Trinidadian life and his eventual willingness to join that bastion of social privilege, "the club where only whites and the island's élite went" (169), despite his earlier protestations that he would do no such thing.

6. In his discussion of Selvon's final novel, *Moses Migrating* (1983), Jeremy Poynting observes a similar link between sex with white women and water, commenting: "There is, [in *Moses Migrating*], I believe, a deliberate echo of the scene in *I Hear Thunder* when Adrian makes love to the white wife of his best friend in the sea, when Moses makes love to Bob's wife Jeannie in a similar maritime fashion" (264).

7. This is both a very stereotypically Indian name and also that of the wife of Rama, in the Hindu epic, the *Ramayana*. She is both the central female character of that story and serves as a model of wifely virtue within Hindu mythology, meaning that there is a knowing quality to Selvon's naming of this character.

8. Selvon's description of how, when bathing with the other women, "Urmilla lay modestly on the stones and refused to get up and show herself" (82) also raises questions about the extent to which Urmilla's development can be viewed as a process of modernization, as much as his own label of creolization. See Mohammed, "The 'Creolisation'", and Hosein, "Modern Navigations".

9. This is a direct echo of Tiger's father in *A Brighter Sun*, who tells his son: "you must look for Indian friend, like you and you wife. Indian must keep together" (47).

10. Although the childhood friendship between Adrian and Afro-Caribbean Mark features strongly in *I Hear Thunder*, the strength of this bond is called into question as Adrian predicts that one day, Mark's social climbing will mean that: "I wouldn't be surprised if you pass me straight on the street" (40).

CHAPTER EIGHT

Cascadura Lovesongs:
Displacing Indo-, Afro- and Other-
centricities in Selvon's Romance

J. Vijay Maharaj

[N]ot just Felicity village on the Caroni plain, but Selvon Country.

– Derek Walcott, "The Antilles: Fragments of Epic Memory"

A brief review of the papers in *The Samuel Selvon Collection* held by the Alma Jordan Library at the University of the West Indies, St Augustine, reveals that critically speaking, Samuel Selvon's beginnings were not, to put it mildly, propitious. For the most part, his representation of life in Trinidad and Tobago was viewed as ostensibly "authentic" but – possibly for that very reason – simplistic, a view interestingly reproduced on the back cover of the welcome re-publication of *Those Who Eat the Cascadura* in 1990, which mentions "great charm and a fresh earthy naiveté" as characteristics of the text. Scholars who were personally familiar with the nuances of Caribbean life and "the complex little worlds" (Rohlehr "Literature and the Folk" 54) of West Indian societies represented in Selvon's writing were not happy with this early critical direction and Susheila Nasta's *Critical Perspectives on Sam Selvon* (1988) provided a timely intervention by consolidating Selvon's own views on his work as well as those of persons familiar with the background of his stories.

Nonetheless, as recently as 2001, Roydon Salick found it necessary to publish *The Novels of Samuel Selvon* in response to "those [readers of Selvon] who have no intimate or firsthand knowledge of Trinidadian dialect" and engage in "a critical imperialism, in which the dicta influencing criticism are being set outside the Caribbean by individuals who have no significant experience of the region or the culture" (3). Salick's concern, as expressed, seems to give credence to Belinda Edmondson's argument that "[p]art of the 'romance' of Caribbean studies is the belief that attends so much work on so-called Third World societies: that is, that you must live it to theorize it" although "[t]he question of what 'living it' really means […] is never really settled" (5). Readings of Selvon's work have been subject to a struggle between those who claim to have "lived it" and critics who have, in line with Elizabeth Deloughrey's appraisal of Caribbean and Pacific literature, confronted its "lack of translatability [and] profound localness" and turned to "the signs of orality in these texts, such as the broad language registers of the creole continuum" (ix). Attempts to engage with this "localness" seem to have inspired Selvon's standard appellation of "calypsonian".[1]

Despite concerns about the fit of the "calypso" christening, there are certainly good grounds for it. As Gordon Rohlehr notes, on the basis of extensive research done on the continuities between Africa and the Caribbean: "elements of improvised praise and blame were transported to the West Indies and Americas from West African singing", along with the "staple themes [...] of early Afro-Caribbean music", including "*picong*, ridicule, improvisation; and the themes of women and love-intrigue" and found their way into calypso (*Calypso and Society* 2). There is an abundance of all of this in Selvon's work, especially in the London novels and short stories. It is no surprise, therefore, that the calypso-lens of critical engagement is deployed in its interpretation. One could say that there is honour in being dubbed a calypsonian, since as the *bona fide* calypsonian, Lord Kitchener, reminds us, calypso is not first and foremost about its linguistic medium: "calypso is about life. It is about sex, violence, love, social and political commentary, it is about jobs, about shelter, about world issues" (qtd. in Guilbault 155). Views expressed via calypso on these subjects often dissented from elitist views in the Caribbean and, as a result, in the past, the genre often faced state censorship. This not only failed to silence calypsonians, it caused them to "express themselves with remarkable freedom and [they] continue to be the bearers of and commentators on a living folklore, most of which had become forbidden by laws passed" (Rohlehr, *Calypso and Society* 125).[2]

If Selvon's works are read in light of Rohlehr's idea of the calypsonian as a communicator of "living folklore", we find within them a revolutionary perspective, despite the views of Selvon's friends, who insisted the author was politically uncommitted.[3] In looking again at Selvon's work, this essay answers to the region, treats him as "bearer of and commentator on a living folklore" and identifies what he is singing in *Those Who Eat the Cascadura* about life, sex, love, colonial labor, violence and world issues. In other words, it proposes to re-state Selvon's social and political commentary in the pedantic prose of literary criticism and to contextualize it in view of the concerns and issues of the historical periods in which his novel is embedded and set.

Considering the Politics

Salick states that the composition of the narrative of *Those Who Eat the Cascadura* began in 1948 "almost at the beginning of Selvon's literary career" in the short story "Johnson and the Cascadura", later "reprinted in *Foreday Morning*" (*The Novels* 59). It evolved into the 1957 short story, also called "Johnson and the Cascadura", published in the collection *Ways of Sunlight*. This version is "almost five times as long", and full of "new information [...] for the benefit of a foreign/ British audience", but also "more complex, more tightly structured, and much more interesting" than the first (61). The final version appeared in 1972, "when *Those Who Eat the Cascadura* was published" (59). In the twenty-four-year gestation period of the novel, Trinidad and Tobago moved from colonized status, to independence, to disenchantment with postcolonial politics. As the novel's narrator reminds us, one widespread consensus in the contemporary Caribbean is that: "years of colonial servitude had roots that nothing simple like the island's independence or the cry of black power could eradicate" (122). And it is to the task of eradication that the novel is directed.

The legacies of colonial servitude are many. One of the most important is usefully articulated by Shalini Puri as, "the persistence and active redeployment of colonial stereotypes". Puri argues that colonial stereotyping is intrinsic to postcolonial politics and involves a racialization of identity that is evident in calypsos. She claims that racialization works to "produce for dominant cultural nationalist discourses [...] the fiction of one seamless and monolithic racial community with common interests pitted against another" similarly constructed ("Race, Rape" 121). This racialization of identity, most prominently African and Indian, but also white Euro-American, Chinese, Dougla and other categories, is the cause of a great deal of unhappiness and contributes to endemic rivalry, antagonism and corruption in the region.

This is the context against which Caribbean literature is produced. However, instead of concentrating solely on the turf war raging on the ground, most creative writers work toward rapprochement. In *Cascadura*, conflict is captured in the interpersonal relationships of the characters and the psychological profiles in which they are embedded. Rapprochement, on the other hand, is informed by concerns such as those of Frantz Fanon, who worried that "[i]nside a single nation, religion splits up the people into different spiritual communities [...] [T]his religious tension may be responsible for the revival of the commonest racial feeling" (*Wretched* 129). Grounds for subverting this problem are given in the novel's portrayal of the syncretism of Caribbean religious sensibilities. This is achieved mainly through the characterization of Sarojini and Manko and their access to the power of love. One may say, moreover, drawing on a Jungian lexicon, that *Cascadura* develops a unique feminine sensibility and delicately attempts to articulate the nebulousness of a largely unconscious sense of the religious.[4] Coincidentally, as a supplement to the views expressed by Lewis MacLeod in chapter three of this collection, this perspective shows that for some characters, the religious "is registered in terms" besides "an endlessly deferred and inconclusive movement into [...] masculine certitude and authority".

Selvon's most overt act of rapprochement inheres in the foregrounding of the cascadura. Salick observes that the cascadura features in all versions of this story but he complains that Selvon correctly describes how the fish is caught and prepared but is "*mistaken* about the meaning of 'creole'", as the preparation relates to a procedure which "is indubitably Indian" (*The Novels* 61, emphasis added). I argue, conversely, as this essay will demonstrate, that Selvon's "creole" cascadura, especially if creole is taken in Brathwaite's sense of "nativization", is quite deliberate ("Caliban, Ariel" 42). Moreover, the conception of "creole" at work in *Cascadura* pre-empts Antonio Benítez-Rojo's and Edouard Glissant's theorizations of creole and creolization as intricately syncretistic, impossible-to-disentangle cultural interconnections, for which terms like "rhizomatic" and "transversal" are appropriate. This simultaneously allows *Cascadura* to problematize dominant national Creole discourses and to centre the creoleness or syncretism of obeah as well as "popular" Hindu practices while troubling "official" Hinduism.[5]

To follow the argument, one must recall that, if one posits an entity called "Indian culture", it can hardly be considered homogeneous; nor can any of its many religions. Hinduism certainly does not refer to a monolithic theology and is problematic to define. Gavin Flood identifies the problem as having to do with Hinduism's lack of a "founder", the absence of a "unified system of belief", "soteriology" and "bureaucratic structure" (6). William M. Reddy concurs and adds an absence of "orthodoxy" to the factors, while focusing also on recent retractions from Orientalist suppositions about the composition of the religion to which the name "Hinduism" is now given (234–35). The elusiveness of the term is compounded in the Caribbean where, as Steven Vertovec points out, "inadvertent permutation, deliberate alteration or innovation, and structurally necessary modification" have occurred ("Official" 227). Vertovec notes elsewhere that this was inevitable in the process of transplantation because "[u]nder such conditions, believers are often compelled to realize that the routine habitual practice, rote learning and 'blind faith' underpinning previous contexts [...] are no longer operational" (*The Hindu Diaspora* 149). Some modifications were politically motivated and influenced by self-orientalizing changes to Hindu identitarian thought on the Indian sub-continent. As Ashis Nandy puts it, "colonialism tried to supplant the Indian consciousness to erect an Indian self-image which, in its opposition to the West, would remain in essence a Western construction" (72). In "Orientalism and the Modern Myth of Hinduism", Richard King states that this involved an insistence on Vedic origins and a demand to return to them, as well as concomitant rejection of medieval aspects of thought and worship.

This Western-inspired Indian construction proved useful to organized groups of Indian migrants in the Caribbean that sought state recognition, but their efforts were affected also by the activities of Christian churches, resulting in new forms of worship and the emergence of what Carolyn Prorok calls the "Trinidadian temple" ("Evolution" 83). Such a temple, conforming quite precisely to Prorok's accounts, is depicted in minute detail in *Cascadura*. The book highlights the fact that the point of primary worship is "a giant *pepal* tree which spread clusters of deep-green heart shaped leaves protectively over a Hindu temple [...] [T]his tree [...] was worshipped and the yard around its roots was hallowed ground" (53). Prorok identifies three periods of temple building that generated the final Trinidadian style. The first, in the period of indentureship, comprised small shrines in places where someone sensed a particular emanation of supernatural power. The second, between 1921 and 1944, in the immediate post-indenture period, Prorok names "the Koutia". She claims: "A Koutia in India usually has no sacred significance attached to it [...] but in Trinidad it took on the function of assembly hall" not unlike the arrangement of consecrated altar and pews in churches of the Catholics or other Christian groups ("Evolution" 80). The last construction phase, between 1945 and 1960, like the second, was less spiritually than socially and politically attuned and, as Selvon notes, geared towards asserting a presence that matched the Christian via the "fanciful" and the "picturesque [...] high domes or steeple-shaped facades" (*Cascadura* 54).

In his descriptive passage, Selvon captures the progression of the temple through all three phases. The first is evident in that the *pepal* tree, the sacred banyan of Hinduism and Buddhism, is given pride of place as the centre of worship. It speaks to a religious sensibility that emanates from the unconscious to make super-sensory contact with force fields of power in the environment. The attached hall is an aspect of the second or third, an additional structure built to imitate more elaborate social forms. The first is otherworldly; the others clearly of this world only. The foregrounding of the landscape in relation to religious worship is in keeping with many other aspects of the environment so emphasized as sources of self-understanding throughout the text – most importantly, the titular cascadura. Selvon also pays attention to the importance of popular practices and attitudes associated with the landscape which result from people's deeply felt needs, fears and concerns. These have very little to do with the pandit and the "assembly hall" which represent the official. According to Vertovec, popular Hinduism comprises "a considerable set of beliefs and practices [which] fall far outside the 'official' forms of Hinduism". It is "usually directed toward therapeutic or protective ends, and include[s] [...] *ojha* (black magic, often blended with Creole forms, called *obeah*)" ("Official" 239). The community's relations to the banyan tree are representative of these features of the popular, as they are outside the administration of the official pandit. Additionally, Selvon also recognizes, as Prorok observes, that the syncretistic whole has become symbolic of the community's identity, "ritually invested with the emotional, political, and social moments that capture a people's recognition of their own history, their own identity. They answer the question, 'Who are we?' with [...] 'Trinidadian Hindus'" ("Transplanting Pilgrimage" 295). Selvon thus calls attention to the fact that despite efforts to narrowly delineate an entity called Caribbean Hinduism, the religion continues to encompass many substantial unrecognized elements. His representation of people's affective relationship to their Hindu identity at the same time reveals concern about the growing hegemony of the official version, which, as Vahni Capildeo's contribution to this collection demonstrates, has now become for many the only version known and accepted as "authentic". It also registers disquiet about the State's relegation of Hinduism to its official version only, the consequent assignment of Hindus to the role of political opponents because of the link between the official religious structures and political activity, and subsequent erasure of the diversity of Hindu traditions in the national imaginary.

Among the elements coming under the pressure of erasure in both national and official Hindu discourses, one that is of central importance in the novel, is the very rich tradition of erotic love, "the Sufi and Bhakti mystico-religious traditions" as Lalita Sinha expresses it (xvii), which in Sinha's and other conservative views is solely a spiritual pathway. This tradition is characterized by an intricate, age-old syncretism. Selvon draws on these elements to make its formulas the basis of a unique love story with bearing on community formation in Trinidad and Tobago and, by extension, on individual subjectivity in an increasingly multicultural world.[6]

A Cascadura Lovesong

Selvon's understanding of religion thus seems in accord with King's argument that "the literary bias in Western notions of religion does not accurately reflect the diversity of human experience" (*Orientalism and Religion* 62). Moreover, for Selvon, a religious sensibility "irradiates every aspect of life [...] [T]here is no fundamental distinction between 'religion' and the rest of life, and there is no cultural production which lies altogether outside the ambit of religion" (Oldmeadow xi). This understanding firmly ensconces the text within a developing discourse on the syncretism of Caribbean religions in general in which, as Victoria Carchidi points out, religion is understood "not as a single-stranded, 'pure' and purely derivative form, but as something that, alive to the needs of the people, draws syncretically upon a variety of different traditions" (180).

In its inscription of these facets of Caribbean religious culture, *Cascadura* can itself thus be seen as a "syncretic artefact" about "syncretic artefacts". As Antonio Benítez-Rojo explains:

> A syncretic artifact is not a synthesis, but rather a signifier made of differences [...] [S]yncretic processes realize themselves through an economy in whose

> modality of exchange the signifier of *there*—of the Other—is consumed
> ("read") according to local codes that are already in existence; that is, codes
> from *here*. (21)

The centrality of cascadura, which is native to the region, signifies the "code from here". Before any of the characters, most of the culture and much of the vegetation were "here"; the cascadura was, is, and most likely will always be, "here".

Fiona Darroch argues that migrants to the Caribbean contribute equally to the development of a religious sense: "Historical and communal memories combine [...] to form a unique mythic plane where the Hindu goddess Kali, the Ashanti spider-god Anancy, and the Christian Virgin Mary all dwell" (ix). In *Cascadura*, on the other hand, Selvon posits that something more and less than combining occurs, and emphasizes that the landscape to which Caribbean migrants came is the node around which the process of becoming proceeds. In other words, as he does in all his works, here Selvon is insisting that a religious self is relational, among humans certainly but also importantly between people and the larger natural setting in which they find themselves. The cascadura as symbol of the primacy of the environment therefore remains central to the story in every version. The cascadura is Selvon's "fixed point", to use Mircea Eliade's terms; it "defines the locus of reality" in the text and the projected future for Caribbean living (qtd. in Darroch 9). Around the nativeness of the cascadura, however, a number of changes revolve.

Salick emphasizes that Selvon's conceptualization of the story begins with only an anonymous male protagonist who "enjoys nature and life, and [...] wishes to be immortal" (*The Novels* 60). These desires for a feeling of oneness with life and the landscape and for immortality are fulfilled by Selvon's introduction of erotic love, which eating the cascadura serves to ensure, in the second story. The erotic love component is then substantially expanded and projected onto an exploration of interpersonal relationships in general by the final version, in which the cascadura symbolically represents the naturalness of belonging and speaks to the many types of relationships Selvon imagines. The male protagonist develops as a consequence, to use Salick's term, from "libertine" to "concerned lover" (62). In fact, the Garry Johnson of *Cascadura*, a freelance writer who does "travel things occasionally" (Selvon, *Cascadura* 33) can be seen as Selvon's means of including the modernist hero, living in the shadow of death and defeated by feelings of hopelessness, aimlessness, nostalgia and melancholy Garry is unable to rise out of this emotional morass because of "accepted precepts and concepts, dogmas and proven convictions [...] controlling his mind as rigidly if it were set in concrete" (99). The text suggests that his salvation is possible if he learns through the experience of love how to rid himself of these chains.

In a similar manner the female protagonist, introduced in the second version where she is called Urmilla, becomes Sarojini, the lover, and a rooted agent in the course of her life in the third version, the *Cascadura* novel. She moves in fact from an Urmilla who unites with Garry through a traditional Hindu marriage ceremony to a Sarojini who is unbounded by any received traditions except those she makes herself, inspired by her affective, intuitive responses to the land and people with which she interacts. Out of such awareness, she makes love to Garry without formal sanction because she recognizes in their mutual responses the indefinable something for which she has been waiting and longing. Selvon's representation of Sarojini's agency in this way would please many feminist scholars. Certainly their relationship negates what Simone de Beauvoir condemns in male-female relations. While it may be possible to see their relationship in terms of sex, "absolute sex, no less", it would be difficult to show that Sarojini "is defined and differentiated with reference to man and not he with reference to her; she is the incidental, the inessential as opposed to the essential". It would be equally difficult to show that only Garry "is the Subject, he is the Absolute" while Sarojini "is the Other" (de Beauvoir 16).

It is important to recognize, therefore, to adapt Anthony Giddens's words from his explorations of how modernity and capitalism at once incite, produce, and regulate erotic desire, that in *Cascadura* "[s]ex […] speaks the language of revolution […] revolutionary hopes […] [are] pinned to sexuality by […] [Selvon,] for whom it represents a potential realm of freedom" (1). But Selvon abjures what Reddy calls the "peculiar dualism" of love and sex as it appears in Giddens' study, which is, as Reddy argues, "unique to Western conceptions and practices" (1). Reddy insists, in fact, that in the "non-European context […] the conceptions, practices, or rituals surrounding sexual partnerships [do not] rely on an opposition between true love, on the one hand, and desire", which is "conceived of as appetite […] on the other" (2–3). He argues rather that "the Sanskrit *shringara rasa* or the Heian *koi* or *monoomoi* refer to a longing for a sublime sexual partnership that is reciprocal and that excludes coercion" (3).

A great deal depends therefore on the ability to interpret the characterization of Sarojini as embodiment of female sexuality in terms of non-Western concepts of love which are unmarked by the mind-body split of Western philosophy. In *Cascadura* she does not function merely to "sustain desire" or "satisfy hunger" or "renourish […] a 'future event'", which is Luce Irigaray's complaint about Emmanuel Levinas's account of the erotic relation in *Totality and Infinity* ("Questions" 110). Via the figure of Sarojini, *Cascadura* also addresses Irigaray's central concern about Levinas's account of the erotic, which is that he views lovers via a gendered lens, distinguishes between the lover and the beloved and gives a specific sex role to each – the lover is male and the beloved is female (*Ethics* 205–206).

In *Cascadura*, Sarojini and Garry are both given the roles of lover, with Sarojini often in the lead. Garry "knew only an exhilaration that was tinged with fear and wonder. It was as if something was happening to him over which he had no control [...] [i]t was partly like that with her too, only [...] [s]he was calm as if everything had been resolved. She knew exactly where she was taking him" (75). In addition, the desiring of the two for the experiences they share is harmoniously reciprocal. As in the representation of love in Nizami's *Laila and Majnun* or Jayadeva's *Gita Govinda*, which belong to the "Sufi and Bhakti mystico-religious traditions" (Sinha xvii), "the nature of the union of the lovers", as Sinha claims, indicates that "each reflects, and is reflected in, the other [...] [T]heir relationship is a union of mutuality and complementarity" (64). To position his female protagonist like this required that Selvon relocated her out of the humdrum politics of Indo-Caribbean women's sexuality, which have been extensively criticized by feminist scholars as a creation of the unholy union between colonial authorities and the architects of Indian religious reconstruction.[7] He does not, however, transfer her out of an Indian frame; rather, he moves towards an entrenchment in alternative medieval Indian (equally applicable to Hindu and Islamic) traditions of love which remain alive and well outside of the official discourses of Caribbean Hinduism (as well as Islam, as evident for example in the under-studied popularity of *ghazals* or Urdu love poems).

Initially, their involvement can be comfortably fitted into the formulaic scenes of a Bollywood movie, in which Indian erotic traditions are appropriated and transformed by nationalist expectations. Garry experiences "a shock of wonder" at their first meeting and a "sudden, flooding urge to reach out and touch her [...] [a] powerful and instantaneous [...] emotion", while Sarojini goes into a "panic" and becomes "nervous and fluttery" (36–37). At their next meeting, Garry calls her name as she is "[d]ancing the cocoa" (71) with other women, and "she was going to jump off and run and run far into the cacao and hide behind the wings of an immortelle root" (70). As he approaches, she imagines that "[s]he fled far away" and is therefore "surprised to find she could only sway." The encounter crescendos with "Sarojini dancing with the white man [...] Kamalla started to hum an Indian air [...] The others joined in" (71).

Later, however, eschewing the conventionalities that confine the Bollywood film industry, Selvon reaches towards older erotic traditions to depict their relationship in ways that can be superimposed flawlessly on to *Laila and Majnun* or the *Gita Govinda*. This is evident, importantly, in the setting in which their lovemaking mainly occurs. Selvon uses flashback to recall the "hidden, wild garden" (76) that Dummy discovers and shares with Sarojini (75). Apart from the tamala tree of the *Gita Govinda* being replaced with the immortelle as a "code from here", the description could have come directly from those other stories of ecstatic love. Just as "[t]he love story of Radha and Krishna takes place in an idyllic Indian forest in the season of spring" (Sinha 53), that of Garry and Sarojini takes place in an idyllic Trinidadian forest in the coolness of a hidden citrus grove. Similarly too, although it is in the open air, there is complete privacy and a movement towards a centre "Here [...]. Here [...]. Here [...]. Here" (75), such as in the mandala created by the lovers in the *Gita Govinda* and "as in *Layla* [...] they are in a paradise" with "imagery [...] fashioned from elements like trees, thickets, rivers" (Sinha 61). As Sinha notes: "Taken together, these nature images in the depiction allow the reader to virtually see, touch, hear, smell, and taste the abundance. Further, these sensory images convey a super-sensory state of being" (61). They are of the untamed order of "birds and butterflies" (Selvon, *Cascadura* 75), peepal trees and cascadura that do not inhabit the domain of the estate world.

This is not, however, where the comparisons end, the scenes of lovemaking also reproducing the wild ecstasy and tenderness of the Indo-Persian texts. The range of the depictions is wide. It includes at one end of the spectrum the tenderness of "slowly he laid beside her and took her in his arms. He felt everything but lust" (76); at the other: "He could sense some urgency and excitement in her, but even so he was not prepared when halfway through the blacksage she flung herself on him and bore him to the ground" (112). This latter scene could have been taken directly from the *Gita Govinda*:

> Held-captive by her arms, pressed by the weight of her breasts, pierced by her finger-nails, the cup of his lower-lip bitten by her teeth, crushed by the slope of her hips, bent-down by her hand on his hair, crazed by the trickling-flow of honey from her lower-lip, the lovely-beloved somehow obtained delight – so, oh! [T]he way of love is paradoxical! (Siegel 282)

In this light, Selvon's depiction of Sarojini can be seen as related to one of the first portrayals of an Indian woman in Caribbean literature, that is, John Edward Jenkins's 1877 *Lutchmee and Dilloo: A Study of West Indian Life*. In this novel, Jenkins introduces his female protagonist as she sings a "free paraphrase of the *Gita Govinda*" in order to Orientalize her as the exotic Other and thus establish a hierarchical difference between Indians and others in order to rationalize the civilizing mission (31–32). Selvon's construction can be seen as writing back to the Orientalizing of erotic Indian traditions.[8] Therefore, almost one century after Jenkins, Selvon's depiction of a comparable figure is directed at establishing difference from European civilized sensibilities but for the purpose of promoting the distinction between East and West as a basis for questioning the outcomes of the civilizing mission, contemplating human freedom through love and a new Indo-Caribbean female subjectivity.

In addition, it is clear that Selvon understands, like Michel Foucault, that to end a regime of sexual oppression involves "nothing less than a transgression of laws, a lifting of prohibitions, an irruption of speech, a reinstating of pleasure within reality, and a whole new economy in the mechanisms of power" (5). Such a "new economy" is given in the contrast between Garry and other male characters on the one hand, and Sarojini and other female characters on the other. White/ Indo-Caribbean gendered relations are evident in the ease with which Roger enters Kamalla's hut and has her perform sexually to satisfy solely his needs. Their sexual interaction is markedly different from the mutual satisfaction of Sarojini and Garry and remarkably like the behaviour of the chickens in the estate yard:

> When a cock succeeded in a mount it spread its wings and the feathers
> separated and opened out to help it maintain balance, and afterwards . . . only
> a few moments . . . the hen would give a kind of shudder and ruffle its feathers
> as if adjusting its dress, and carry on pecking at the ground as if nothing had
> happened. (12)

The relationship's banality and animalistic undertones ensure that no one is ever aware of its existence, just as no one knew of the relationship between Roger and Sarojini's mother. The new relational economy that Selvon is working towards is clear from the way their relationship's veiling from public view is not transmitted on a similar level of metaphoricity and imagery as Sarojini's and Garry's. The money that Roger throws at Kamalla and Sarojini, in contrast to the lack of monetary exchange between Garry and Sarojini, also speaks to another "economy". Kamalla is in the relationship not because of her desire for Roger but out of a desire for the commodities that his money buys. The requirement of pretending to be a corpse that the relationship demands is a well-engineered metaphor for her self-commoditization. Similarly, any woman on the estate, Kamalla or any of the cocoa-dancers, would have entertained a relationship with Garry or Roger because of the desire for an economically, socially and politically privileged white subjectivity. Sarojini, on the other hand, has little desire for such privileges. In Aimé Césaire's terms, therefore, one may say that Sarojini is rendered as civilized and the others as "decivilized"; he avers: "colonization works to *decivilize* the colonizer, to *brutalize* him in the true sense of the word, to degrade him, to awaken him to buried instincts, to covetousness, violence, race hatred, and moral relativism" (35, original emphasis). The "decivilized" are represented like "[t]he fowls [who] ate greedily and fought although there was enough for all" (Selvon, *Cascadura* 12).

Because Selvon wishes to depict a subjectivity like Sarojini's, he needed to change her name. Sarojini is not only the name of the Indian poet Sarojini Naidu, who writes eloquently of love, and after whom Selvon may well have named his protagonist; it also means "lotus" or "she who sits on the lotus" – a goddess.

More importantly, the name change is significant because Sarojinis – lotuses – and cascadura belong to the same environment and in their superimposition in the novel "the signifier of *there*—of the Other—is consumed". In Hinduism, the lotus is a symbol of the atman, for want of a better term, the "soul", because it grows in mud, draws in and becomes suffused from root to petals with matter from its environment like the spirit in the material world, but rises unsullied out of it, not unlike the cascadura that scavenges in the mud from which it protects itself with a hard armour-plating that conceals its delicate, and sought after, flesh. Sarojini transcends the limitations of birth and environment and fulfils their hidden potentialities by the seemingly foolish refusal to give up the one good she has discovered in her world – the capacity to love and a longing for a sublime love with one unique other. This tenuous thing, however, protects her from all negativities and ensures the fulfilment of Manko's prediction that "you going to be happier than you ever was in your life" (20). It also gives her the strength to defy Ramdeen yet sympathize with him. It also allows her to pointedly inform Prekash that "I wear what I like, when I like, how I like [...] The day ain't come yet when you, nor no man, could tell me what to wear" (67).

The developments in the story through its various versions reveal Selvon's increasing concern to treat with fundamental issues of existential importance. In this regard, the resolution of the plot also moves from death in the first to a happy-ever-after resolution in the second to an open-ended ambiguity about the possibility of conventional happiness in the third and final. *Cascadura*, in fact, leaves the shadow of death intact. In this way, the protagonists' triumph and blessing becomes their embrace of the chance to love fully despite the shadow. Salick claims that *Cascadura* comprises "the stuff of romance" but hastily withdraws as though to say so is to say something derogatory; he qualifies: "But it is not unbridled romance, for there is ample evidence of Selvon the realist everywhere" (*The Novels* 66). His recoil is reminiscent of Brathwaite's critique of "romantic rhetoric" in the work of a writer who does not "know very much about Africa necessarily, although he reflects a deep desire to make a connection" (*Roots* 211). This is indicative of widespread prejudices about love and romance and an undervaluing of their importance in a wide cross-spectrum of thought during much of the twentieth century. Reddy rightly identifies this as a legacy of the scientism and reification of rationality in Enlightenment thinking as well as the medieval Christian Church's abhorrence of earthly love (1). But it may well be a sign also of the chauvinism of early Caribbean criticism and much of the peri-Independence male-authored literature.

Cascadura, on the other hand, displays an "ethical commitment to love" which, as Kelly Oliver remarks, albeit in a re-reading of Fanon, "is necessarily part of a politics of liberation [...] The transformative power of love is a social and political power" (42–43). Therefore, notwithstanding the prevailing prejudices, Selvon writes a love story centred on, as Salick puts it, his "most complete heroine" (70). Given this representation of Sarojini, one may consider that Selvon constructs a "national heroine" that parallels Brathwaite's resuscitation of Nanny of the Maroons to restore a "sense of an intimate, emotional connection with [the] past" (*Wars of Respect* 3). The risk Selvon takes in presenting a story that may not be taken seriously signifies the importance he attaches to its telling. Central to the act is Sarojini's subjectivity, out of which her loving flows. It is made an ideal, revealing the horror of the psychological pathologies of others, which affect their ability to relate to others. In *Cascadura*, the political is thus irreversibly personal, and vice versa: each has an impact on the ability to live in community and to facilitate egalitarian relationships.

Obeah, Love and Conflict

Another character who works in a similar fashion in *Cascadura* and commands as much attention as Sarojini is Manko. In fact, if we were to arrange the characters on a pyramid of narrative approval, Sarojini would occupy the pinnacle, Manko would come immediately after, Garry would follow and others would be scattered underneath. As storyteller, Manko can be seen as "the Brer Anansi figure [...] in Selvon's fiction" of which Rohlehr speaks, but in *Cascadura,* the figure stands for more ("Literature and the Folk" 64). Manko is also known as the "obeahman" and African-derived religion in the text revolves around him, as the centring of Indian-derived religion revolves around Sarojini. As with Sarojini, Selvon makes sure that Manko's Africanness is immediately apparent via mundane details of the quotidian, as in the style of his house (87).

Moreover, as with the portrayal of Sarojini's unconscious access to a tradition that she may not be able to articulate, the text establishes an ordinariness for Manko's obeah, in the manner of magical realism, by its unobtrusive penetration into plantation routines. In the midst of chickens being fed and teeth being brushed, the narrator tells us: "It would not be too difficult, with the powers [Manko] had, to go into a coma and appear lifeless" (14). This introduction to Manko's powers acts as a reminder of the long history of belief in the supposedly paranormal, in phenomena that are not validated by reason but are accepted on empirical evidence. Manko is not sure where his special powers come from but is aware of their efficacy. Likewise, Sarojini substantiates her belief in Manko's power against Prekash's opinion of it as "stupidness" with evidence to the contrary: "You remember the other day when that baby was sick in the village, and the doctor couldn't do nothing? Ain't it was Manko who give she bush-tea to drink and make she better?" (19).

A lot of effort has been put into countering ambivalence about and disparagement of obeah and other African-derived practices in the Caribbean by re-inscribing them as "a complex of shamanistic practices [...] conducted by ritual specialists" (Brown, *The Reapers* 145) and "directed toward what the slave community defined as socially beneficial goals" (Bilby and Handler 155).[9] This re-evaluation of obeah, intended to undo its colonial denigration and policing, can be seen as underwriting Selvon's representation. However, Selvon complicates the picture by making integral the shamanistic, spiritually-grounded elements of obeah while at the same time undermining the notions of ritual specialty and the primacy of a community orientation. He places greater emphasis on the unique unfolding of capacities latent within Manko, who makes up rituals mainly to satisfy the psychological needs of those he assists.

More importantly, Selvon gives to Manko a philosophy of life that has marked Hindu overtones of karma and its laws of acceptance, which are also inherent to the concept of divination: "He was constantly advocating acceptance of what was decreed and had to happen" (93). Thus, Selvon moves Manko's being out of the Afrocentricity of studies dedicated to the subject of obeah and into the same syncretism in which he inscribes Sarojini's Hinduism. In this way, *Cascadura* manifests David Dabydeen's notion of "a continuum of slave and indenture experience", in which the subject stands "with one foot planted in Africa [...] [and] one foot planted in India in an equally ambiguous way" (qtd. in Dawes 204). Selvon's representation of Manko, as a result, runs counter to the hegemony of nationalist narratives geared towards revivifying African cultural retentions while others are debarred from the national imaginary.

But Selvon also foregrounds the power of love that underwrites syncretism in the tension-filled rectangle made by Manko, Prekash, Sarojini and Garry. One of the most important ways this happens is in the impossibility of accepting fate when love is at stake. Sarojini's love for Garry and Manko's love for Sarojini, albeit of different varieties, cause Manko to want to intervene in Garry's fated death and "tempt [him] to pit his puny knowledge against the might of powers which controlled a man's mission" (93). Manko's dilemma is, of course, an existential one that every man and woman face as they confront the impossibility of divining with certainty what the universe requires of them. In Manko's particular situation, it is the inability to distinguish whether it is hubris or fate that makes him want to help Garry to get rid of "a tiny bit of shrapnel" (34).

Unfortunately, this dilemma is compounded by Manko's distaste for people and things of the white world and his carefully maintained distance from them. This aversion can be viewed as a failing. It leaves him vulnerable to behaving at the most unexpected times like a racist and evidences a problem to which Dabydeen and Nana Wilson Tagoe allude in their view that "the West Indian finally becomes schizophrenic under the pressure of racism" (149). For Manko, it begins with a conception of "blackness". As Stuart Hall reminds us in "New Ethnicities", in the British context "the term 'black' was coined as a way of referencing the common experience of racism and marginalization [...] as a singular and unifying framework based on the building up of identity across ethnic and cultural difference" (441). As Selvon shows, however, in multi-cultural, multi-ethnic places like Trinidad and Tobago, it can also become an instrument of exclusion, doing as much damage to those it includes as those it excludes because it is part of the constant reshaping of racialized identities, the original Caribbean sin.

One instance in which exclusion is evident is when Manko foresees that "something wrong with that man", long before Garry's arrival. But he "can't rightly tell at the moment" what it is (23). His problem of vision, as it turns out, is about his distance, in more ways than one, from the object on which he trains his concentration. This is unmistakable in his response to Sarojini's query about whether Garry "is a good man"; Manko replies: "He is a good man. Though good is good with white people, and is a different thing with black people" (23). Manko has not met Garry but he assumes that he knows him because of his racialization of the man. This initial response to Garry characterizes all Manko's interactions with him, and reveals what Fanon calls "a third-person consciousness", perpetually on the defensive against a world he perceives as constantly challenging him to declare a position (*Black Skin* 110–11). His reactions are, of course, depicted as not unwarranted, given Caribbean history, Roger's smooth insertion into it, and Garry's subsequent entanglement in it despite his need for Manko's power. Garry accepts Manko's help only in response to Sarojini's obviously greater need for him to do so. Nonetheless, his recuperation depends on his ability to determine "how could he bring himself to hope an old black man untutored and uncivilized, could help when the best medical resources had failed" (99). The text leaves the problem unresolved. Even so, Manko is depicted as less than the man he is capable of being in his interactions with Garry. This is particularly palpable when Sarojini protests that "I not black"; "I is Indian" and Manko retorts "You still black" and informs her that her complexion "don't make no difference" (23).

That difference can be made a lethal weapon is not overlooked. It is obvious, for example, in the way Prekash uses it to manipulate Ramdeen into an attempt to crush the relationship between Sarojini and Garry. Although Prekash protests his love for Sarojini, he has no compunction in likening her to "a George Street whore" or in describing her relationship with Garry in the following terms: "You don't see how bad it reflect on the whole Indian generation for this girl to fling sheself like that at a *white* man." Prekash also calls on Ramdeen to "think of our religion and customs" (97, original emphasis). Ironically, the only custom to which he is shown to adhere is the conviction, which he shares with Eloisa, that

Roger "was a good man who gave him bread and butter," and therefore, "Prekash followed him, unaffected by any thought of freedom from the white man's grip" (28). His proud assertion of Indianness in the circumstances is unconvincing. He is in fact represented as a classic mimic. However, as Gayatri Gopinath argues: "within a colonial system of gender, possessing a viable masculinity is intimately tied to the ownership of property in the form of an idealized domestic space." Given that this is "invariably denied to the colonized male subject [...] 'mimic' masculinities of colonized men are [...] desperate attempts to become real [and are] the only forms of identification available" (73). Prekash can therefore be seen as desperately fighting for a fantasy because his sense of selfhood depends on it. His fight is, however, at the expense of the person who is central to its fulfilment and this makes him incapable and unworthy of the love he so desperately wants and disrespectful of others he perceives as different.

"[T]here are certain general features to racism," as Hall argues, "[b]ut even more significant are the ways in which these general features are modified and transformed by the historical specificity of the contexts and environments in which they become active" ("Gramsci's Relevance" 435). As Selvon depicts it repeatedly, in Trinidad and Tobago those modifications and transformations are related to the ongoing racialization of identity which serves to "decivilize" the population. *Those Who Eat the Cascadura* instead conceives identity as open, in a state of intercultural negotiation, and in a process of becoming. It is in how the story ends, however, that Selvon's final statement on the issue is evident.

The End: The Power of the Cascadura

Gerald Prince in the *Dictionary of Narratology* defines "end" as follows:

> The final incident in a Plot or Action. The end follows but is not followed by other incidents and ushers a state of (relative) stability [...] [T]he end occupies a determinative position because of the light it sheds (or might shed) on the meaning of the events leading up to it. The end functions as [...] the magnetizing force, the organizing principle of narrative: reading (processing) a narrative is, among other things, waiting for the end. (26)

The end of *Cascadura* is determinedly the daily banality of estate life. The "Come, kip, k-i-p" with which the novel opens (12), calling the chickens for food, is the same when Sarojini returns to the estate after Garry's departure at the end (180). By Prince's measure, the end would reveal that the story has been about nothing of any great importance to the quotidian. Therefore, recourse to Paul Ricoeur's sense of end is apropos: "It is in the act of retelling rather than in that of telling that this structural function of closure can be discerned" (60).

In the act of retelling undertaken here, the end occurs when Manko warns Sarojini against paying attention to the Alistair Macmillan couplet that speaks of the magical power of eating the cascadura: "Listen girl [...] it was some stupid Englishman what say that. White man don't know nothing about obeah" (164). What sticks in Sarojini's mind, however, is the couplet's idea of "native" (163); she senses in it a magic of more ancient lineage in this landscape than Manko has at his command, which suggests that Manko's powers from "there" have not yet been consumed by "here". To his surprise, Manko sees in consequence that "spirits were being manifested, taking shape, mobile as smoke drifting in air, and he had no idea where they came from, or why" (163). The final manifestation of power in the novel thus belongs to an entity that exceeds the will of those who have come via their various pathways to the Caribbean. The novel suggests that they ignore it at their peril.

This allegorical message of the cascadura's power is reiterated through another "native" symbol in the novel, the samaan tree, through which Selvon's philosophy of postcolonial community formation can be read: "the giant samaan tree [...] harboured and supported several species of wild vine and orchids [...] and even small trees [...]. All these, as if by common consent, flowered in the morning, and there were so many hues and sizes and shapes that only by bulk could the samaan tree itself be identified" (55). This arboreal image disrupts the narrative discourse and renders the text "fugitive", in Benítez-Rojo's sense, as

> constituting a marginal catalog that involves a desire for nonviolence [...]. If we look at the Caribbean's most representative novels we see that their narrative discourse is constantly disrupted, and at times almost annulled, by heteroclitic, fractal, baroque, or arboreal forms, which propose themselves as vehicles to drive the reader and the text to the marginal and ritually initiating territory of the absence of violence. (25)

The living community of the samaan tree, presages the vision of human community toward which the text works. It is a community in which diversity and difference are non-threatening. The samaan tree itself can be viewed as representative of an ontological core that Selvon posits for the mature human being and for society – a core he interestingly bestows to the least socially important characters, Sarojini and Manko. It is in their manifestation of a religious consciousness informed by love that Selvon builds a samaanic core and sings songs of love that belong to the "living folklore" of all the region's peoples.

NOTES

1. See, for example, Betjeman, Hicks, Levy, Lingle and the review "Plea for the Lonely".
2. The extent to which these views of calypso are relevant to Trinidad and Tobago today is a question worth raising.
3. See for example Clarke, et. al., "Sam Selvon: A Celebration".

4. Carl Jung's view of the importance of what he referred to as the "feminine" in religious sensibility is of course well known as is his argument regarding the eclipse of the "feminine" with the rise of Christianity. See Smith Barusch's *Love Stories of Later Life*.

5. Ingalls, in the foreword to *Divinity of Krishna* for example, asserts: "The *Bhagavata* [the main text on which the tradition draws in the Caribbean] draws from all classes, as it does from all of India's intellectual traditions [...] What is important to the *Bhagavata* is to feel God, to be moved by Him" (xii). See also Edwin Bryant.

6. See for example Mehta; Puri, "Race, Rape"; and Niranjana, "Left to the Imagination" and *Mobilizing India*.

7. For more on this, see Maharaj, *A Caribbean Katha*.

8. The literature on Orientalizing Indian erotics is voluminous. See for example Sangari and Vaid, Bhattacharya, and Das.

9. See also for example Bellegarde-Smith, Fernandez-Olmos and Paravisini-Gerbert, Houk, Hurston, Stewart and Thornton. See also Paton for an interesting discussion of the struggle this entails.

CHAPTER NINE

"English Brother or Not": British State-National Critiques and the Moment of *Pressure*

Joseph Jackson

One reason for a lack of critical attention to *Pressure* (1975) from scholars of Samuel Selvon, despite its significance as a foundational black British film text, is the relative difficulty in classifying the work as part of a Selvon canon. Written during one of the more febrile moments of race consciousness in British history and the product of a collaboration with filmmaker and Black Power activist Horace Ové, *Pressure* is clearly not a single-authored text. Nor can it be considered fully in isolation. The story of *Pressure* is the story of two progenitor figures and three interrelated outputs, the film itself one of two texts emergent from an initial script, *The Immigrant,* co-authored by Selvon and Ové. The genesis of these *Pressure* texts are outlined in Selvon's handwritten note on the cover of the manuscript of *The Immigrant* held at the University of the West Indies:

> This is the original script of the feature film PRESSURE. The work was officially intended for a BBC TV drama-documentary. The TV project collapsed. Horace Ové (who works with films) went on to make the film PRESSURE. I used my research material to write an original drama for radio, MILK IN THE COFFEE, which was broadcast by the BBC. (Selvon and Ové, 1)

Selvon's moderate disavowal here, reaffirmed later in conversation with Peter Nazareth, where he acknowledges that "I collaborated on the script [but] did not have a great deal to do with the actual shooting of the film" (434), further disrupts an easy assignation of the full film text of *Pressure* to Selvon's body of work. Analyzing *Pressure* as part of a critical response to Selvon therefore requires a methodological manoeuvre: examining the whole quasi-triptych that constitutes its moment while deploying other Selvon works in comparative focus. In this way, Selvon the author can function as an organizing principle for interpreting the triptych as social text. The *Pressure* texts provide a political critique of Britain that is consanguine with Selvon's individual pieces from that period and earlier, and resist the priority the British state has in preserving a certain political status quo. By exploring modes of experience and social relations that expose or counter state-national priorities, these works disrupt the principles behind the state's management of race, represented by a narrative of crisis and a process of cultural classification that is a precondition for political multiculturalism.

I refer to Britain as a "state-nation" above because of the role the state plays in establishing and managing British national values, coherence, and stability, while neglecting, or actively curtailing, actual national experience in the form of civic participation, popular sovereignty, and representative democracy. Selvon has recently been highlighted as reimagining an English nation in counter-British terms. For Elizabeth Maslen, his novel *The Lonely Londoners* "offered subversive readings" of the national condition of England, and "call[ed] for a conscious act of revision" for a moribund Englishness yoked to the declining post-imperial British state (45). Echoing Maslen, Michael Gardiner argues that the novel emphasizes a rebellious democracy amongst those marginalized within the state-nation, where the characters [...] often-exaggerated civility [...] reiterates Englishness in a familiar-yet-unfamiliar experiential form" (90), while as black immigrants they occupy "the place of civic collectivists who find themselves to be a state-national scapegoat" (91). *The Lonely Londoners* thus advances the project of reclaiming England from the national narratives of the state, which, for the sake of British state-national stability and continuity, consign England to either a pastoral, elegiac "pastness" or reject Englishness as white-supremacist and/or ethno-cultural. The *Pressure* texts extend this, directly dramatizing the conflict described by Gardiner between civic participation and a state politics of race; this is played out in the opposition between meaningful social relations, solidarity, and grassroots political organization, and the institutional power of the state form most readily evoked through the police. The texts critique the role of state management in the discursive production of race, with respect to both the incipient classifying practice of political multiculturalism and the narratives of crisis and moral panic prevalent around blackness in the 1970s.

The Immigrant and *Pressure* revolve around the changing political consciousness of Anthony, the son of Trinidadian migrant parents who begins the narrative as a subdued representative of colonial mimicry and ends it as a radical and informed political actor. The spur for this transformation is his inability to find a job despite his credible school-leaving qualifications: he is rejected at interview, where racial profiling is insinuated; he enviously regards the wage-enabled freedom of his white friends; he is caught up in the small-scale criminal enterprises of his disenfranchised black peers. Anthony's older brother Colin organizes a group dedicated to black political consciousness and solidarity. Eventually Colin's persistent agitation of his brother bears fruit and Anthony attends a Black Power meeting, which is violently broken up by the police. The closing scenes of both the film and screenplay track the aftermath of the meeting, where Anthony's increasingly vocal opposition to racism is channelled through greater involvement in the protest movement, and which triggers a familial and intergenerational reckoning in his household over the migrant experience. *Milk in the Coffee*, Selvon's single-authored radio play, dispenses with Colin and the explicit Black Power motif, but retains the race politics of the 1970s approached through unemployment, demands for integration, and police racism experienced by the protagonist – now "Andrew", but in other respects similar to *Pressure*'s Anthony.

The historical frame for the triptych is contemporaneous with Selvon's *Moses Ascending*, published in 1975, a critical period in Britain's post-war narrative of race, where the reconfiguration of race from biological to cultural classification was providing firm foundations for subsequent strategies in the state definition and management of culture. The immediate background to this transition can be seen in the 1968 Race Relations Act, which not only codified the framework through which discrimination could be prosecuted, but also validated the existence of categories of "racial origin" to empower that framework. Subsequently, both the Commonwealth Immigration Act (1968) and its successor, the Immigration Act (1971), saw a renegotiation of the criteria and basis for British citizenship, or more accurately, subjecthood, as rights were withdrawn from previously entitled Commonwealth citizens; these measures are an indication of exactly how, in the words of Ben Pitcher, "the state [is] the single most important social actor in the politics of race" (4). This new phase in race politics not only effectively legislated for the division of the UK population into racial-cultural groups, but also nourished a developing post-war British nationalism based on culturalism and ethno-cultural homogeneity – the so-called "new racism" (Barker). Nowhere is an ethnicized vision of Britishness more starkly displayed than in Enoch Powell's infamous April 1968 speech in Birmingham, the racialized "Rivers of Blood". This oration led to Powell's symbolic ejection from the Conservative shadow cabinet, as his successors went about simultaneously castigating and implementing his vision. Powell's centrality to British discourses of race can hardly be overstated, but it is important to recognize the role of his ethnicizing vision in propping up the state-national vision of Britain in the 1970s, maintaining a compliant Englishness and warding off the dangers of devolutionary fragmentation in the post-imperial void. As Tom Nairn describes, writing in 1977, the political career of Powell was determined most acutely by one project:

> Powell's basic concern is with England and the – as he sees it – half-submerged nationalism of the English. His real aspiration is to redefine this national identity in terms appropriate to the times – and in particular, appropriate to the end of empire. England's destiny was once an imperial one; now it has to be something else. (258)

Powell's ideological programme was on the surface incoherent and reactionary, an "incredible patchwork of nostrums", stretching to "economic laissez-faire, Little England, social discipline, trade before aid, loyalty to Ulster, and racism" (260). It was the final nostrum that bore the greatest weight in Powell's mission to restore

England, one that he perceived as integral to the continuation of a "great nation" ideal, but importantly one that presented no challenge to the integrity and continuity of the British state and establishment. In that moment, as Nairn points out, "England need[ed] another war" and Powell's state-national scapegoats were already lined up as the opposing combatants:

> The only *new* experience, going sharply counter to tradition, [had] been that of the coloured immigration of the 1950s and 60s. Hence, as Powell realized, it [had] become possible to define Englishness vis-à-vis this internal "enemy", this "foreign body" in our own streets". (274)

The racism of the 1970s, the backdrop to the dramatic sequences that occur in *Pressure*, is thus intrinsically linked to the crisis of English nationhood caused by the negation of imperial destiny and the associated threat to British state-national legitimacy posed by the prospective development of an alternative English national consciousness.

Discourses of race underwritten by state actors such as politicians, the police and the BBC, and pertaining to black criminality and law and order, are central to *Pressure*; as Kobena Mercer argues in a rare critical response to the film, its narrative arc and characterization constitute "a counterreply to the criminalizing stereotypes generated and amplified by media-led moral panics on race and crime in the seventies" (57). In this respect, *Pressure* substantially anticipates the comprehensive racial critique presented by Birmingham's Centre for Comparative Cultural Studies in *Policing the Crisis* (1978) (Hall et al). In its analysis of the racialization of street crime and the concomitant invention of a moral panic around mugging, *Policing the Crisis* diagnosed the state's discursive management, which was already shaping a British public understanding of race in the 1970s. This managerial strategy is enmeshed with the rise of a British politics of multiculturalism, a system that Pitcher describes as "a form of state practice" (4) in which the assertion of pluralism "actually conceals a highly prescriptive agenda which imposes the state's own definition of community and sets out the terms of legitimate belief and behavior that may occur within it" (8–9). This description is particularly apposite in the context of the British state-nation, where multiculturalism can be seen as the natural extension of cultural management established by the race legislation of the preceding decades.

State-institutional attitudes to culture and race are unavoidable features of *Pressure*, resulting not only from a narrative focus on various manifestations of racism in its historical moment, but from the conditions of its production and release. Publicly funded through the British Film Institute (BFI) and completed in 1975, the film was mothballed for three years on account of "scenes showing police brutality" (Ward). Despite this, the film was released to US audiences in 1976, suggesting different priorities in film censorship at work. For Mercer, the BFI's original decision to fund *Pressure* resulted from the context of racial discontentment, where "political expediency—the need to be seen to be doing something—was a major aspect of the benevolent gestures of many public institutions, now hurriedly redistributing funding to black projects" (77); the banning of what must have been an unpalatable final result suggests a further level of state sanction, maintaining control over a narrative of race. This is particularly important in a period of racialized moral panic, where only certain expressions of dissent were permissible, especially where the police were concerned. The modern BFI position on *Pressure*, outlined by Julia Toppin on the organization's *Screenonline*, makes no reference to the temporary ban, but acknowledges "how forthright and critical the film is of the British system, in what were very sensitive times", and that "*Pressure* remains a key Black British film, which helps to demonstrate how modern multi-cultural Britain was shaped". The tone of Toppin's writing encapsulates how the energies of a strident political critique of state power and institutional privilege such as *Pressure* can be diverted into reinforcing a certain vision of Britishness, where criticism is tolerated – even encouraged – before being subverted and absorbed into resolved, unitary, "modern multi-cultural Britain". Toppin's reference to "Black British" is also inflected with a sense of disempowerment: this is the black Britain of equal opportunities declarations, classification and measurement, where *Pressure* can be safely quarantined within a narrow band of ethnicized concerns. The deeper political and social implications of the film – for collective action, citizenship, institutional racism, and a state politics of ethnicization – are diminished when equated with sectionalism in this manner.

Of course, blackness as objectification and as a rallying point for anti-racist political action is a key element in *Pressure*. An indicative irony of the screenplay *The Immigrant* is that the protagonist, Anthony, is not an immigrant at all; contrarily, in the odd formulation of Toppin, he is "born in Britain and is British". Anthony's experience mirrors the immigrant in his progressive, Fanonian realization of the "fact of blackness", illustrated using a series of contrasts between his overtly Anglo-British cultural choices and his experiences of racism. He prefers fish and chips to patty and his mother's Trinidadian cooking, and bacon and eggs to avocado; to the chagrin of his brother, he is a patron of mainstream nightclubs; his initial panicked reaction to the possibility of trouble with the police – "Oh God, oh God … the Police … the Police! They coming? They coming? Are they here?" (54) – speaks of a bourgeois sensibility, reminiscent of Harris from *The Lonely Londoners*, that valorizes respectability and order. His older brother Colin bemoans that "I just can't get him to think black" (38). Before the intervention of the police, Anthony's slow-burning politicization takes place initially through the casual racism he finds in the employment market. While his lesser-qualified white friends are employed, Anthony finds himself profiled as fit only for manual labour, sent to the welding yard to be greeted with "Bloody hell! Those geezers up at the Exchange always doing the same thing. I ain't got no jobs here for anybody with 'O' levels. They bloody well know that" (48). This exchange with the welding yard foreman is part of a succession of encounters in which Anthony's education and intellect are mismatched or rejected by potential employers, and his gradual disenchantment accompanies a realization of the material conditions and political decisions that underpin them, contextualizing the film's later introduction of the British Black Power movement. Paul Gilroy observes that the 1971–72 sitting of the Home Affairs Select Committee, part of the remit of which was to examine the rise of Black Power movements in Britain, made "no direct connection between the rise of Black Power and unemployment" (*There Ain't* 113). This constitutes a delinking of social unrest, political organization, underlying economic conditions, and the racism that amplified those conditions. Anthony is presented as a willing volunteer for assimilation as a British state-cultural citizen who gradually turns to alternative forms of political expression and participation, and whose struggles not only reintroduce but amplify those links.

The emphasis on colour in the scripting of on-screen characters in *The Immigrant* gives an indication of the importance of racial signposting to *Pressure's* political counter-narrative, and makes clear the implications of the visual depictions. Anthony encounters "one of his old BLACK SCHOOLMATES, who is standing around with a WHITE GIRLFRIEND" (22); a "BLACK WELDER with torch in hand" is juxtaposed with "a WHITE WOMAN TYPIST and a WHITE CLERICAL WORKER" (48); later, there are "YOUNG CHILDREN both WHITE and BLACK playing without any hang-ups" (59). The dialogue presents a similar emphasis, where capitalization draws out the racialized conflicts in the narrative. This is epiphanic in the moment of Anthony's outrage in the closing scenes of *The Immigrant*, where police intimidation of his family forces a reconsideration of his own political position:

> God is a WHITE MAN, and it is the WHITE MAN who has done this to us.... and they ain't the only people in the world ... They ain't no fucking LORDS AND MASTERS ... We are human. BLACK PEOPLE are fucking human beings too! (75)

On the surface, Anthony's angry denunciation of white superiority, echoing the recurrent binary of black and white, seems at odds with Selvon's moderate stance on an explicit black politics. Nevertheless, these elements in *The Immigrant* can be traced elsewhere in contemporaneous and earlier Selvon works; in *Moses Ascending*, for example, Mervyn Morris has argued that "[r]acial discrimination is assaulted in passage after passage" ("Introduction" ix). The racial segregation of work into black/heavy labour and white/administrative labour is reminiscent of Cap's visit to the railyard in *The Lonely Londoners* (examined perceptively by Lisa Kabesh in "Mapping Freedom"). The power of sexual desire and romantic involvement to both transgress and entrench racial classification, the black boy/white girl motif referenced here and acted out by Anthony himself, echoes in numerous other Selvon works, not least *Milk in the Coffee*. The emphasis in dialogue conveyed by the capitalization of "BLACK PEOPLE" in the script recalls a stylistic tactic in *The Housing Lark* (1965), where "OUR PEOPLE", capitalized, is used to refer to Caribbean migrants in London by the characters Poor (107), Teena (113, 133), and also by the narrator (110, 115, 128, 152). The treatment of racialized experience in *The Immigrant* is thus, throughout, expressed in a mode consonant with Selvon's other writing, reflecting his influence on the collaborative work.

Establishing Selvon in the thematic concerns of *Pressure* is less clear-cut when considering the most pressing political articulation of race in the film, which comes through conflict between a repressive police force and an incipient Black Power movement. Here, it seems more credible to find the hand of Ové, active in the Black Power efforts of the late 1960s and early 1970s. *Pressure* dramatizes the history of encounter between Black Power and the police in Britain, drawing on examples of civic organization such as the Mangrove Demonstration of August 1970. This march was in opposition to repeated police raids, conducted under the pretence of targeting the sale of drugs, on the Mangrove restaurant in Notting Hill, popular with the area's black community and political activists. Ové was involved in documenting the protest through photography, and later the Mangrove restaurant itself would play a cameo role in *Pressure*. Robin Bunce and Paul Field's biography of Darcus Howe extensively details the moment of the demonstration as marking a watershed in the state's awareness of black political activism:

> The Mangrove Demonstration sent shockwaves through the British polity. Black Power, which had been such a potent force in the United States and the Caribbean, was finally flexing its muscles in Britain. The press were horrified, ministers demanded immediate briefings and the Metropolitan Police, determined to stamp out black radicalism, took it as a cue to launch a series of raids on the leaders responsible for the protest. (105)

This account indicates the way racialized policing was part of a reaction to political agency that not only threatened a racial status quo, but seemed to provide a template for action against the larger political structures that enabled it. This culminated in the trial of the Mangrove Nine, where several of the defendants, including Howe, opted to represent themselves in court; their subsequent acquittal not only a triumph for solidarity in the face of institutional police racism – recognized in closing remarks by the judge – but also a distinctive act of self-determination in the face of British sovereignty massed in the courts, the police force, and the media.

In contrast to Ové's direct participation in this phase of British Black Power, Selvon's London novels treat black consciousness and political organization with a degree of ambivalence or scepticism that can also be traced in the substance of the *Pressure* texts. Moses's laughing dismissal of Galahad's Fanonian turn in *The Lonely Londoners* – "that is a sharp theory, why don't you write about it" (89) – is the first indication, and in the inconsistent Galahad of *Moses Ascending*, as Susheila Nasta describes, "the political activist is ridiculed by the narrator's wider vision which penetrates beneath his Black Power 'glad rags' and the use of the latest political jargon to expose a still profoundly vulnerable awareness of self" ("Setting up Home" 93). This sceptical position surfaces in *The Immigrant,* where amidst the preparations for the final protest, there is a glimpse of the same humor as Galahad's posturing in the misjudged outrage of Junior's placard:

> JUDGEMENT HAS COME
> MERCY IS GONE
> BLOOD! BLOOD! BLOOD!
> ALL WE WANT IS <u>DEATH</u>
> TO ALL WHITE PEOPLE! (83, original emphasis)

Out of place among banners impeaching the police and calling for solidarity, the Old Testament exaggeration of the message is rendered doubly ridiculous in the closing visuals of *Pressure*, where the placard is carried solemnly by a white man.

Despite this ambivalence, Morris provides a useful corrective when he points out that "[r]esistant to Black Power, Moses nevertheless allows us several indications of the white racism to which Black Power is one response" ("Introduction" ix). This more moderate position is an effective barometer for *The Immigrant*, where the narrative is ambivalent towards racial-political radicalism, but occurrences of white racism informed by the ethno-cultural imperatives of the state abound. While pretensions and violent binaries are satirized, solidarity remains a key resource in the struggle against racism. Anthony's scepticism towards the ameliorative potential of Black Power in relation to poverty and unemployment prompts an angry response from Colin, his activist brother:

> You don't see Black Power feeding them, eh? That's why I just come from the pig's house trying to get Jacko out… Cha! I'm trying to get a lawyer to go down and arrange some kind of bail [...] that's what Black Power is all about! Something constructive! Not going around thiefing tins of cornbeef! (62)

Colin's speech argues for effective collectivist action, which Gardiner diagnoses as characteristic of the boys" lifestyle in *The Lonely Londoners,* and which challenges the divide-and-rule priorities of the state, symbolized by the "pig's house". The ambivalence towards Black Power in Selvon and elsewhere is indicative of the paradox this generates, where solidarity produces a democratic collective that draws its coherence from the racial-ethnic dividing lines prescribed by the managerial state.

Continuing with his identification of a subtle shift towards the political in Selvon's work, Morris notes that "[t]he police, a negligible element in *The Lonely Londoners*, are a particular focus in *Moses Ascending*" ("Introduction" ix), a focus which is paralleled in *The Immigrant*. In advance of *Policing the Crisis*, the police are the chief antagonists who manufacture crisis around street encounters and political mobilization. The notorious "suspected person" or "sus" laws are aired, where "TWO POLICEMEN have a BLACK YOUTH against the wall, with his hands above his head. One of them is briskly frisking the YOUTH" (31). The break-up of the Black Power meeting, the catalyzing event in Anthony's radicalization, involves a particularly violent police intervention, featuring "TWO YOUNG GIRLS [being] savaged by the dogs" (70), the arrest of an "ELDERLY BLACK WOMAN [...] (in great fright and distress)" (70), and the interrogation of suspects to a soundtrack of "[s]houts and screams and blows as if people are being beaten" (72). In the aftermath of consecutive raids on the meeting and a subsequent "drugs" raid on Colin and Anthony's parents' house, the imbrication between state-media reports and police interests is brought home by the drifting sound from the television set, where "the raid is mentioned very briefly stating that TEN Police were beaten up at a Ladbroke Grove Black Power Benefit, and five have been detained in hospital" (87, original emphasis). The racial character attached to the conflict ties this particular state narrative to Pitcher's description of a multiculturalism that is both "prescriptive" and allows for the literal policing of "legitimate beliefs and behaviour" (9). Here, the Black Power Benefit is repurposed as an example by the state, its collectivism and political agitation positioned outside the parameters of permissible dissent through an equivalence drawn between black political organization and violence against benevolent order.

The dream sequence near the conclusion of *Pressure* alludes to a fantasy of violent retribution against the police, where Anthony imagines himself knifing a squealing shape beneath a blanket which is then revealed as a pig. The scene itself provoked consternation: David Wilson's review described it as the film's "only serious miscalculation", though he inaccurately describes Anthony as "stabbing a white man who metamorphoses into a pig" (141) which is, as Stewart Home points out, "a fantasy of the critic's own making". Although a directly retributive reading of this scene is persuasive, this "pig" is more convincing as "[t]he Big White Brother PIG [that] tells everybody what to do!" (85), the ultimate object of Anthony's maturing ire: an established ruling elite that is representative of an Orwellian pig-state (two years later, Pink Floyd's *Animals* would depict pigs in the same way). This reading is backed up by the surroundings in which Anthony perpetrates the pig-stabbing – a dim but opulent bedroom inside a country house, the grounds of which he has symbolically broken into and wandered among, in an enactment of the 1970s "crisis" of the threatening black male figure. His transgressive penetration into aristocratic splendour, and into the sanctity of the white domestic space, is strongly contrasted to the spatial reality of his own home – a small flat above his father's shop – and the decrepit accommodation of his black friends. This transgression is representative of a challenge to prescriptive state-national modes of experience which are regulated spatially, explored elsewhere in *The Immigrant*'s spatial construction of London. For Gardiner, the boys' exploration of London – Charing Cross, Piccadilly Circus, Marble Arch, Bayswater – provides some of the most important civic aspects of *The Lonely Londoners*: appropriating imperial spaces, tramping and contravening state-delimited boundaries, celebrating lived experience, and laying a claim to place (90–91). *The Immigrant* continues this fictional engagement with the London cityscape in its naming of London locations: the youth club situated in "the Metro in Ladbroke Grove" (14); the exploratory perspective as "[w]e follow them in the Portobello road" (35); protestors encroaching on the sacred institutional authority of the Old Bailey (89). Home describes the influence of Godard and Buñuel in the Portobello Road scenes in *Pressure*, "with passers-by deliberately stepping into frame and leering towards the camera"; acts of traverse and transgression in a spatial sense – cruising, loitering, fleeing the police, roaming in areas of white privilege – are underscored by a cinematic style that approximates the unpredictable, and unmanageable, everyday of London street life.

Just like navigating the space of the street, negotiating the domestic sphere of the house is a recognizable trope in Selvon's writing. Drawing on the Moses novels and *The Housing Lark*, Roydon Salick notes that "worrying about rent and accommodation were critical elements in Selvon's metropolitan immigrant experience" (*The Novels* 113), while for James Procter, migrant living space in *The Lonely Londoners* provided both an "exclusionary environment" and "a site of congregation and public change", an "important repository for group consciousness" (45, 46). The focus on the quality and availability of housing for migrants in post-war black British writing is itself a reflection of certain state priorities. Ové has pointed out that governmental "active" indifference towards the rapacious practices of "slumlords" such as Peter Rachman "had created a huge avenue for Rachman to move into. Because nobody wanted to house all these black workers that they'd brought over from the Caribbean to do the dirty work for them" (Green 344). The quasi-collectivist home spaces of *The Lonely Londoners* decay generationally to a new level of dereliction in *The Immigrant*, where Jacko and the boys live in two rooms, a "dirty, dingy basement in a dilapidated derelict of a house [...] [The other room] is in even worse condition, cluttered with rubbish and rubble of all kinds" (52). The set directions make clear the poverty, impermanence and marginality of young black life in London:

> the shabby, dirty room in which there is only an old rusty paraffin heater, two single beds with dirty sheets, a wobbly table, two old chairs. The only window is barred off with pieces of box wood as there is no glass....A naked bulb hanging from a limp electric cord....The wallpaper is hanging off the walls. The ceiling is cracked and flaking, etc. (54).

The bare language of the scene-setting in the script directly evokes the destitution of the boys. This is the story of housing policy from the other side of Powell's emotive "white flight" neighbourhood in the Birmingham speech. In one sense, there is an upwards trajectory to the question of housing traceable through the London novels: the difficulty in securing, maintaining, and heating rented properties in *The Lonely Londoners* progressing through the perils of acquisition in *The Housing Lark*, to tentative ownership in *Moses Ascending*. Considering the return to impoverished living conditions in *Pressure*, seen in the experience of Jacko and his new generation of "boys", the corrosive effects of the government's management strategy of "active indifference", effectively leading to segregated slum-formation, are starkly illustrated.

Despite its urgent demand for "waking up" and mobilization, *Pressure* ends with a resonant scene of bedraggled and thwarted protest in the rain outside the Old Bailey. Arranged against the full institutional power of the British legal system, encapsulated in the Central Criminal Court of England and Wales, the tone of the final lines is unmistakeable in *The Immigrant*, where the protestors are described as walking "In circles… and circles… and circles …" (89), a heavy-handed suggestion of the "circularity" of black experience in Britain that Nasta has identified in the London novels and the plays of *Eldorado West One* ("Introduction", *Eldorado* 7–8). These images provide a particularly stark illustration of frustrated activism when compared to pictures taken by Ové at the Mangrove Demonstration, which capture some of the scale and energy of the Black Power movement earlier in the decade. The most explicit articulation of the political inertia of Britain is left to Anthony, newly politicized and, through the immediacy of personal experience, now aware of the state's responsibility for the promulgation of racialized thinking through institutional and discursive power:

> If you look at it this way, who runs the country? Who has the Power? Who has the Army? and the Police Stations? Who runs the Schools … and the Educational System? Who controls all the jobs??? Just a handful of people … just a handful of people have all this power and they tell everybody what to do! (85, original emphasis)

Where *The Immigrant* ends on a note of frustrated pathos, the closing moments of *Pressure* include a slight but indicative variation on the script. Rather than closing with the protest, the camera angle rises from street level before resting on the imposing dome of the Old Bailey, surmounted by a gilded statue of Justice.

The shot lingers and fades, leaving the protestors, and the film, presenting an unanswered question to the literal and figurative architecture of the British justice system. This final scene appropriately extends the disproportionate, criminalizing response to "constructive" civic collectivism; although the ideological force of Black Power in the film remains caught between political empowerment and racial re-inscription, the focus on the institutional quality of British racism and its common purpose alongside state-national priorities is maintained.

The differences between *Pressure* and *Milk in the Coffee* are more pronounced than the differences between the former and *The Immigrant*. Selvon chose radio as the medium for his own interpretation of the material that had constituted *The Immigrant*, and justified it to Peter Nazareth by favourably, and pointedly, comparing radio plays to visual performance: "I like writing radio plays. I think drama for radio is much more imaginative, and I can do that much better" (Nazareth 433). As one of the first writers to make contact with Henry Swanzy and *Caribbean Voices* at the BBC in London, Selvon's literary career in Britain had been launched from a platform provided by his stories for radio; during his time in Britain, over 20 of his plays were broadcast by the BBC (Nasta "Introduction" *Eldorado* 4). Describing "Caribbean Voices" as "the greatest thing that ever happened", Selvon said his experience with radio plays cemented a relationship with the oral and aural in his experiments with nation language, and he described his novels as an attempt "to convert this oral impression into a visual one, so that the page becomes a tape recorder as it were" (Thieme and Dotti 117, 119).

Unlike *The Immigrant*, *Milk in the Coffee* successfully navigated the censors and was broadcast on BBC Radio 4 in June 1975. Although the BBC has a non-partisan remit, as a state broadcaster it has historically been unwilling to go beyond low-level engagement with British politics to present a critique of the state-form of which it is a part. With *Pressure* languishing in the archives of the BFI, *Milk in the Coffee* presented a sufficiently tolerable vision of British society to be optioned by the corporation. That is not to say that the play is politically anodyne or apolitical. The narrative shares many features which could demarcate Selvon's influence on the original screenplay: a *bildungsroman* set out according to a generational divide between migrant father and "native" son, with "sus" searches and implied police brutality, prejudiced working environments, and the recurring juxtaposition of Trinidad and England. The play communicates an acute awareness of the wider background of British politics at the time, particularly the incipience of Thatcherite politics. Andrew's father Ralph, "bitter and bigoted" according to the abstract (1), seems to adopt a post-consensus conservative position where he announces that "I don't believe in all this welfare and culture thing, that's the truth. Maybe if I had wallop him and give him a few thumps when he was growing up, I would of knock all that <u>Englishified</u> stupidness out of him" (54, original emphasis). Ralph is a parody, railing against "Englishified stupidness" at exactly the moment that the British post-war political consensus is aligning with his suspicion of welfare. The generational schism recurs elsewhere, as the black teenager Charlo, describing his relationship with his parents before he "cut out", explains that "I tell them it's all their bloody fault [...]. Right? They just left the children to their own resources, and fend for themselves" (20). Charlo's words presciently indicate the changing shape of British political consensus, the betrayal of post-imperial promises to Commonwealth migrants, and the development of a Thatcherite ideology of individualism. The breakdown of familial and intergenerational bonds and obligations are here suggestive of the neglect of social relations – the absence of meaningful, civic participation and communality – within the state-national reality of Britain. Charlo and Andrew, second-generation Caribbean migrants with denuded cultural-historical resources to fall back on, are in a unique position to perceive the extent of this national disintegration.

The politics of race that is channelled through the Black Power movement in *Pressure* is invested in *Milk in the Coffee* in the drama surrounding a gollywog doll. The presence – and destruction – of the doll stands in for many of the explicit representations of race and racism in the film. The gollywog is initially introduced through Gran, who keeps her childhood toy as a memento of Trinidad. Its discovery in the household precipitates an angry exchange between Andrew and his father. For Ralph, the gollywog is "blighting [his] luck" and "bringing trouble in [his] household" (23), an "evil voodoo thing" (24) which represents "how the white people who educate you see all of we" (23, original emphasis). Consequently, he hacks it to pieces with a kitchen knife. This violence towards the doll crystallizes a number of Ralph's anxieties and frustrations: resentment of his mother-in-law's naivety, and her imposition on him; impotence in the face of racism; and anger at the memory of Trinidad and his experience of migration. Ralph's destruction of the doll is clearly mirrored in Andrew's subsequent encounter with the police, where he is profiled, stopped and searched. They find a second gollywog doll, bought as a replacement for his grandmother's, which is then similarly cut apart, "[slashed] to shreds" (34), by a penknife-wielding police officer searching for drugs. Here, the tearing of the doll *is* suggestive of a voodoo-like metaphorical function, where the violence visited on the crudely realized black body encapsulates the dynamic of the racialized stop-and-search and "law and order" panics, and prefigures the assault Andrew suffers at the hands of the same police officers. Despite the different valences of the respective gollywog incidents, they are consciously aligned by Andrew, who laments "the hate, man, the hate [...]. My dad, when he slashed it up [...] and that fuzz did the same thing [...]. They both had that hate in their eyes" (44). In the eyes of Andrew, for whom the gollywog is "only a rag doll" (23), the slashing evidences the "hate" of an entrenched and oppositional race consciousness, tending towards violence, which admits no progressive resolution.

The gollywog is also the subject of an impending government ban on the grounds of racial sensitivity: Ralph flatly states that "black people don't like the idea and the government should eradicate them" (23). The credibility of Ralph's sentiments is diminished by the social and economic conditions faced by Andrew over the course of the play, victimized by the police and proscribed from certain forms of employment. Indeed, as Andrew points out in response to the gollywog debate, "I'd have thought the government could attend to some more pressing problems. Like employment, for instance. I'm not the only black boy looking around for something decent to do" (23). Recalling the extensive narrative interrogation of employment, socio-economics and unrest in *Pressure,* Andrew's words juxtapose the management of the British state-national brand, symbolized in the gollywog ban, against substantive political action. This "legislating for sensitivity" also chimes with Mercer's diagnosis of a kind of racial-political expediency in the actions of the state in the 1970s. A prototypically British state-multicultural position, such a policy masks the material conditions and state practices that underpin the continuation of racial typographies under a veneer of attentiveness to cultural difference – one that maintains division even as it presents an inadequate attempt at resolution.

The conclusion to *Milk in the Coffee* sees Andrew and his white girlfriend Brenda symbolically entering a new nightclub together, connoting a future of new experience and resolution in the face of racism. However, the contrasting conclusion of *Pressure* seems to capture institutional failures and state-national management in Britain in the mid-1970s more accurately. During the time the film spent in limbo, Selvon moved to Scotland to take up a creative writing fellowship at the University of Dundee. This period, a first step away from England, is equated by Kenneth Ramchand with "a growing dissatisfaction with life in the mother country [that] prompted him to leave, never to return", culminating in another migration to Canada in 1978 ("Selvon, Samuel Dickson"). Selvon's departure from Scotland came immediately before one of the strongest illustrations of British state intervention in democratic process: the 1979 referendum on the introduction of a devolved Scottish Assembly, which was defeated on a government-introduced technicality that required support from an arbitrary 40 percent of the electorate rather than a simple majority. The temporary suspension of normal first-past-the-post practice marked another chapter in the state's continued shoring-up of the British-nation concept in the post-war period. Like the civic and democratic claim for self-determination from Scotland, the collectivist politics and social critique of *Pressure* represent a challenge to a state-national ideal of integrity, unity, and perpetuation. The moment of *Pressure* thus threatens not only a state-sanctioned narrative of race, but also the state-sanctioned definition of civic belonging and national experience permissible in the context of England during the post-war and post-imperial decline of the British state form.

CHAPTER TEN

"Playing Mas Isn't Playing the Ass":
Moses Migrating as "Farce en Noir"

Malachi McIntosh

"The present, in truth, is a farce"

– Samuel Selvon, *An Island Is a World*

Samuel Selvon's final novel, and thus his career as a novelist, ends with an arresting scene. In the closing pages of *Moses Migrating*, Moses Aloetta, the book's protagonist, narrator, and Selvon's most frequently recurring character, lands in London after winning first prize for "Most Original Individual Costume" at the Trinidad carnival. Moses's carnival costume is a portrayal of Britannia on the face of a coin, and he exults, both before and after receiving his honour, in his opportunity to act as a faithful emissary of the mother country on post-colonial Trinidad's biggest stage. Despite his own fealty to Britain, Moses returns to his country of residence to receive something other than an open-armed welcome. He explains:

> We touch down at Heathrow about six o'clock in the morning, and there was a cold breeze blowing, and a flake of snow brush my cheek lightly [...].

> I clutch my passport tightly as I shuffle up in the queue to Immigration, and hand it to the officer.

> He open it and peer inside. "Just one moment sir," he say, and get up to go to the office.

> "Hold on," I say, and open my plastic carrier bag and take out the silver cup first prize what I get in Trinidad for my loyal impersonation of Britannia. "I have this to declare," and I hold it up, like Arthur Ashe hold up the Wimbledon Cup when he win the tennis, for all the peoples in the airport to see. Only to me it was like holding up the Holy Grail.

> "That's quite all right, sir," the officer say smoothly, "I won't keep you a minute," and he go off to the office with my passport, leaving me holding the cup in the air like I was still playing charades. (193–94)

Those five paragraphs, barring the eight words elided by the ellipsis ("on the exact spot where Doris slap me"), form the entirety of the novel's final scene.

Moses, surprised at the start of the narrative to find his British citizenship revoked in the wake of Trinidadian independence, despite his "more than twenty years" living in Britain (29), is left stranded at its end, "brandishing his 'holy grail' […] as proof of his loyalty to the realm" and stripped of the ability to either move ahead or to regress (Tiffin 138). Moses's choice of "Holy Grail" to describe his prize is, as Helen Tiffin hints in the preceding quotation, a direct reference to the imagined national past in which he seeks to claim a stake, his words asserting that, like Ashe at Wimbledon, he has acted as his country's champion on a foreign stage and has thus proven his fit within it and his right to return. The immigration officer is unswayed, his simple speech-act, "That's quite all right, sir", refusing to recognize the worth or even the existence of the carnival prize. In just five words, he saps Moses's performance of all of its signifying force, shows the hollowness of Moses's belief in the justice of the mother country and renders the prize's display an empty, suspended semaphore.

In many ways, the conclusion of *Moses Migrating* is a fitting finale for Selvon's literary career. It places the main character from the novel that made his name in a transitional space akin to the "fog" and "blur" of the sleeping city of London from which he first emerged (*The Lonely Londoners* 23); it deposits this same character in a location between London and Trinidad, the main settings of all of Selvon's work; and, in addition, and most importantly, the scene allegorizes Selvon's most abiding fixation: the status of World War-era Caribbean people based abroad. From Boysie in *A Brighter Sun,* through to Foster and Rufus in *An Island Is a World*, to Mark in *I Hear Thunder,* to the central cast of *The Lonely Londoners, The Housing Lark, Moses Ascending,* and the *Pressure* triptych (see chapter nine), Selvon continually used his fiction to reflect on the concept that this single scene encapsulates. We receive at the end of *Moses Migrating* a snapshot image of an immigrant asserting a right to belong and requesting equal treatment, but having both things denied; we have, in short, in just a handful of paragraphs, a distillation of Selvon's thirty-year engagement with Caribbean migrants' quests for recognition.

That Difficult Final Novel

While the conclusion of *Moses Migrating* perfectly echoes Selvon's preoccupation with im/emigration across his oeuvre, the pages that precede it are easy to take as anomalies within that same body of work. The novel's narrative tracks the fulfilment of the desire to return to Trinidad expressed but repeatedly deferred by Moses in *The Lonely Londoners.* It begins simply and suddenly with the declaration, "I don't rightly recollect when it was the idea of going back home hit me" (29), and then moves at a rapid clip to depict Moses's journey to and sojourn on the island of his birth. The book, unlike Selvon's other Moses novels, is rigidly plotted: first, Moses travels by boat in the company of Bob and Jeannie, the man from the Midlands and his young bride introduced in *Moses Ascending*; next, he reunites with the woman who raised him, Tanty Flora, and falls in love with her current ward, Doris; and finally he participates in carnival, wins his cup, abandons Doris and returns to England and the limbo space depicted above. From this distance the plot recalls the journey and return structure of some of Selvon's other works but at the closer level of narrative form the book offers us something else. As noted by its critics, within *Moses Migrating*'s pages, "Selvon recirculates and reanimates racist and colonialist clichés and stereotypes" (Tiffin 131), he offers comedy that is often "coarse and broad, sexist and sexual" (Ramchand, "Comedy as Evasion" 98) and he "maintain[s] a sense of detachment" (Fabre, "Moses and the Queen's" 391) from his main character, who appears at times to be an "absurd anglophile" (Poynting 260) riven by "self-delusions" (Sindoni 280). While all of these features can be detected in one or another scene or character in *Moses Migrating*'s predecessor texts, the novel combines them into an unstable, contradictory, and somewhat resistant mix, one that slips free from Roydon Salick's three broad categories for all of Selvon's work as either "peasant", "middle-class" or "immigrant" (*Samuel Selvon* 53) to reside in a space in between.

Moses Migrating is almost immediately difficult to fix. After announcing his desire to return to Trinidad, Moses decides to pen a letter to Enoch Powell, the staunchly anti-immigrant Conservative Party representative, to support his proposed programme of repatriation. He declares to Powell that

> [t]hough I am deciding to return to Trinidad it is grieving me no whit and it is only your kind offer to subsidise such black immigrants as desire to return to their homelands that will make it possible for me [...]. As proof I have no ill-feelings or animosity for your sentiments re blacks, and in gratitude for your assistance, if I open a business when I go home I will call it Enoch-aided Enterprises, or some such title that will show what your true feelings are, and not like the newspapers and television that try to defame you, though I would not bother with that so much if I were you, as they do the same thing to black people (29–30).

I quote the passage above at length to showcase the way in which it swerves from a sense of straightforward false consciousness, Moses's lack of "ill-feelings" or "animosity" for Powell despite the nature of the man's racist rhetoric, to something more elusive. The passage challenges us to make sense of Moses's "gratitude" for "assistance" – which could either be heartfelt or a kind of tactical flattering. It adds additional instability through the parenthetical "or some such title" – which may or may not reveal Moses's lack of real commitment to his proposal. The letter's claim that Powell's defamation by the press is characteristic of an unscrupulous media that also unfairly attacks black people, is simultaneously a way of showcasing the scapegoating of the black British community by the press and a sign of support for Powell's race-baiting tactics. We can be tempted to take these uncertainties as a kind of complicated irony aimed at the politician by the character, but it is followed by no recognition on the character's part of anything besides full commitment to Powell's programme. Thinking of this kind proliferates in the text, Moses often failing to recognize the contradictions within his thoughts about England and its people.[1] The challenges of how to take him, a character who seems to be something of a "fantasist" (Nasta, "Introduction" *Moses Migrating* 11) but who acts as our sole window into the narrative world, is the challenge of how to take the novel itself. Where the Moses of *The Lonely Londoners* was clearly both jaded and enticed by England, and the Moses of *Moses Ascending* was clearly trying to get by in England without causing much fuss, the Moses of *Moses Migrating* is unclear – he seems to both overflow with unearned fealty to England and simmer with unacknowledged contempt.

The oddities of Moses's representation have demonstrably affected the book's critical reception. Writing about the novel in 1995, Tiffin explained that, while

> [a] number of critics have noted the complex tonal modalities of *The Lonely Londoners* and examined the subversive strategies of *Moses Ascending* [...] *Moses Migrating* has generally been ignored or dismissed as a lesser sequel to the 1975 novel, having little to add beyond the prolongation, into the 1980s, of the adventures of a now popular Trinidadian character. (130–31)

Almost a decade later, these words still apply. Of the three novels that compose the Moses trilogy, *Moses Migrating* is, without question, the least frequently read and analyzed, and by far the most often derided. There is a clear hierarchy of critical interest in these texts, one made manifest through the MLA International Bibliography. The online database currently registers twenty articles or book chapters on *The Lonely Londoners,* seven on *Moses Ascending* and zero on *Moses Migrating.* While the list misses several important critical texts that touch upon the work, including Tiffin's and several others I will reference, the novel's current status on the website perfectly encapsulates its reputation.

For most critics the book is a problem, if not an outright failure. Roydon Salick, in his recent book-length summary of Selvon's career, offers a model for this kind of thinking when he calls it the "darkest" of the trilogy, a text in which "approbation and sympathy pale into censure, humour is replaced by cynicism, and irony and sarcasm give way to incremental satire". In his eyes, this is all a result of the fact that Selvon had "grown tired of his protagonist" and was thus content for the character "to continue to make a consummate ass of himself" (*Samuel Selvon* 91). Kenneth Ramchand, in "Comedy as Evasion", says similarly, albeit more softly, that "the pattern of growth and hope that ran subtly through *The Lonely Londoners*" is present in *Moses Migrating* but ultimately "denied and devalued" (95), thus distancing the final novel from the rest of the trilogy in a mode that is replicated and intensified by Victor Ramraj who calls it "less a continuation of *Moses Ascending* than a separate work, even though there are brief initial references to some minor issues and situations in the earlier novel" ("The Philosophy" 82). Even the most generous readings of the text still offer a sense of it as a "lesser sequel". In Jeremy Poynting's "Samuel Selvon, *Moses Migrating*", for instance, a detailed engagement with the book begins with a description of it as "one of Samuel Selvon's entertainments, an apparently frothy concoction which contains a good deal more nourishment than might be at first suspected" (260), a summary that seems to offer as much as it withdraws.

The thoughts of the critics above are all responses to some of the difficulties of the text, difficulties which seem to stem from the nature of its composition. Selvon claimed to have finished the book in his 1979 interview with Peter Nazareth, a full four years before it appeared in print. In that conversation, he says of the drafting process that

> I really and truly never thought in terms of writing for Trinidadians as such or people in the Caribbean except for my latest novel, which I have just completed, which is kind of a sequel to *Moses Ascending*. And yet I have difficulty now because I think that I have turned away from the English reader in the Caribbean and it has made a difference in the actual style and quality of the writing. I will have to look at it carefully again. This is one novel that I may have to revise. (424)

Later in the same interview, Selvon states that he had "always been thinking, perhaps unconsciously, of an English audience" and the switch to writing for Trinidadian readers required him "to adjust [Moses's] thoughts, adjust the way he moves". "I found some interest in this," he continues, "but I'm not quite sure about this experiment, I will have to think a bit more about it to see if I have really accomplished this or not" (425). Selvon's struggle to find an adequate form for the work seems to have necessitated several iterations. We get a clue of this both from the differences between the manuscript and the typescript of the novel housed at the Alma Jordan Library and from Michel Fabre's 1982 description of an unpublished draft that concludes with "Moses tak[ing] leave of Doris at the airport" (391) a scene altered in the novel released one year later.

In light of all of this it would be strange to characterize the novel as anything other than challenging, with Selvon's protracted struggles to "adjust" Moses confounding critics with the nature of his adjustments. While the novel is by no means difficult to read – as is implicit in Poynting's portrayal of it as an "entertainment" – it is difficult to *read*, to analyse in search of a clear sense of effects and intentions. One of the largest impediments facing any assessor is the book's use of humour, which ranges from the convoluted ironies of the Powell letter to long sections of "crude", "broad", "sexist and sexual" comedy. The latter kind of humour can feel disjunctive and, as a result, is dismissed by both Ramchand and Ramraj as "farce" – as, at best, a "simple if resourceful revelation of incongruity after incongruity" (Ramchand "Comedy as Evasion" 88), and, at worst, just "slapstick" that saps our "sympathy" for the main character (Ramraj "The Philosophy" 83).

In his article, "'You Have to Start Thinking All Over Again'", Lewis MacLeod maintains that the lack of a clear political stance in the "idiosyncratic fictional worlds" of Selvon's works have confused critics and led them to comment only on those elements of his texts that conform to prefabricated, valorizing ideas about Caribbean people (157, n. 1). While this is a poor characterization of Ramchand's analysis of *Moses Migrating*, much work on the book confirms this diagnosis by attempting to posit it as a reflection on Caribbean "authenticity", or otherwise struggling with the fact that it offers something other than the showcase of cultural resilience found in Selvon's earlier London-set texts and features a returning migrant with an odd allegiance to Britain. I want to argue that if we take the author's words as an opening, and think of the book as one written for a new aim of addressing a Trinidadian readership, we can find our way to an appreciation of what it does differently from the rest of the Moses trilogy rather than downplaying or finding frustration in what it fails to do the same. Of all the unique features of *Moses Migrating*, its comedy is particularly ripe for reconsideration. To think of the book on its own terms, and in its full complexity, it is necessary to recognize how its deployment of bawdy, bodily humour is central rather than tangential to its aesthetic. With attention thus directed, we find many gestures beyond realism to the genre that both Ramchand and Ramraj dismiss. If we take the book on its own terms, as a novel that repeatedly pushes its humour into the realms of farce – not farce as designation of comedic or representational failure, but farce as a defined theatrical form – we can discover within its play the serious core that sits at the centre of its performances.

Moses Takes the Stage

In her seminal study of farce in theatre, Jessica Milner Davis describes the form as featuring works that are "short and often episodic in structure" characterized by "broad, physical, visual comedy", "slapstick" and "more or less coherently funny narrative[s]" and "whose effects are pre-eminently theatrical", created "solely to entertain" (1). Farce presents "archetypical" characters like "impotent old fathers", "languishing ladies, wives or daughters", "buxom servant girls", "smooth and potent lovers" and "clownish servants" (15) in works where "[v]erbal and literary artifice is simply overwhelmed by physical action" (17). To read these descriptions and fail to see reflections of *Moses Migrating* is a demanding task indeed. The book is, as its critics make clear, home to the type of comedy and episode-based structure that Davis describes and is, too, populated by a largely archetypical, supporting cast with Jeannie, Bob and Tanty, to just take three, easily slotted into categories like "insatiable ingénue", "ignorant Midlander" and "maternal market woman". The book is also profoundly theatrical, with tropes of performance thread through a narrative where, in replication of Davis's thoughts on farce, character's words make as much meaning as their actions. More important than all of this though, the novel contains the central feature of farce through its many centuries of development and mutation. It reflects the form's "values":

> to the young and the bold goes the enjoyment of sex; to the old and the timid its
> frustrations; to the slow-witted, defeat is due, and to the clever, an immediate
> advantage. But that advantage is [...] temporary in nature, and when the rebels
> overreach themselves, the thrust of the joke is reversed. (Davis 42)

Moses Migrating clearly conforms to the "[s]ymmetrical patterns" common to the genre, which hinge on reversals of fortune and reestablishment of the status quo (Davis 43, 84), a feature easily seen in Moses's return to the periphery in the text's final section.

The connections between the book and farce on stage are close not only at the level of representation, but also in the arena of reception. Farce is, notably, an undervalued genre. As Peter Holland explains of the form during the Restoration, in words that directly address the critics of *Moses Migrating*, many deride farce because "it breaks realism and represents impossible characters" (119). Holland argues that in their dismissals, critics fail to take into account the fact that "farce has its own logic", that it "refut[es] the demands of contemporary theories with their high valuing of the 'natural,' of the necessity of mimetic accuracy" (118). *Moses Migrating* lacks the developed engagement with the felt experience of *Windrush*-era migrants given in *The Lonely Londoners*,[2] it jokes constantly and sometimes crudely about the human body, and it features the kind of wordplay common to the bawdy joke – such as when Jeannie arrives in Trinidad, confuses it with Hawaii, and tells her sometimes-lover Moses that "I was disappointed I never got my lei" (83) – but it is through all this that it presents its most important ideas.

In order to better develop a sense of the function of the text's debts to farce and thus reassess the role played by its comedy, it is necessary to re-examine its oft-cited fixation on costuming and disguise. The central role of masks and acting in the novel is asserted early on when Moses "don[s] waistcoat, and spats, and evening jacket, and brushe[s]" his "bowler [hat] to a shine" to get ready for dinner with Bob and Jeannie, the absurdity of this outfit for a casual meal with friends made plain when "Bob hail me in jeans and Afro-shirt and a pair of sandals what show his dirty toenails. And Jeannie flounce up in an open-neck shirt—open-breast, really—and red cotton slacks" (31). From this scene onward, the putting on and taking off of clothing, and the alterations in behaviour that it inspires, comes to characterize the interactions between these three characters and acts as the central source of the comedy of their shared episodes. Shortly after Moses puts on his waistcoat, Bob and Jeannie show Moses their "tropical gear" for their Trinidad trip, which consists of "what you see film stars wear on safari", including "a great elephant gun" (37–38); later, Moses dresses as Bob when the latter is incapacitated with seasickness and Moses cuckolds him, taking on Bob's conjugal role as he takes on his clothes (66); and throughout, Jeannie is described in a range of outfits that expose her body, from her "open-breast" shirt, above, to a "flimsy flesh-coloured bikini" (95), to a "red cotton halter—no bra—white shorts—no panties—and sandals" (128), her near-nude costumes almost always presented as a prelude to comedic sexual play.[3]

The book's interest in costumes connects to a wider theme of performance which is crucial to the relationship between Moses and all others and repeatedly frames his meetings with Jeannie and Bob. The importance of performance is presented, almost as guide to what follows, from the very outset of the text. In the dinner party scene described in brief above, Jeannie "perform[s] the ceremony" of serving food, a "ceremony" – a word which cannot but connote artifice – which features Jeannie and Moses struggling to put into practice putatively upper-class rituals like extending a finger while sipping their drinks (33–34). At the same dinner, Bob asks Moses to comment on a Pinter play shown on the BBC (32) – depositing a seed of the theme of performance, a seed fed shortly thereafter by the description of he and his wife as attired like "film stars" in their safari outfits. At the end of the text the costuming and acting of these three characters continues, if not culminates, in carnival, first at Jouvert, where Moses's costume is a "composite" of donations from Bob and Jeannie and others (176), and then at the climax with Moses, Bob and Jeannie dressed as Britannia, a slave and a handmaiden, respectively.

As Moses declares in his narration, within this text clothing "maketh the man" (73) – and also often forms the basis of the comedic scene. When Moses, Bob and Jeannie meet, the comedy is obsessive about the covering and uncovering of the body and fixated on what can and cannot be concealed. Out of this stems its "broad" nature – its serial preoccupations with sex, food, fluids and skin – but underneath it is a sustained interest in vulnerability, the fragile interior that performance and clothes try to hide and which is always open to exploitation. This sentiment moves to the surface most notably when a costumed Bob receives a splinter while dragging Moses's carnival platform, pauses his performance, and receives a "cheer" of delight at his revealed wound from the surrounding crowd (187).

From "Comedy as Evasion" to "Farce en Noir"

While Kenneth Ramchand is sceptical of Selvon's achievement in *Moses Migrating* in the essay "Comedy as Evasion", his overarching assessment that "the pattern of growth and hope that ran subtly though *The Lonely Londoners*" (95) is present in the book but ultimately "denied and devalued" opens up an avenue for a deeper analysis of Selvon's farce-indebted and performance-obsessed aesthetic. Ramchand's frustration with the novel's deployment of the features of farce is centred on what he takes as its sustained subversion of everything, its "deflating of the emotions associated with [...] sacred moments in a life (departure, arrival, falling in love, belief, etc)" (104). He sees in *Moses Migrating* glimmers of "the philosophical Selvon of the early novels" (96) – the man he describes in the first chapter of this collection – and the book fails, in his reading, because it palpates the serious issue of a migrant's return but aborts a full exploration, evading a full engagement and instead presenting the "easy course" (106) of a "parodic treatment" (105). Maria Grazia Sindoni, writing three years later, in implicit disagreement with Ramchand, argues that the theme of migrant return *is* adequately sustained throughout the text, Moses's "ambivalence", showcasing the "problems of identity for immigrants" and the impossibility of return to origins (280). Where Ramchand's presentation and eschewal of the humour in the work is detailed, Sindoni's treatment is somewhat light, but despite the gaps between them, both readings can be combined to offer a rounded understanding of the farcical within the text.

Drawing on Ramchand's registration of the oscillations of the book in and out of seriousness, we must recognize that *Moses Migrating* does not fully conform to Davis's general definition of farce; it is something other than sustained "broad, physical, visual comedy [...] intended solely to entertain" and it is not a consistently or "coherently funny narrative" (1). The novel presents only a handful of moments of pure farce: the dinner party scene above; Moses's sustained liaison with Jeannie on the ship to Trinidad; and Moses's sex with and re-costuming of Jeannie in the sea. These scenes are interwoven with destabilizing episodes which hinge on an ironic distancing from Moses and his perspective, as in his opening letter to Enoch Powell – moments where humour can, at times, be hard to fix. The novel also, significantly, contains moments where humour seems to be eschewed altogether, in particular when Moses interacts with Tanty and Doris. The book is thus not a straightforward farce: it is a hybrid, one that closely aligns with a peculiar farce form that Davis identifies.

In *Farce*, Davis writes of a particular manifestation of the form, common to the "English" tradition (92), which seeks to engage the sympathy of its audience. Where farce is usually "comedy with self-awareness left out" (88), some farces fail to maintain detachment from their characters and in them "[i]t begins to matter, for example, whether a match is really a love-match and not just a physical match [...] whether any feelings have really been hurt" (89–90). These farces offer "mixtures of laughter and sympathy, or the rapid alternation between the two", which can create "black humour – alarm, and even terror" (93). She dubs this form, ironically due to the description's fit for *Moses Migrating*, farce "en noir" (93). Davis's idea of "laughter and sympathy" fits perfectly for this text, as does the concept that, within the "farce en noir", stakes rise and feelings matter, as they do in the Doris and Moses love affair. Unlike Selvon's other works, where "laughter and sympathy" also famously feature, in *Moses Migrating*, the pendulum swings rapidly from comedy to solicitude, with Moses often switching from an apparently unselfconscious fool – the farcical figure par excellence – to a pitiable man who worries about his life and its meaning, sometimes within a single scene.

Returning to and following Sindoni, as we did Ramchand, we must recognize that these switches occur as a part of a coherent presentation of migrant's return – the book's events suggesting a sense of "impossibility" at the core of Moses's life. Selvon places his main character in cabin "13B" (50) on the boat that brings him back to Trinidad – a direct echo of the address of his migrant players in *The Housing Lark* – and also makes him a face in a nameless crowd in Port of Spain (104), a crowd akin to the one we see at the end of *The Lonely Londoners*. Both things function as intertextual signals of the recapitulation and reversal of the theme of accommodation found in the earlier works. This book, from beginning to end, stresses Moses's liminality. It has Galahad refer to the character at the outset as a man out of phase, "retired from the scene", a "Rip Van Winkle" (30), then proceeds to position Moses in several baldly liminal locations: he is frozen on a "gang-plank" mounting the ship to take him to the Caribbean (50); he is first paused and then stuck on the ladder between the lower and upper levels of the same ship (57, 68); he is made external to all groups at a bar while travelling (75); is reluctant to leave the empty ship once it has docked (82); describes himself as born into a marginal space, as an abandoned orphan dropped in a waste dump (84); and, at the end, is stuck at immigration holding his "Holy Grail" (194). Over and over again, we find Moses on the outside trying to get in; wrestling to get acceptance from the English, from his Caribbean cabin-mate Dominica, from Tanty and Doris, from the Trinidadian newspaperman Lennard, and from the carnival audience and carnival judges. Despite his central role as the voice of the text, Moses always seems somehow to be orbiting rather than sitting at the centre of things, a fact underscored by his supplementary position in respect to the three couples that feature in the novel: Bob and Jeannie, Tanty and Doris, and Galahad and Brenda.

The pathos of Moses's position and his pathological desire to move inward is the prime source of the text's moments of comedy and its moments of sympathy. Moses's literal and figurative struggle to enter into and find accommodation within the Jeannie/Bob dyad leads to all of the comedic scenes mentioned above, while his efforts to find a space in the home and lives of Tanty/Doris lead to their opposite: moments of confusion, loss and diminishment – the novel's only moments of pure pathos. When the character first encounters Tanty, she questions his voice, claiming, "[y]ou sounding strange, Moses. You learn to talk like white people?" (88) distancing him from herself at the level of his expression in a first-person narrative where Moses's words are the only substance of his self. She follows this statement with a further distancing by nation in addition to race, claiming, "[y]ou don't sound Trinidadian to me no more [...] Maybe as you been away so long" (88). She continues throughout the text to stress Moses's difference, most often through reference to his assumed wealth and social status in Britain, rendering him, always and irrevocably, an outsider. Doris behaves very similarly in her scenes. She dismisses Moses variously as rich and too committed to white people throughout the book, and "slip[s] away" at the end of the novel after the night they spend together, leaving Moses alone when he wakes (182). Moses reads Doris's resistance as the "way" of "Caribbean girls [...even] if they like somebody, they tease them all the time" (124–25), but the only time Doris fully accepts Moses is at carnival, in an "all o' we is one" scene which, like that in Selvon's *I Hear Thunder*, is as effusive as it is effervescent. As Moses advances, Doris retreats, and both she and Tanty summon the textual and personal "self-awareness" that Davis presents as the antithesis of farce's aims. In the final pages of the narrative, Moses laments that he denies Doris in his departure from the island like Peter denied Christ (193). What the character fails to recognize is how many times he himself has been denied by Doris, and by everyone else.

While critics have mentioned Moses's peripherality in terms similar to mine, it has yet to be noted how this is presented, serially, as the result of others' actions. Although he arrives in Britain as a citizen and lives there for two decades, he is unable to receive a British passport when he leaves for Trinidad (39) and is denied recognition as arriving in England as a citizen (93). Bob consistently refuses to see him as an equal, even after discovering his own black ancestry (191). Jeannie's interactions are almost solely requests for sex. Galahad and Brenda, whenever present, see Moses only as a fool. Doris suspects his intentions almost from beginning to end. Even his taxi driver takes him for a foreigner (162). Moses is not British to the British characters and not Trinidadian to the Trinidadians. In her reading of the text, Sindoni argues that its core idea is that "obedience to Western systems of beliefs and values on the part of the ex-colonial is [...] the worst legacy of the colonial experience" (280–81), but the text clearly depicts Moses shuttling between the "Western" and the "Caribbean" Sindoni renders as its opposite – his attempts to prove his Trinidadian/Caribbean credentials, to find space within those "beliefs and values", made as much, if not more fraught than his parodic allegiance to Britain. Moses's carnival performance becomes a chance to reconcile his longing for acceptance in both spaces; it grants him, in his words, the chance to fulfil his "two most important desires at one time [:] Britannia on one side, Doris on the other, and yours truly in the centre. We three was not a crowd!" (134).[4] The days of carnival do offer this but in their wake everything evaporates.

The abject "impossibility" of Moses's position – the "alarm", in Davis's words, generated by his bizarre allegiances and the farcical actions and pathos that they summon, stems from the abject paradox that is the centre of the text. According to the conditions set by the Trinidadian characters and the British characters in *Moses Migrating*, Moses can neither be British nor Trinidadian, even though he is already both. By performing the role of one, he invalidates his claim to the other. In this world, to be British is to be white, culturally chauvinistic and selectively xenophobic; to be Trinidadian is to be non-white with a single way of speaking and a burgeoning sense of nationalism. To try to be and believe as both things within these matrices is absurd, farcical, untenable. To defend the Britain of the National Front as valued because "I was hungry and they gave me fish and chips; I was thirsty and they gave me a cuppa" (156) is eminently nonsensical; to state that "I do not understand why white people do not keep their arses quiet with their Bank holidays in their own countries and let black people get on with their Carnival" after travelling to carnival as a proud Briton with two white friends (189) is as hypocritical as maintaining faith in the value of whiteness while hoping your embodiment of Britannia as a black man "might even strike a blow for Race Relations" (155). These serial contradictions seem to me to be exactly the point. The text presents a world where the terms set for blackness and Britishness, Trinidadianness and Englishness are mutually exclusive – where an attempt to perform all identities can only end in farce.

The comedy of the novel, then, acts as a way to register the options presented to Moses: be British and hate your origins or be Trinidadian and somehow erase the changes made in you while abroad. It is self-conscious comedy that constantly flags its own oddity, registering its many distortions through the knottiness of Moses's thinking and in the many moments of detached laughter that accompany it. Throughout the text characters are described as either not laughing at events or laughing at each other without pleasure. Early on, Moses's whiskey, rather than Moses himself, laughs at Jenny's suggestion to join her and Bob in Trinidad (34); he does "not laugh" at Bob's and Jeannie's absurd safari costumes (37) and he laughs when he loses his British citizenship (39). This laughing which either doesn't occur or is inappropriate to circumstances, or, like the whiskey laugh, is distanced and made strange, is heightened by the arrival of Dominica and his "kind of Caribbean laughter, derisive and mocking, what put you in your place", the kind of laugh a Caribbean person does when he "can't talk" (52). This "Dominica laugh" signals not mirth or entertainment but bile and the loss of words. Later on in the novel Moses goes on to perform it, this laugh of an "insecure jester" (59), and also has it aimed at him. The novel heaves with laughing characters and, by drawing attention to their laughter, by spelling it out on the page, and by creating, through Dominica, a kind of acrimonious non-amusement that is nonetheless expressed as a laugh, it complicates its own farcical play. The effect of the characters' laughing or not, derisively or not, constantly asserted in the text, is something akin to the switch of the non-diegetic laugh track of a sitcom with diegetic giggling; like characters on a TV screen cracking up after their own jokes and/or sometimes announcing they will not laugh and/or sometimes laughing mockingly at each other's joking; it is a wry recognition that begs assessment of the comedy displayed. We are, as readers, asked not simply to absorb the humour but also to assess its humorousness – to question whether or not the laughter described – of whatever kind – is warranted.

These prods, the text's endless foregrounding of its own comedy, assert a sense of intentionality behind its farce. In her reading of the text, Giselle Rampaul takes the laughter in *Moses Migrating* as akin to that in *The Lonely Londoners*: she describes it as "a means of survival and a defiance of [Caribbean peoples'] wretched lot and, therefore […] an empowering gesture" (313). It is hard to see this in the text, especially when Moses is mocked at a bar (103) or when Dominica aims his signature laugh at Bob because he knows, and Bob doesn't, that Jeannie is having sex with Moses behind his back (145). The laughter in *Moses Migrating* seems, rather, a reminder of Sam Vásquez's claim that "despite identifiable commonalities […] and the sense of community that jokes can imply, jokes are largely subjective. Furthermore, *one can joke without laughter and one can laugh when one does not get the joke*" (9, emphasis added). In short, it showcases how comedy can *undermine* community, exclude individuals and *dis*empower people because being able to laugh at or with implies status. In this text laughter registers conflict more often than it does community and it features not only as the tool of the weak against the strong. All of this reveals the double valence of Moses's ostensibly praise-giving self-description that "[i]f all the men in the world was a pack of cards, and you shuffle the pack, I would come out the joker" (74). The joker is, of course, a joker – a comedian, a jester, an entertainer – but it is also the odd one out, the card that can in some games act as other cards but never fully become them, the card which is, in most games, left out altogether.

In on the Joke

In her book on farce, Davis describes comedy as

> drawn from the most human of strivings: our continual impulse to rebel
> against convention and morality and our continued efforts to master our own
> bodies and our physical environment. Most often, the joke entails the failure
> of the attempt; but it is a failure which must also touch the audience, since the
> joke is on us all as members of the human race (22).

For Davis, farce is all this and more: it goes a step further; it deletes the ameliorative
effects of the resolution of tension in comedic narratives, denies development
and forces recognition of the scale of the struggle to master ourselves and what
surrounds us. In farce, "[p]eace can be bought only by submission, or by the kind
of growth in character that farce-structures are designed to exclude" (101). Owing
to this, she argues, "[d]espite its gaiety, despite its cruelty" readers must recognize
that "farce is a serious theatrical genre" (102).

If we take *Moses Migrating*'s movement in and out of farcical episodes as
integral to its form rather than a series of representational aberrations, we can
discover within it similar seriousness. The book refuses to grant us the stability
of a more orderly representational mode and denies realism's standard promise
of sustained individual development. It gives us, instead, something disjunctive,
difficult, fragmented. While the book follows in the wake of Selvon's many other
reflections on the status of Caribbean emigrants, it presents us with a character
very different from the "nostalgic dreamer"-figure (Wyke 113) we find in his other
novels. The Moses of *Moses Migrating* does share some of the characteristics of
Selvon's earlier leads, not least his positioning within a journey-return narrative,
but he is distinct, placed in a bizarre kind of farce that uses distancing strategies
as it appeals to our sympathy, that creates comedy and pathos from human
vulnerability, that asks us to laugh while questioning why we are laughing. The
book uses Selvon's signature short episodes and experimental narrative voice(s) to
present a sense, in echo of James Loxley's summary of the insights of performance
theory, that performance often "shapes societies" and acts as "the very stuff of our
ordinary lives" (154).

Moses is given two options, to fit into a Britishness that equals whiteness or
a Trinidadianness that conflicts with his history, and he tries to do both. The
narrative that details his attempt to perform these conflicting roles contains
all the absurdity of a man acting while wearing two masks. The pathos of its
scenes with the Doris/Tanty dyad and the comedy of its episodes with Bob and
Jeannie can easily be seen as a gap between two ways of being – one system within
which Moses is a pitiable outsider and another where his sole role is that of an
entertaining plaything – neither of which can be fully reconciled.[5]

If we follow Selvon to read the book as addressing a Trinidadian audience for the first time, presenting to them a man born in Trinidad but matured abroad, who can find no space for accommodation within Trinidad after independence, we can then see within its experimental aesthetic a struggle to express the marginalization of a particular generation of migrants, those who left too early and returned too late. We can take this as a supplement to his career-long critique of the opportunities for migrant settlement, re-directed at his former home. Roydon Salick has read *Moses Migrating* as a reflection of Selvon's contentment to let his most famous fictional creation "continue to make a consummate ass of himself" (*Samuel Selvon* 91), but I think, in light of all above, that it is far better to follow the words of one of the minor characters in the novel and recognize that farcical performances can be far more than just that; that within and through this text, "[p]laying mas isn't playing the ass'" (134) – or at least, it is not that alone.

NOTES

1. For developed discussions of the gap between Moses's statements and his recognition of their implications, see Sindoni (308); and Looker (190).
2. *Londoners* is so fully focused on rendering this experience that the history of its criticism has become a history of seeking evidence of the realities of *Windrush*-era migrants' lives within it. See Procter (47).
3. If we follow Kate Houlden's argument in chapter seven, it is hard to escape a sense that this book sees a return by Selvon to a rendition of a white woman as, primarily, a sex object. Jeannie is not quite as empty as Doreen in *Turn Again Tiger*, and wholly lacks the latter's sense of threat to the main character, but she is no Petra (of *The Plains of Caroni*); from beginning to end in the novel, she is almost exclusively associated with fantasies of sex.
4. It is interesting that Doris here is positioned as the opposite to Britannia – rather than the opposite to Jeannie, her most obvious foil – in a paralleling act that suggests Doris is a stand-in for the Trinidadian nation. This idea is supported by the fact that Moses describes Jeannie as incapable of acting as the symbolic version of Britain (158). While Jeannie is frequently counter-posed with Doris in the book, she does not have the symbolic weight of the Trinidadian character.
5. While the carnival scene ostensibly shows Moses's recognition by the two audiences he longs to woo – the British and the Trinidadian – it culminates in pivotal failures to communicate with representatives of both groups. First, he fundamentally fails to convey his desire to marry Doris despite consummating their affair (180–81). Next, he goes on, as we have seen, to fail to receive any significant recognition from the immigration officer to whom he shows his prize. Thus, while the carnival scenes read as fusion and consummation, these are ephemeral, fleeting, purely physical connections.

AFTERWORD

Continuing to Defy Categories:
Unusual Encounters with Samuel Selvon

Susheila Nasta

© National Portrait Gallery, London

S ince 1994, when Sam Selvon sadly passed away on a trip home to Trinidad, there has been a growing swell of international interest in his work. This has ranged from single-author studies, to several anthologies, to a recently published poetry collection which opens a window on Selvon's verse, to attempts to reissue out-of-print novels, to requests for translation, stage and film rights.[1] At the same time, following the new turn in modernist studies, many contemporary scholars have begun, belatedly, to read his work through wider-angled spectacles, locating him as one of the key writers to creolize the post-war metropole and a writer who was to challenge the once tightly guarded interface between metropolitan and colonial modernisms.[2] Whilst such recent work has partially been stimulated by Selvon's now undisputed reputation as one of the most important Caribbean and British writers of his generation, this shift in critical attention is also due to a number of other factors. Such elements of Selvon's multifaceted literary persona have always been available but seldom, until recently, noted.[3]

There have always, of course, been many Selvons. This became blatantly apparent when I visited the London National Portrait Gallery in 2011 to see a retrospective exhibition of the work of Ida Kar, an Armenian photographer famous for her intimate studies of an eclectic range of mid-century artists and writers formative to twentieth-century modernity. Featured amongst her remarkable portfolio of over forty black-and-white images of 1950s writers based in London and Paris was a wonderful portrait of Sam Selvon. Having known Sam for many years, both as critic and as a friend, the image jumped out at me, at the same time posing a number of intriguing questions.

Dated 1956, the picture seems to have coincided with the publication of Sam's famous and now iconic novel of West Indian migration, *The Lonely Londoners*, which received wide acclaim in its time and later.[4] I was stunned by the power of this evocative photograph, which depicted Sam, a handsome young East Indian Trinidadian man of thirty three, sitting in his London study lined by several shelves of books. But even more exciting was how Kar's early framing of Sam anticipated with prophetic foresight the potentiality of a major writer who would only come to be fully recognized in the world of international letters several decades later.[5] As Caryl Phillips explained in 1999, Sam's significance for him was not because he was a writer from the Caribbean who had already mapped the black migrant terrain of "belonging" and "unbelonging" so relevant to his own generation in the 1970s; nor was it because of Selvon's linguistic agility as pioneer in the formation of an invented Caribbean vernacular sensibility. What made Sam matter was his depth of imagination and breadth of perception. As Phillips was to put it:

> If I were to point a student towards writing which captures the rhythm, texture, and tone of London as the austere fifties were about to give way to the swinging sixties, I would not send them to the plays of John Osborne or Arnold Wesker, or the prose of David Storey or John Braine. For acuity of vision, intellectual rigour, and sheer beauty of language they would have to be supplicants at the pages of Selvon. (36)

Already in 1956, then, Kar, unlike the majority of literary reviewers of the period, had placed Sam alongside many now established world artists and writers. These ranged from European existentialists such as Jean-Paul Sartre and Jean Cocteau to already established figures such as T.S. Eliot or Somerset Maugham and the then upcoming voices of Doris Lessing, Laurie Lee, Iris Murdoch, Eugene Ionesco and Colin MacInnes. Amongst the group were also numerous world painters and sculptors such as Jacob Epstein, Henry Moore, Barbara Hepworth, Feliks Topolski, Marc Chagall and F.N. Souza. Notably, there were no other writers from the Caribbean in the group, which surprised me given the number in London at the time. Also, apart from the Indian-born painter F.N. Souza and Selvon himself, there were no other artists of colour on display.

Whilst I was aware that Kar, a migrant herself, had a particular interest in featuring bohemian artists from outside the so-called "mainstream", I inevitably began to wonder how Sam had got involved with this particular photo shoot and with the photographer.[6] Interesting too were some of the names on the books that filled the shelves behind him. Though difficult to decipher, one could just make out a range of twentieth-century authors from William Faulkner to J.D. Salinger, George Orwell, Joyce Carey, Ernest Hemingway and Alberto Moravia, as well as popular works such as *The Willing Flesh* (released in English translation in 1956) by the German author Willi Heinrich. Sam had always told me he had been an avid reader and described the many nights he spent feeding this passion during the "night watch" as wireless operator for the Naval Reserve during the war. Like many other colonials, he was fully versed – despite the subject matter of some of his most popular short stories and novels – in the English classics. I knew he was keen on the Romantic poets and that he was also taken as a young man with reading existentialist philosophy, the poetry of T.S. Eliot and some of the other Euro-American moderns, an aspect that has recently been commented on in relation to his innovative experiments with form and voice in *The Lonely Londoners*. Yet, whenever audiences asked Sam to name books which influenced him as a writer, he was always reticent. Apart from pointing to the need (perhaps developed during his apprenticeship at the *Trinidad Guardian* as a journalist) to observe the subjects of his fiction very closely, he repeatedly stressed there had not been any value for him in reading the work of others. In fact, he often said that if a writer had to explain his work, he might as well not write.[7]

Selvon's presence amidst Kar's community of other twentieth-century moderns reflects interestingly on the objectives of this collection. There is frequently a tension between the ways in which trends in critical thinking, often shaped by political or cultural movements, situate the work of writers who almost always see the imaginative forces driving their works very differently. Moreover, as several of the essays in *Beyond Calypso* demonstrate, the uneven evolution of Selvon's now distinguished reputation in the world of Caribbean and twentieth-century letters has been especially subject to such containments. It is not my intention, as is common in afterwords of this kind, to comment in detail on the many rich and provocative perspectives offered between these covers. For me, it is more than clear that the shared objective of these essays, to move beyond the well-trodden tracks of Selvon criticism and expose a writer whose talents and connections to other artists active in his time far exceed his established stature as apogee of the Caribbean vernacular voice and "father of black British writing", is not only timely, but long overdue.

The publication of this volume was sparked in the first instance by a conference held at the University of Warwick in July 2011. I am delighted that these many different readings not only revisit some of Sam's most overlooked works but also continue to mark out his place as a multitalented but often under-read writer who was, nevertheless, to pioneer a revolution in thinking which long predated the hybrid and mulatto poetics so familiar in the contemporary writings of those who have followed on from him. As Sam's friend, the late Stuart Hall, was to famously reflect in 1987, the complex cultures of his global Caribbean heritage had long anticipated what was to become a new direction in Western metropolitan culture:

> Now that, in the postmodern age, you all feel so dispersed, I become centred. What I've thought of as dispersed and fragmented comes, paradoxically, to be *the* representative modern experience! ("Minimal Selves" 33–34)

Yet on many occasions towards the end of his life, Sam lamented how the increasingly narrow agenda of critical discourse had inadvertently placed his work into convenient pigeonholes. As fiercely contested issues around race, national politics and identity took pre-eminence both in the Caribbean and Britain, he regretted that the wider dimensions of his writing and the reach of his vision as self-professed "citizen of the world" were misread.

As he intimated in 1992, in a "Special Preface" belatedly added to the American edition of his last published novel, *Moses Migrating* (1983):

> It have a lot of myths and legends and nancy stories that circulate since I, Moses Aloetta Esq., presented my credentials to the literary world. Some people think I am an arsehole, some people say I am an enigma that never arrived, the chosen few consider me a genius [...].
>
> So laugh your guts out. But remember there is more in the mortar than the pestle. (25, 28)

Characteristically playing the artful dodger and presenting a commentary on his own reception through the eyes of one of his best-known characters, Selvon was of course being more than playful. Moses's pointed flagging of the critical hurdles Selvon himself had to negotiate, whether as apogee of the Caribbean vernacular or as the much-cited voice of the black British community, while failing (like Moses here), to adequately carry the burden of representation, or be the "genius" who actually "arrives", is interestingly reflected in the observations of an influential millennial essay by Gillian Beer. Advocating the urgent need for critics to sidestep the canon and attempt new "narrative swerves" in order to circumnavigate the ever-returning grand narratives of history, Beer called for a return to the figure of the "trickster", not as the ancient character from medieval legend or Afro-Caribbean folklore, but instead as the reinvented epistemological shape of the archetypal modern. As she puts it, such a vehicle is flexible, not "simply a conman" but "a figure elusive", a "Tiresias without guilt, transformative, *per*formative" a "survivor who pays no deference to class or sex because tricks defy categories" (4).

Though Beer's objectives derive originally from a different context, they are pertinent to the aims of this new collection of essays, which seeks to "invert common critical practice[s]", just as Selvon himself adopted unorthodox strategies over the course of a long career to shift away from the expectations imposed on his art. Although Beer's notion of the "trickster" as flexible new conduit for the modern might be seen to invoke a return to the easy critical shorthand evident in the steady interest in Selvon's "calypso" aesthetic, its implications are far more liberating. As Selvon himself often made plain, his various personas, whether as novelist, playwright, poet, journalist or essayist, were intimately linked to his pleasure in literary ventriloquism and consistent desire to move beyond and explode the limitations of narrow stereotypes. As evident in *The Housing Lark* (1965), the canonical epistemological authority and orthodox "English" history of "Hamdon Court" (deliberately misspelt) is implicitly interrogated by the banter of his characters, who make it plain that it is their linguistic agility and consequent ability to conjure new worlds that will ensure their survival.

> It don't matter what the topic is, as long as words floating about, verbs, adjectives, nouns, interjections, paraphrase and paradise, the boys don't care. It like a game, all of them throwing words in the air like a ball, now and then some scandalous laugh making sedate Englishers wonder what the arse them black people talking about. (126–27)

It is perhaps worth returning here to reflect on what prompted Selvon's composition of Moses's addendum. Outraged by a public assault on his artistic freedom in London in 1986, when a woman attacked him on stage for overstepping the mark in his parodying of black women during a satirical reading from *Moses Ascending* (1975), he later toured the Caribbean, defiantly reading out extracts from his belatedly written retort. Interestingly, when Selvon returned to Britain in 1993 to join a prestigious Arts Council Literature Tour, he did not re-present his "Special Preface" but instead chose a series of other readings that cumulatively undercut any neat categorization of his writings as representative of a "politically correct" or deviant migrant voice. As I introduced him in five Northern cities, he read works I had never heard him perform before. This is not to say that he was in any way avoiding the parodic satire for which he had previously been so rudely condemned. As always, drawing the audience in with the edgy, fast-paced humour of some of his best known Trinidad and London stories, Sam soon shifted gear by moving to passages in Standard English from early works such as *An Island Is A World* (1955) or by reading from his 1957 love poem to life and to London, "My Girl and the City". At the same time he offered rare glimpses of his voice as a young writer in formation, reading from non-fictional pieces such as "As Time Goes By" or "Little Drops of Water".[8] And though Selvon usually returned to more familiar territory at the close: either reciting the almost choric jazz scene from the end of *The Lonely Londoners*, when Moses wonders if he, like them "fellars" in "France" (140), can ever write books, or instead winning laughs with an iconoclastic extract from *Moses Ascending*, it became clear by the end of the tour that Sam had deliberately set out on a course to divert British audiences from any overly simplistic political or cultural judgments.

These readings sadly turned out to be the last events Selvon would take part in. When I encountered him again at the National Portrait Gallery in 2011 as part of Ida Kar's exhibition of what were then largely up-and-coming moderns, I was delighted. It seemed not only, however paradoxical the setting, that Selvon had finally "arrived", but also that the breadth, significance, range and potentiality of his work – an element he unusually highlighted in those final readings I witnessed on that 1993 tour – had already been captured by Ida Kar fifty years earlier. As I pondered why it had taken so many decades for this major writer to begin to be fully appreciated, some important lines from "My Girl and the City", the extract Sam had read to an audience in Hull, began to reverberate. Only later did I realize that the expression of the anxieties of this particular artist as a young man, evoked in his early perambulations in a city that would both stimulate his literary talents and betray him, tallied perfectly with the image by Ida Kar I had encountered:

> Once again I am on a green train returning to the heart from the suburbs, and I look out the window into windows of private lives flashed on my brain. Bread being sliced, a man taking off a jacket, an old woman knitting. And all these things I see […].

> When I was in New York, many times I went into that city late at night […] it lighted up with a million lights, but never a feeling as on entering London. Each return to the city is loaded with thought, so that by the time I take the Inner Circle I am as light as air.

> At last I think I know what it is all about. I move around in a world of words. Everything that happens is words. But pure expression is nothing. One must build on the things that happen; it is insufficient to say I sat in the underground

and the train hurtled through the darkness and someone isn't using Amplex. So what? So now I weave, I say there was an old man on whose face wrinkles rivered, whose hands were shapeful with arthritis but when he spoke, oddly enough, his voice was young and gay.

But there was no old man, there was nothing, and there is never anything. (175–76)

NOTES

1. There have been several author-specific studies published in the last two decades, including most recently Roydon Salick's *The Novels of Sam Selvon* and *The Poems of Sam Selvon* (ed). As executor of his literary estate, I have received several requests for the rights to Selvon's work, ranging from proposals to film *Those Who Eat the Cascadura* to several proposals to stage or film *The Lonely Londoners*.
2. See especially the following general studies: J. Dillon Brown, *Migrant Modernism*; H. Adlai Murdoch, *Creolizing the Metropole*; Peter Kalliney, *Commonwealth of Letters*; and Sukhdev Sandhu, *London Calling*.
3. It remains surprising that, despite the publication of a range of Selvon's writings in *Critical Perspectives on Sam Selvon*, ed. Susheila Nasta, and *Foreday Morning: Selected Prose (1946–1986)*, ed. Ken Ramchand and Susheila Nasta, that so few have begun to comment, until recently, on the wide range of Selvon's lesser known works.
4. This novel is the only work by Selvon to have remained in print since it was first published in 1956 and is now a Penguin Modern Classic selling on average over 6,000 copies a year.
5. This discussion of the portrait is a shortened version of my essay, "An Unexpected Encounter with Sam Selvon at the National Portrait Gallery".
6. More detail provided in essay above.
7. Personal correspondence, 4 April 1983.
8. See Nasta, *Critical Perspectives*.

CONTRIBUTORS

Lorna Burns is Lecturer in Postcolonial Literatures in the School of English at the University of St Andrews. She is the author of *Contemporary Caribbean Writing and Deleuze: Literature Between Postcolonialism and Post-continental Philosophy* (Continuum, 2012), and co-editor of *Postcolonial Literatures and Deleuze* (Palgrave, 2012) and of a special issue of the *Journal of Postcolonial Writing* (2013) on the Guyanese writer Wilson Harris.

Vahni Capildeo (b. Trinidad) writes poetry and prose. Her books include *No Traveller Returns, Undraining Sea, Dark & Unaccustomed Words, Utter* (inspired by having been an Oxford English Dictionary lexicographer), and *Measures of Expatriation* (Carcanet, forthcoming). She has been widely anthologized, e.g. in *London: City of Disappearances* (ed. Iain Sinclair), the *Oxford Book of Caribbean Verse*, and *New Poetries VI* (Carcanet, 2015). A former Rhodes Scholar with a DPhil in Norse and translation, Capildeo has taught at universities including Glasgow, Leeds, and Sheffield. She is interested in multilingual and interdisciplinary collaborations, and the global curation and communication of work. She served as a Forward Prizes Judge (2014) and is Contributing Editor for the *Caribbean Review of Books* and Contributing Adviser for *Blackbox Manifold*.

Denise deCaires Narain is a Senior Lecturer in English at the University of Sussex where she specializes in postcolonial and Caribbean women's writing and postcolonial feminist theory. She has published widely on Caribbean women's writing, including two monographs: *Contemporary Caribbean Women's Poetry: Making Style* and *Olive Senior*. She is currently working on a monograph, *Strange Intimacies: Representing the Servant in Postcolonial Women's Texts*.

Alison Donnell is a Professor of Modern Literatures in English in the Department of English Literature at the University of Reading, UK where she is also Head of the School of Literature and Languages. She has published widely on Caribbean and black British writings, including *Twentieth-Century Caribbean Literature: Critical Moments in Anglophone Literary History* (Routledge, 2006) and a major new *Companion to Anglophone Caribbean Literature* (Routledge, 2011) co-edited with Michael A. Bucknor. She is currently completing a monograph entitled *Caribbean Queer: Desire, Dissidence and the Constructions of Literary Subjectivity.* She is a Founding Editor of *Interventions: International Journal of Postcolonial Studies* and is on the editorial board of *Journal of West Indian Literature*, as well as a Trustee and Director of *Wasafiri*.

Kate Houlden is a senior lecturer at Anglia Ruskin University. She has published widely on questions of gender and sexuality in postwar Caribbean literature and postcolonial writing. Her book *Sexuality, Gender and Nationalism in Caribbean Literature* is forthcoming with Routledge (2016) and she has a co-edited collection, *Popular Postcolonialisms* in development.

Joseph Jackson is an Assistant Professor in Twentieth-Century and Contemporary Literature at the University of Nottingham. His research interests are in race and ethnicity, nationhood and language, particularly in the context of postwar British fiction, the Scottish novel, and in comparative Caribbean studies.

Lewis MacLeod is an Associate Professor in the Department of English at Trent University. Some of his research focuses on the transition between modern and postmodern cultures/literatures, the function of ritual in secular cultures, as well as the connections between the poetics of narrative omniscience and the politics of surveillance. His work has appeared in a number of books and journals, including: *Modern Fiction Studies, Narrative, Critique, Mosaic, ARIEL, LIT, Yearbook of English Studies, The Journal of West Indian Literature*, and *Studies in the Literary Imagination.*

J. Vijay Maharaj lectures at the University of the West Indies St Augustine campus – to undergraduates about poetry, drama and prose fiction and to postgraduates about theory, fiction and film. Her primary research interests are theoretical and methodological approaches for opening up literary and social texts so as to translate them into practical, ethical action in the present.

Malachi McIntosh is a lecturer in English at the University of Cambridge and a Fellow of King's College. His book *Emigration and Caribbean Literature* was published by Palgrave MacMillan in 2015.

Susheila Nasta is the editor of *Wasafiri*, the magazine of international contemporary writing, which she founded in 1984. A literary activist, she is currently Chair of Modern Literature at the Open University. Her early publications focused particularly on Caribbean writing, especially the work of Sam Selvon as well as women's writing from Africa, the Caribbean and South Asia. Her 2002 monograph, *Home Truths* (Palgrave) was one of the first studies of the migrant imaginary in South Asian fiction in Britain. Since 2007 she has directed a large research project on the South Asian British presence from 1858-1950. Recent publications include *India in Britain* (Palgrave, 2012) and *Asian Britain: A Photographic History* (Westbourne Press, 2013). She is currently working on a group biography provisionally entitled, *Across the Tracks: The Bloomsbury Indians*. She is literary executor for Sam Selvon and received an MBE in 2011 for services to black and Asian literatures.

Kenneth Ramchand is Professor Emeritus and First Professor of West Indian Literature of the University of the West Indies (UWI), and Emeritus Professor of English, Colgate University, Hamilton, New York. He served for over twelve years as an Independent Senator in the Senate of the Republic of Trinidad and Tobago. A Fellow of the Guggenheim Foundation, and Leverhulme Fellow at Warwick University, he has served as President of the University of Trinidad and Tobago (UTT) and Director of the Academy at UTT for Arts, Letters, Culture and Public Affairs. Professor Ramchand's research interests are in the sphere of education, Caribbean literatures and indigenous cultural and artistic expression. His work and his contributions have seen him rewarded with the conferment of the Chaconia Medal (Gold) of the Republic of Trinidad.

BIBLIOGRAPHY

Works by Samuel Selvon

A Brighter Sun. 1952. Harlow, UK: Longman, 1985. Print.

"Autobiographical Essay 1." *The Samuel Selvon Collection.* Alma Jordan Library, The University of the West Indies, St Augustine, Trinidad and Tobago. Item 88. Typescript.

"Autobiographical Essay 3." *The Samuel Selvon Collection.* Alma Jordan Library, The University of the West Indies, St Augustine, Trinidad and Tobago. Item 90. Typescript.

"Autobiographical Essay 5." *The Samuel Selvon Collection.* Alma Jordan Library, The University of the West Indies, St Augustine, Trinidad and Tobago. Item 91. Typescript.

"Discovering Tropic." *The Blue Horizons. Caribbean Voices: An Anthology of West Indian Poetry.* Vol. 2. Ed. John Figueroa. London: Evans Brothers, 1970. 160–64. Print.

Foreday Morning: Selected Prose (1946–1986). Ed. Kenneth Ramchand and Susheila Nasta. London: Longman, 1989. Print.

The Housing Lark. 1965. Washington, DC: Three Continents, 1990. Print.

I Hear Thunder. London: MacGibbon and Kee, 1963. Print.

"In the Cemetery." *The Evening News* [Trinidad]. 28 Feb. 1948. Print.

An Island Is a World. 1955. Toronto: TSAR, 1993. Print.

The Lonely Londoners. 1956: Harlow, UK: Longman, 1985. Print.

Milk in the Coffee. 1975. *The Samuel Selvon Collection.* Alma Jordan Library, The University of the West Indies, St Augustine, Trinidad and Tobago. Item 168. Typescript.

Moses Ascending. 1975. London: Heinemann, 1984. Print.

Moses Migrating. [n.d.]. Alma Jordan Library, The University of the West Indies, St Augustine, Trinidad and Tobago. Item 172. Typescript.

Moses Migrating. 1977. Alma Jordan Library, The University of the West Indies, St Augustine, Trinidad and Tobago. Item 173. Manuscript.

Moses Migrating: A Novel. 1983. Boulder, CO and London: Lynne Rienner, 2009. Print.

"My Girl and the City." *Ways of Sunlight*. 1957. Harlow: Longman, 1987. 169–76. Print.

The Plains of Caroni. London: MacGibbon and Kee, 1970. Print.

The Poems of Sam Selvon. Ed. Roydon Salick. Royston, UK: Cane Arrow, 2012. Print.

"A Special Preface by Moses Aloetta Esq." *Moses Migrating*. Washington: Three Continents, 1992. 25–28. Print.

Those Who Eat the Cascadura. 1972. Toronto: TSAR, 1990. Print.

"Three into One Can't Go — East Indian, Trinidadian or West Indian? Samuel Selvon Discusses the Question of an East Indian Identity." *Wasafiri* 3.5 (1986): 8–11. Print.

Turn Again Tiger. 1958. London: Heinemann, 1979. Print.

Ways of Sunlight. 1957. London: MacGibbon and Kee, 1961. Print.

"The West Indian Patchwork." *The Geographical Magazine* 2/6 (1955): 516–19. Print.

Selvon, Sam and Horace Ové. *The Immigrant*. 1975. *The Samuel Selvon Collection*. Alma Jordan Library, The University of the West Indies, St Augustine, Trinidad and Tobago. Item 78. Typescript.

OTHER SOURCES

Appiah, Kwame Anthony. *Cosmopolitanism: Ethics in a World of Strangers*. London: Penguin, 2007. Print.

Barker, Martin. *The New Racism: Conservatives and the Ideology of the Tribe*. London: Junction Books, 1981. Print.

Barratt, Harold. "An Island is Not a World: A Reading of Sam Selvon's *An Island Is a World*." *Ariel: A Review of International English Literature* 27.2 (1996): 25–34. Web. 27 Oct. 2014.

———. "Sam Selvon's Tiger: In Search of Self-Awareness." *Something Rich and Strange: Selected Essays on Sam Selvon*. Ed. Martin Zehnder. Leeds: Peepal Tree, 2003. 27–38. Print.

Beer, Gillian. "Narrative Swerves: Grand Narratives and the Disciplines." *Women: A Cultural Review* 11.1–2 (2000): 2–7. Print.

Bellegarde-Smith, Patrick, ed. *Fragments of Bone: Neo-African Religions in a New World*. Illinois: University of Illinois Press, 2005. Print.

Benítez-Rojo, Antonio. *The Repeating Island: The Caribbean and the Postmodern Perspective*. 2nd ed. Trans. James E. Maraniss. Durham, NC and London: Duke University Press, 1996. Print.

Benson, Ann D. "Honesty, Humor in Selvon Novel." Rev. of *A Brighter Sun*, by Samuel Selvon. *Boston Herald* 1 Feb. 1953. *The Samuel Selvon Collection*.

Alma Jordan Library, The University of the West Indies, St Augustine, Trinidad and Tobago. Item 363. Print.

Bentley, Nick. "Black London: The Politics of Representation in Sam Selvon's *The Lonely Londoners.*" *Wasafiri* 18.39 (2003): 41–45. Web. 14 Dec. 2011.

Betjeman, John. "First Love without Self Pity." Rev. of *The Lonely Londoners*, by Samuel Selvon. *Daily Telegraph* 21 Dec. 1956. *The Samuel Selvon Collection.* Alma Jordan Library, The University of the West Indies, St Augustine, Trinidad and Tobago. Item 365. Print.

Bhabha, Homi. *The Location of Culture.* London: Routledge, 1994. Print.

Bhattacharya, Narendra Nath. *History of Indian Erotic Literature.* Delhi: Munshiram Manohar, 1975. Print.

The Bible. New International Version. *BibleGateway.com.* Web. 20 Aug. 2014.

Bilby, Kenneth M. and Jerome S. Handler. "Obeah: Healing and Protection in West Indian Slave Life." *Journal of Caribbean History* 38.2 (2004): 153–83. Print.

Birbalsingh, Frank. "Indian-Trinidadian Women Writers: An Overview." *Wasafiri* 28.2 (2013): 14–19. Print.

———, ed. *Passion and Exile: Essays in Caribbean Literature.* London: Hansib, 1988. Print.

Bogue, Ronald. *Deleuze on Literature.* New York and London: Routledge, 2003. Print.

Bourdieu, Pierre. *The Rules of Art: Genesis and Structure of the Literary Field.* Trans. Susan Emanuel. Cambridge: Polity Press, 1996. Print.

Brathwaite, Edward Kamau. "Caliban, Ariel and unProspero in the Conflict of Creolization: A Study of the Slave Revolt in Jamaica in 1831." *Comparative Perspectives on Slavery in New World Plantation Societies.* Ed. Vera Rubin and Arthur Tuden. New York: Academy of Sciences, 1977. 41–62. Print.

———. *Contradictory Omens: Cultural Diversity and Integration in the Caribbean.* Kingston: Savacou Publications, 1974. Print.

———. *Roots.* Ann Arbor: The University of Michigan Press, 1993. Print.

———. *Wars of Respect: Nanny, Sam Sharpe and the Struggle for People's Liberation.* Kingston, Jamaica: API, 1977. Print.

Brittan, Arthur. "Masculinities and Masculinism." *The Masculinities Reader.* Ed. Stephen M. Whitehead and Frank J. Barrett. Cambridge: Polity, 2001. 51–55. Print.

Brown, J. Dillon. *Migrant Modernism: Postwar London and the West Indian Novel.* Charlottesville and London: University of Virginia Press, 2013. Print.

Brown, Vincent. *The Reaper's Garden: Death and Power in the World of Atlantic Slavery.* Cambridge, MA and London: Harvard University Press, 2008. Print.

Brown, Wayne. "A Greatness and a Vastness: The Search for God in the Fiction of Sam Selvon." *Ariel: A Review of International English Literature* 27.2 (1996): 35–46. Web. 27 Oct. 2014.

Browning, Robert. "Andrea del Sarto." *Selected Poems.* Ed. Daniel Karlin. London: Penguin, 2004. 115–22. Print.

Bryant, Edwin F., trans. *Krishna: The Beautiful Legend of God: Srimad Bhagavata Purana, Book X.* New York: Penguin, 2003. Print.

Bunce, Robin and Paul Field. *Darcus Howe: A Political Biography.* London: Bloomsbury, 2014. Print.

Burns, Lorna. *Contemporary Caribbean Writing and Deleuze: Literature Between Postcolonialism and Post-continental Philosophy.* London: Continuum, 2012. Print.

Butler, Judith. *Gender Trouble.* New York and London: Routledge, 1990. Print.

Carchidi, Victoria. "'Heaven Is a Green Place': Varieties of Spiritual Landscape in Caribbean Literature." *Mapping the Sacred: Religion, Geography and Postcolonial Literatures.* Ed. Jamie S. Scott and Paul Simpson-Housley. Amsterdam and Atlanta: Rodopi, 2001. 179–99. Print.

Césaire, Aimé. *Discourse on Colonialism.* Trans. Joan Pinkham. New York: Monthly Review Press, 1972. Print.

Chatterjee, Partha. "Colonialism, Nationalism, and Colonialized Women: The Contest in India." *American Ethnologist* 16.4 (1989): 622–33. Print.

Clarke, Austin. *A Passage Back Home: A Personal Reminiscence of Samuel Selvon.* Toronto: Exile Editions, 1994. Print.

Clarke, Austin, et. al. "Sam Selvon: A Celebration." *Ariel: A Review of International English Literature* 27.2 (1996): 49–63. Web. 27 Oct. 2014.

Coleman, Daniel. *Masculine Migrations: Reading the Postcolonial Male in "New Canadian" Narratives.* Toronto: University of Toronto Press, 1998. Print.

Connell, R. W. *The Men and the Boys.* Berkley: University of California Press, 2000. Print.

Cools, Janice A. "Masculinity as Prison in Samuel Selvon's *A Brighter Sun*." *Culture, Society and Masculinities* 3.2 (2011): 24–40. Print.

Crichlow, Michaeline A. *Globalization and the Post-Creole Imagination: Notes on Fleeing the Plantation.* Durham and London: Duke University Press, 2009. Print.

Crystal, David. *The English Tone of Voice: Essays in Intonation, Prosody and Paralanguage.* London: Edward Arnold, 1975. Print.

Dabydeen, David. Preface. *India in the Caribbean.* Ed. David Dabydeen and Brinsley Samaroo. London: Hansib, 1987. 9–12. Print.

Dabydeen, David and Nana Wilson-Tagoe. *A Reader's Guide to West Indian and Black British Literature.* Kingston-upon-Thames, UK: Rutherford Press, 1987. Print.

Dandeker, Christopher. *Surveillance, Power, Modernity: Bureaucracy and Discipline from 1700 to the Present Day*. Cambridge: Polity, 1990. Print.

Darroch, Fiona. *Memory and Myth: Postcolonial Religion in Contemporary Guyanese Fiction and Poetry*. Amsterdam and New York: Rodopi, 2009. Print.

Das, Veena. *Critical Events: An Anthropological Perspective on Contemporary India*. Delhi: Oxford University Press, 1996. Print.

Davis, Jessica Milner. *Farce*. London: Methuen, 1978. Print.

Dawes, Kwame. "Interview with David Dabydeen, 1994." *The Art of David Dabydeen*. Ed. Kevin Grant. Leeds: Peepal Tree, 1997. 199–221. Print.

Dawson, Ashley. *Mongrel Nation: Diasporic Culture and the Making of Postcolonial Britain*. Ann Arbor, MI: University of Michigan Press, 2007. Print.

de Beauvoir, Simone. *The Second Sex*. Ed and trans. H. M. Parshley. London: Vintage, 1997. Print.

deCaires Narain, Denise. "Wilson Harris: Dreaming to Change the World; Writing to Change Our Dreams." *Stabroek News*. 1 April, 2001. 12–13. Web. 27 Oct. 2014.

———. "Naming Same-Sex Desire in Caribbean Women's Texts: Towards a Creolizing Hermeneutics." *Contemporary Women's Writing* 6.3 (2012): 194–212. Print.

Deleuze, Gilles. *Essays Critical and Clinical*. Trans. Daniel W. Smith and Michael A. Greco. London and New York: Verso, 1998. Print.

———. *Kafka: Toward a Minor Literature*. Trans. Dana Polan. Minneapolis: University of Minnesota Press, 1986. Print.

———. *The Logic of Sense*. Trans. Mark Lester. London: Continuum, 2004. Print.

———. *Masochism: Coldness and Cruelty*. Trans. James McNeil. New York: Zone Books, 1991. Print.

———. *Negotiations: 1972–1990*. Trans. Martin Joughin. New York: Columbia University Press, 1995. Print.

———. *Pure Immanence: Essays on a Life*. Trans. Anne Boyman. New York: Zone Books, 2001. Print.

Deloughrey, Elizabeth M. *Routes and Roots: Navigating Caribbean and Pacific Island Literatures*. Honolulu: University of Hawai'i Press, 2007. Print.

Diawara, Manthia. "A Conversation with Édouard Glissant aboard the Queen Mary II (August 2009)." *Afro Modern: Journeys through the Black Atlantic*. Ed. Tanya Barson and Peter Gorschülter. Liverpool: Tate Liverpool, 2010. 58–63. Print.

Donnell, Alison. "Caribbean Queer: New Meetings of Place and the Possible in Shani Mootoo's *Valmiki's Daughter*." *Contemporary Women's Writing* 6.3 (2012): 213–32. Print.

———. *Twentieth-Century Caribbean Literature: Critical Moments in Anglophone Literary History*. London: Routledge, 2006. Print.

Dyer, Rebecca. "Immigration, Postwar London, and the Politics of Everyday Life in Sam Selvon's Fiction." *Cultural Critique* 52 (2002): 108–44. Web. 13 Dec. 2011.

Edmondson, Belinda J. "Introduction: The Caribbean: Myths, Tropes, Discourses." *Caribbean Romances: The Politics of Regional Representation.* Ed. Belinda Edmondson. Charlottesville, VA and London: University Press of Virginia, 1999. 1–11. Print.

Edmondson, George. "Easy Calypso Rhythm Dragged Writer from Rut." *Richmond News Leader.* 19 Feb. 1980. 12. *The Samuel Selvon Collection.* Alma Jordan Library, The University of the West Indies, St Augustine, Trinidad and Tobago. Item 382. Print.

Ehrenreich, Barbara. *The Hearts of Men: American Dreams and the Flight From Commitment.* London: Pluto, 1983. Print.

Fabre, Michel. "Moses and the Queen's English: Dialect and Narrative Voice in Samuel Selvon's London Novels." *World Literature Written in English* 21.2 (1982): 385–92. Print.

———. "Samuel Selvon." *West Indian Literature.* 2nd ed. Ed. Bruce King. London: Macmillan, 1995. 152–62. Print.

Fanon, Frantz. *Black Skin, White Masks.* Trans. Charles Lam Markmann. London: Pluto, 1986. Print.

———. *The Wretched of the Earth.* Trans. Constance Farrington. Harmondsworth: Penguin, 1990. Print.

Fernandez-Olmos, Margarita and Lizabeth Paravisini-Gebert, eds. *Sacred Possessions: Vodou, Santería, Obeah, and the Caribbean.* New Brunswick: Rutgers University Press, 1997. 283–88. Print.

Flood, Gavin. *An Introduction to Hinduism.* Cambridge: Cambridge University Press, 1996. Print.

Forbes, Curdella. *From Nation to Diaspora: Samuel Selvon, George Lamming and the Cultural Performance of Gender.* Mona, Jamaica: The University of the West Indies Press, 2005. Print.

Foucault, Michel. *The Will to Knowledge: The History of Sexuality Vol. I.* Trans. Robert Hurley. London: Penguin, 1998. Print.

Freer, Scott. "The Victorian Criminal Underworld and the Musical Carnivalesque." *Neo-Victorian Studies* 2.1 (2008/2009): 52–77. Print.

Gardiner, Michael. *The Return of England in English Literature.* Basingstoke: Palgrave Macmillan, 2012. Print.

Giddens, Anthony. *The Transformation of Intimacy: Sexuality, Love and Eroticism in Modern Societies.* Stanford, California: Stanford University Press, 1992. Print.

Gikandi, Simon. *Writing in Limbo: Nationalism and Identity: Culture and the Imagination in a Caribbean Diaspora*. London: Zed Books, 1996. Print.

Gilmore, David. *Manhood in the Making: Cultural Concepts of Masculinity*. New Haven: Yale University Press, 1990. Print.

Gilroy, Paul. *Postcolonial Melancholia*. New York: Columbia University Press, 2005. Print.

———. *There Ain't No Black in the Union Jack: The Cultural Politics of Race and Nation*. London: Routledge, 1992. Print.

Glissant, Édouard. *Caribbean Discourse: Selected Essays*. Trans. J. Michael Dash. Charlottesville, VA: University Press of Virginia, 1989. Print.

———. "Creolization in the Making of the Americas." *Race, Discourse, and the Origin of the Americas: A New World View*. Ed. Vera Lawrence Hyatt and Rex Nettleford. Washington, DC: Smithsonian Institute, 1995. 268–275. Print.

———. *Faulkner, Mississippi*. Trans. Barbara Lewis and Thomas C. Spear. New York: Farrar, Straus and Giroux, 1999. Print.

———. *Poetics of Relation*. Trans. Betsy Wing. Ann Arbor, MI: University of Michigan Press, 1997. Print.

Gopinath, Gayatri. *Impossible Desires: Queer Diasporas and South Asian Public Cultures*. Durham, NC: Duke University Press, 2005.

Green, Jonathon. *Days in the Life: Voices from the English Underground, 1961–1971*. London: Pimlico, 1998. Print.

Guilbault, Jocelyne. *Governing Sound: The Cultural Politics of Trinidad's Carnival Musics*. Chicago and London: The University of Chicago Press, 2007. Print.

Hall, Stuart. "Gramsci's Relevance for the Study of Race and Ethnicity." *Stuart Hall: Critical Dialogues in Cultural Studies*. Ed. David Morley and Huan-Hsing Chen. London and New York: Routledge, 1996. 411–40. Print.

———. "Lamming, Selvon and Some Trends in the West Indian Novel." *BIM* 6.23 (1955): 172–78. Print.

———. "Minimal Selves." *Identity*. Ed. Lisa Appignanesi. London: Institute of Contemporary Arts, 1987. 25–34. Print.

———. "New Ethnicities." *Stuart Hall: Critical Dialogues in Cultural Studies*. Ed. David Morley and Huan-Hsing Chen. London and New York: Routledge, 1996. 441–49. Print.

Hall, Stuart, et. al. *Policing the Crisis: Mugging, the State and Law and Order*. London: Macmillan, 1978. Print.

Hallward, Peter. *Absolutely Postcolonial: Writing between the Singular and the Specific*. Manchester: Manchester University Press, 2001. Print.

Harney, Stefano. *Nationalism and Identity: Culture and the Imagination in a Caribbean Diaspora*. London: Zed Books, 1996. Print.

Hicks, John H. "Calypso in Britain." Rev. of *The Lonely Londoners*, by Samuel Selvon. *St. Louis Post-Dispatch* 3 Feb. 1956. *The Samuel Selvon Collection*. Alma Jordan Library, The University of the West Indies, St Augustine, Trinidad and Tobago. Item 402. Print.

Holder, G.A. "*An Island Is a World*: Samuel Selvon." *BIM* 6.23 (1955): 202. Print.

Holland, Peter. "Farce." *The Cambridge Companion to English Restoration Theatre*. Ed. Deborah Payne Fisk. Cambridge: Cambridge University Press, 2000. 107–26. Print.

Home, Stewart. "Pressure." *Metamute.org*. Mute Publishing. 25 Oct 2005. Web. 01 Sep. 2013.

Hosein, Gabrielle Jamela. "Modern Navigations: Indo-Trinidadian Girlhood and Gender Differential Creolization." *Caribbean Review of Gender Studies* 6 (2012): 1–24. Web. 19 Aug. 2014.

Hosein, Gabrielle Jamela, and Lisa Outar. "Indo-Caribbean Feminisms: Charting Crossings in Geography, Discourse, and Politics." *Caribbean Review of Gender Studies* 6 (2012): 1–10. Web. 19 Aug. 2014.

Houk, James. *Spirits, Blood, and Drums: The Orisha Religion in Trinidad*. Philadelphia: Temple University Press, 1995. Print.

Hurston, Zora Neale. *Tell My Horse: Voodoo and Life in Haiti and Jamaica*. New York: Harper and Row, 1990. Print.

Ingalls, Daniel H. H. Foreword. *The Divinity of Krishna*. By Noel Sheth. New Delhi: Munshiram Manoharlal, 1984. Print.

Irigaray, Luce. *An Ethics of Sexual Difference*. Trans. Carolyn Burke and Gillian C. Gill. Ithaca, NY: Cornell University Press, 1993. Print.

———. *This Sex Which is Not One*. Trans. Catherine Porter and Carolyn Burke. Ithaca, NY: Cornell University Press, 1985. Print.

———. "Questions to Emmanuel Levinas: On the Divinity of Love." Trans. Margaret Whitford. *Re-Reading Levinas*. Ed. Robert Bernasconi and Simon Critchley. Bloomington: Indiana University Press, 1991. 109–18. Print.

Jayadeva. *Gita Govinda: The Love Songs of Radha and Krishna*. Trans. Lee Siegel. New York: New York University Press, 2009. Print.

Jenkins, John Edward. *Lutchmee and Dilloo: A Study of West Indian Life*. London and Basingstoke: Macmillan, 2003. Print.

Kabesh, Lisa. "Mapping Freedom, or Its Limits: The Politics of Movement in Sam Selvon's *The Lonely Londoners*." *Postcolonial Text* 6.3 (2011). Web. 01 Dec. 2013.

Kalliney, Peter. *Commonwealth of Letters: British Literary Culture and the Emergence of Postcolonial Aesthetics* (Oxford: Oxford University Press, 2013). Print.

———. "Metropolitan Modernism and Its West Indian Interlocutors: 1950s

London and the Emergence of Postcolonial Literature." *PMLA* 122.1 (2007): 89–104. Print.

King, Richard. "Orientalism and the Modern Myth of 'Hinduism.'" *Numen* 46.2 (1999): 146–85. Web. 05 Feb. 2014.

———. *Orientalism and Religion: Postcolonial Theory, India and "the Mystic East."* London and New York: Routledge, 1999. Print.

Knox, Valerie. "Sugar Power." *The Guardian* [UK] 21 May 1970. n.p. *The Samuel Selvon Collection.* Alma Jordan Library, The University of the West Indies, St Augustine, Trinidad and Tobago. Item 416. Print.

Lamming, George. *The Pleasures of Exile.* London: Michael Joseph, 1960. Print.

Levy, Evelyn. "West Indian Gaiety, Misery in London." Rev. of *The Lonely Londoners,* by Samuel Selvon. *Baltimore Sunday Sun* 1 Dec. 1957. *The Samuel Selvon Collection.* Alma Jordan Library, The University of the West Indies, St Augustine, Trinidad and Tobago. Item 420. Print.

Lingle, Betty. Rev. of *The Lonely Londoners,* by Samuel Selvon. *San Francisco Chronicle* 16 Feb. 1958. *The Samuel Selvon Collection.* Alma Jordan Library, The University of the West Indies, St Augustine, Trinidad and Tobago. Item 421. Print.

Looker, Mark. *Atlantic Passages: History, Community, and Language in the Fiction of Sam Selvon.* New York: Peter Lang, 1996. Print.

Lovelace, Earl. "Calypso and the Bacchanal Connection." *Anthurium* 3.2 (2005). Web. 20 Aug. 2014.

———. *The Dragon Can't Dance.* London: Longman, 1979. Print.

———. *Is Just a Movie.* London: Faber and Faber, 2011. Print.

———. "Reclaiming Rebellion". *Wasafiri* 74 (2013): 69–73. Print.

Loxley, James. *Performativity.* London: Routledge, 2007. Print.

Lyon, David. *Surveillance Society: Monitoring Everyday Life.* Buckingham, UK and Philadelphia: Open University Press, 2001. Print.

MacDonald, Bruce F. "Language and Consciousness in Samuel Selvon's *A Brighter Sun.*" *Critical Perspectives on Sam Selvon.* Ed. Susheila Nasta. Washington, DC: Three Continents, 1988. 173–86. Print.

MacLeod, Lewis. "'You Have To Start Thinking All Over Again': Masculinities, Narratology and New Approaches to Sam Selvon." *Ariel: A Review of International English Literature* 36.1–2 (2005): 157–81. Web. 27 Oct. 2014.

Maharaj, J. Vijay. *A Caribbean Katha: Re-visioning the Indo-Caribbean "Crisis of Being and Belonging".* Basingstoke, UK and New York: Palgrave Macmillan, 2014. Print.

Maslen, Elizabeth. "The Miasma of Englishness at Home and Abroad." *The Revision of Englishness.* Ed. David Rogers and John McLeod. Manchester: Manchester University Press, 2004. 40–51. Print.

May, Larry. *Masculinity and Morality*. Ithaca, NY: Cornell University Press, 1998. Print.

Mehta, Brinda. *Diasporic (Dis)locations: Indo-Caribbean Women Writers Negotiate the* Kala Pani. Mona, Jamaica: University of West Indies Press, 2004. Print.

Melville, Herman. *Billy Budd, Sailor and Selected Tales*. Ed. Robert Milder. Oxford: Oxford University Press, 2009. Print.

Mercer, Kobena. *Welcome to the Jungle: New Positions in Black Cultural Studies*. New York and London: Routledge, 1994. Print.

Mohammed, Patricia. "The 'Creolisation' of Indian Women in Trinidad." *Questioning Creole: Creolisation Discourses in Caribbean Culture*. Ed. Verene A. Shepherd and Glen Richards. Kingston, Jamaica: Ian Randle, 2002. 130–47. Print.

———. "Changing Symbols of Indo-Caribbean Femininity." *Caribbean Review of Gender Studies* 6 (2012): 1–16. Web. 19 Aug. 2014.

MLA International Bibliography. *Proquest LLC*. Web. 10 Aug. 2014.

Mootoo, Shani. *Cereus Blooms at Night*. Toronto: McClelland and Stewart, 1996. Print.

———. *He Drown She in the Sea*. New York: Grove Press, 2005. Print.

———. "On Becoming an Indian Starboy". *Canadian Literature* 196 (2008): 83–96. Print.

Morgan, David H. J. "Family, Gender and Masculinities." *The Masculinities Reader*. Ed. Stephen M. Whitehead and Frank J. Barratt. Cambridge: Polity, 2001. 223–32. Print.

Morris, Mervyn. Introduction. *Moses Ascending*. By Samuel Selvon. London: Heinemann, 1984. vii–xviii. Print.

———. "Some West Indian Problems of Audience." *English* 16.94 (1967): 127–30. Web. 15 Dec. 2011.

Munasinghe, Viranjini. "Theorizing World Culture through the New World: East Indians and Creolization." *American Ethnologist* 33.4 (2006): 549–62. Print.

Murdoch, H. Adlai. *Creolizing the Metropole: Migrant Caribbean Identities in Literature and Film*. Bloomington: Indiana University Press, 2012.

Naipaul, V.S. "'Caribbean Voices." *Critical Perspectives on Sam Selvon*. Ed. Susheila Nasta. Washington: Three Continents, 1988. 110–13. Print.

———. *The Mimic Men*. Harmondsworth: Penguin, 1973. Print.

———. "Turn Again Tiger." *Critical Perspectives on Sam Selvon*. Ed. Susheila Nasta. Washington, DC: Three Continents, 1988. 123–24. Print.

Nairn, Tom. *The Break-up of Britain: Crisis and Neo-nationalism*. London: NLB, 1977. Print.

Nandy, Ashis. *The Intimate Enemy: Loss and Recovery of Self under Colonialism*. Delhi: Oxford University Press, 1983. Print.

Nasta, Susheila, ed. *Critical Perspectives on Sam Selvon*. Washington, DC: Three Continents, 1988. Print.

———. Introduction. *Eldorado West One*. By Samuel Selvon. Leeds: Peepal Tree, 1988. 7–14. Print.

———. Introduction. *Moses Migrating: A Novel*. By Samuel Selvon. Boulder and London: Lynne Rienner, 2009. 1–22. Print.

———. "Setting Up Home in a City of Words: Sam Selvon's London Novels." *Tiger's Triumph: Celebrating Sam Selvon*. Ed. Susheila Nasta and Anna Rutherford. Hebden Bridge, UK: Dangaroo, 1995. 78–95. Print.

———. "'An Unexpected Encounter with Sam Selvon at the National Portrait Gallery" *Wasafiri* 28.2 (2013): 33–35. Print.

Nasta, Susheila and Anna Rutherford, eds. *Tiger's Triumph: Celebrating Sam Selvon*. Hebden Bridge, UK: Dangaroo, 1995. Print.

Nazareth, Peter. "Interview with Sam Selvon." *World Literature Written in English* 18.2 (1979): 420–37. Print.

Newman, Beth. "'The Situation of the Looker-On': Gender, Narration and Gaze in *Wuthering Heights*." *PMLA* 105.5 (1990): 1029–1041. Print.

Niblett, Michael. *The Caribbean Novel since 1945: Cultural Practice, Form and the Nation-State*. Jackson, MS: University Press of Mississippi, 2012. Print.

Niranjana, Tejaswini. "'Left to the Imagination': Indian Nationalisms and Female Sexuality in Trinidad." *Public Culture* 11.1 (1999): 223–43. Web. 14 Jul. 2013.

———. *Mobilizing India: Women, Music, and Migration between India and Trinidad*. Durham, NC and London: Duke University Press, 2006. Print.

Nizami. *The Story of Layla and Majnun*. Ed. and trans. Rudolf Gelpke. New York: Omega Publications, 1997. Print.

Nussbaum, Martha C. "Objectification." *Philosophy and Public Affairs* 24.4 (1995): 249–91. Web. 27 Oct. 2014.

O'Callaghan, Evelyn. *Women Writing the West Indies, 1804–1939: "A Hot Place, Belonging to Us"*. London and New York: Routledge, 2004. Print.

Oldmeadow, Harry. Foreword. *Unveiling the Garden of Love: Mystical Symbolism in* Layla Majnun *&* Gita Govinda. By Lalita Sinha. Bloomington, IN: World Wisdom, 2008. xi–xvi. Print.

Oliver, Kelly. *Witnessing: Beyond Recognition*, Minneapolis: University of Minnesota Press. 2001. Print.

Ové, Horace, dir. *Pressure*. 1975. *Pressure, Baldwin's Nigger: Two Films by Horace Ové*. British Film Institute, 2005. DVD.

Palmer, Colin A. *Eric Williams & the Making of the Modern Caribbean*. Chapel Hill, NC: The University of North Carolina Press, 2006. Print.

Paton, Diana. "Obeah Acts: Producing and Policing the Boundaries of Religion in the Caribbean." *Small Axe* 28 (2009): 1–18. Web. 05 Feb. 2014.

Pavel, Thomas G. *Fictional Worlds*. Cambridge, MA: Harvard University Press, 1986. Print.

Phillips, Caryl. "Following On: The Legacy of Lamming and Selvon". *Wasafiri* 14.29 (1999): 34–36. Web. 27 Oct. 2014.

Pitcher, Ben. *The Politics of Multiculturalism: Race and Racism in Contemporary Britain*. Basingstoke, UK: Palgrave Macmillan, 2009. Print.

"Plea for the Lonely." Rev. of *The Lonely Londoners*, by Samuel Selvon. *Surrey Comet* 12 Jan. 1957. *The Samuel Selvon Collection*. Alma Jordan Library, The University of the West Indies, St Augustine, Trinidad and Tobago. Item 321. Print.

Pouchet Paquet, Sandra. Introduction. *Turn Again Tiger*. By Samuel Selvon. London: Heinemann Education, 1979. vii–xxiv. Print.

———. "Samuel Dickson Selvon." *Fifty Caribbean Writers: A Bio-Bibliographical Critical Sourcebook*. Ed. Daryl Cumber Dance. Westport, CT: Greenwood Press, 1986. 439–49. Print.

Poynting, Jeremy. "Samuel Selvon, *Moses Migrating*." *Critical Perspectives on Sam Selvon*. Ed. Susheila Nasta. Washington, DC: Three Continents, 1988. 260–65. Print.

Prince, Gerald. *Dictionary of Narratology*. Lincoln, NE: University of Nebraska Press, 1987. Print.

Procter, James. *Dwelling Places: Postwar Black British Writing*. Manchester and New York: Manchester University Press, 2003. Print.

Prorok, Carolyn V. "Evolution of the Hindu Temple in Trinidad." *Caribbean Geography* 3.2 (1991): 73–93. Web. 14 Nov. 2013.

———. "Transplanting Pilgrimage Traditions in the Americas." *Geographical Review* 93.3 (2003): 283–307. Web. 14 Nov. 2013.

Puri, Shalini. *The Caribbean Postcolonial: Social Equality, Post-Nationalism, and Cultural Hybridity*. New York: Palgrave Macmillan, 2004. Print.

———. "Race, Rape, and Representation: Indo-Caribbean Women and Cultural Nationalism." *Cultural Critique* 36 (1997): 119–63. Web. 05 Feb. 2014.

Quigly, Isabel. "New Novels." *Critical Perspectives on Sam Selvon*. Ed. Susheila Nasta. Washington, DC: Three Continents, 1988. 109. Print.

Rahim, Jennifer. "The Nation/A World/A Place to be Human: Earl Lovelace and the Task of 'Rescuing the Future.'" *Anthurium*. 4.2 (2006). Web. 25 Jan. 2012.

Ramchand, Kenneth. "Calling All Dragons: The Crumbling of Caribbean Masculinity." *Interrogating Caribbean Masculinities: Theoretical and Empirical*

Analyses. Ed. Rhoda E. Reddock. Mona, Jamaica: University of the West Indies Press, 2004. 309–25. Print.

———. "Comedy as Evasion." *Something Rich and Strange: Selected Essays on Sam Selvon*. Ed. Mark Zehnder. Leeds: Peepal Tree, 2003. 85–106. Print.

———. Introduction. *An Island Is a World*. By Samuel Selvon. Toronto: TSAR, 1993. v–xxv. Print.

———. "Selvon, Samuel Dickson (1923–1994)." *Oxford Dictionary of National Biography*. Oxford University Press, 2006. Web. 01 Dec. 2013.

Rampaul, Giselle. "Voice as a Carnivalesque Strategy in West Indian Literature: Sam Selvon's *The Lonely Londoners* and *Moses Ascending*." *Bodies and Voices: The Force-Field of Representation and Discourse in Colonial and Postcolonial Studies*. Ed. Merete Falck Borch, et al. Amsterdam and New York: Rodopi, 2008. 309–19. Print.

Ramraj, Victor. "Samuel Selvon (1923–1994)." *Canadian Literary Humorists*. Ed. Paul Matthew St Pierre. *The Dictionary of Literary Biography*. Vol. 362. Detroit: Gale, 2011. 227–36. Print.

———. "The Philosophy of Neutrality: The Treatment of Political Militancy in Samuel Selvon's *Moses Ascending* and *Moses Migrating*." *Something Rich and Strange: Selected Essays on Sam Selvon*. Ed. Martin Zehnder. Leeds: Peepal Tree, 2003. 77–84. Print.

Redding, Saunders. "Sex in Trinidad." Rev. of *I Hear Thunder* by Samuel Selvon. *Afro American*. n.p. *The Samuel Selvon Collection*. Alma Jordan Library, The University of the West Indies, St Augustine, Trinidad and Tobago. Item 451. Print.

Reddy, William M. *The Making of Romantic Love: Longing and Sexuality in Europe, South Asia, and Japan, 900–1200 CE*. Chicago and London: University of Chicago Press, 2012. Print.

Ricoeur, Paul. *Time and Narrative, Vol. I*. Trans. Kathleen McLaughlin and David Pellauer. Chicago: University of Chicago Press, 1984. Print.

Roach, Eric. "Enchanting the Word for His Sardonic View of Life." Rev. of *Those Who Eat the Cascadura*, by Samuel Selvon. *Trinidad Guardian* 8 Mar. 1972. 6. *The Samuel Selvon Collection*. Alma Jordan Library, The University of the West Indies, St Augustine, Trinidad and Tobago. Item 457. Print.

Roberts, Kevin, and Andra Thakur. "Christened with Snow: A Conversation with Sam Selvon." *Ariel: A Review of International English Literature* 27.2 (1996): 89–115. Web. 27 October 2014.

Rohlehr, Gordon. *Calypso and Society in Pre-Independence Trinidad*. Tunapuna, Trinidad: Gordon Rohlehr, 1990. Print.

———. "Literature and the Folk." *My Strangled City and Other Essays*. Port-of-Spain, Trinidad: Longman, 1992. 52–85. Print.

Rothfork, John. "Race and Community in Sam Selvon's Fiction." *Caribbean Quarterly* 37.4 (Dec 1991): 9–22. Print.

Rutherford, Jonathan. *Men's Silences: Predicaments in Masculinity.* London and New York: Routledge, 1992. Print.

Salick, Roydon. *The Novels of Samuel Selvon: A Critical Study.* Westport, CT: Greenwood, 2001. Print.

———. "Sam Selvon's *I Hear Thunder*: An Assessment." *Ariel: A Review of International English Literature* 27.2 (Apr 1996): 117–29. Print.

———. *Samuel Selvon.* Tavistock, UK: Northcote House, 2013. Print.

Sandhu, Sukhdev. *London Calling: How Black and Asian Writers Imagined a City.* London: Harper Collins, 2003. Print.

Sangari, Kumkum and Sudesh Vaid, eds. *Recasting Women: Essays in Colonial History.* New Delhi: Kali, 1989. Print.

"The Secret London of Samuel Selvon." *Evening Standard* 29 Mar. 1957. n.p. *The Samuel Selvon Collection.* Alma Jordan Library, The University of the West Indies, St Augustine, Trinidad and Tobago. Item 10. Print.

Sheller, Mimi. *Citizenship from Below: Erotic Agency and Caribbean Freedom.* Durham, NC and London: Duke University Press, 2012. Print.

Short, John Rennie. *Global Dimensions: Space, Place and the Contemporary World.* London: Reaktion Books, 2001. Print.

Siegel, Lee. *Sacred and Profane Dimensions of Love in Indian Traditions as Exemplified in the* "Gitagovinda" *of Jayadeva.* Delhi: Oxford University Press, 1978. Print.

Sindoni, Maria Grazia. *Creolizing Culture: A Study on Sam Selvon's Work.* New Delhi: Atlantic, 2006. Print.

Sinha, Lalita. *Unveiling the Garden of Love: Mystical Symbolism in* Layla Majnun *&* Gita Govinda. Bloomington, IN: World Wisdom, 2008. Print.

Smith Barusch, Amanda. *Love Stories of Later Life: A Narrative Approach to Understanding Romance.* Oxford and New York: Oxford University Press, 2008. Print.

Sommer, Doris. "Irresistible Romance: The Foundational Fictions of Latin America." *Nation and Narration.* Ed. Homi Bhabha. London: Routledge, 1990. 71–98. Print.

Stewart, Dianne M. *Three Eyes for the Journey: African Dimensions of the Jamaican Religious Experience.* New York and Oxford: Oxford University Press, 2005. Print.

Thieme, John and Alessandra Dotti. "'Oldtalk': Two Interviews with Sam Selvon." *Something Rich and Strange: Selected Essays on Sam Selvon.* Ed. Martin Zehnder. Leeds: Peepal Tree, 2003. 117–33. Print.

Thornton, John. *Africa and Africans in the Making of the Atlantic World, 1400–1680.* New York: Cambridge University Press, 1992.

Tiffin, Helen. "'Under the Kiff-Kiff Laughter': Stereotype and Subversion in *Moses Ascending* and *Moses Migrating.*" *Tiger's Triumph: Celebrating Sam Selvon.* Ed. Susheila Nasta and Anna Rutherford. London: Dangaroo, 1995. 130–39. Print.

Toppin, Julia. "Pressure (1975)." *BFI ScreenOnline.* Web. 01 Sep 2013.

Tynan, Aidan. *Deleuze's Literary Clinic: Criticism and the Politics of Symptoms.* Edinburgh: Edinburgh University Press, 2012. Print.

Vásquez, Sam. *Humor in the Caribbean Literary Canon.* New York: Palgrave Macmillan, 2012. Print.

Vertovec, Steven. *The Hindu Diaspora: Comparative Patterns.* London and New York: Routledge, 2000. Print.

———. "'Official' and 'Popular' Hinduism in the Caribbean: Historical and Contemporary Trends in Surinam, Trinidad and Guyana." *Perspectives on the Caribbean: A Reader in Culture, History, and Representation.* Ed. Philip W. Scher. West Sussex, UK: Wiley-Blackwell, 2010. 227–41. Print.

Walcott, Derek. "The Action is Panicky." *Critical Perspectives on Sam Selvon.* Ed. Susheila Nasta. Washington, DC: Three Continents, 1988. 125–26. Print.

———. "The Antilles: Fragments of Epic Memory." Nobel Prize Lecture, 7 December 1992. *NobelPrize.org.* Web. 20 Aug. 2014.

———. "Epitaph for the Young XII Cantos." *Derek Walcott.* Ed. Maria Cristina Fumagalli. Spec. issue of *Agenda* 39.1–3 (2002–2003): 15–50. Print.

———. "Mass Man." *Collected Poems 1948–1984.* New York: Farrar, Straus & Giroux, 1990. 99. Print.

Ward, Paul. "Horace Ové." *Reference Guide to British and Irish Film Directors.* London: BFI, 2006. Web. 01 Sep. 2013.

Warner-Lewis, Maureen. "Sam Selvon's Linguistic Extravaganza: *Moses Ascending.*" *Caribbean Quarterly* 28.4 (1982): 60–69. Print.

Wilson, David. "Pressure." *Critical Perspectives on Sam Selvon.* Ed. Susheila Nasta. Washington, DC: Three Continents, 1988. 139–41. Print.

Wyke, Clement H. *Sam Selvon's Dialectal Style and Fictional Strategy.* Vancouver: University of British Columbia Press, 1991. Print.

Zehnder, Martin, ed. *Something Rich and Strange: Selected Essays on Sam Selvon.* Leeds: Peepal Tree, 2003. Print.

INDEX

www.ingramcontent.com/pod-product-compliance
Lightning Source LLC
Chambersburg PA
CBHW030326020726
47493CB00004B/1171